Volunteer Vacations Across America
Across America
Immersion Travel USA

Sheryl Kayne

The Countryman Press
Woodstock, Vermont

For my daughters, Aviva and Elanit, and
my mother, Ruth Wolff, who at age 86
received a lifetime achievement award for
her over 40 years, and still giving, of
volunteer work in Richmond, Virginia.

ISBN 978-0-88150-864-2

Interior photographs by the author unless otherwise specified
Book design and Composition by Hespenheide Design

Published by The Countryman Press, P.O. Box 748, Woodstock, VT 05091

Distributed by W. W. Norton & Company, Inc., 500 Fifth Avenue, New York, NY 10110
Printed in the United States of America
10 9 8 7 6 5 4 3 2 1

Contents

Foreword

"You make a living by what you get; you make a life by what you give." The speaker is unknown but the message is especially relevant today. More and more people are seeking opportunities to help the people, places, and things that share this planet. From politicians to religious leaders to teachers and parents, we as a society are responding to this global call to service.

For much of my career I have studied, taught, and helped develop tourism. My travels to large cities and small villages throughout the world have afforded me many wonderful opportunities, but the memories that have remained with me are of rolling up my sleeves and working, side by side, with my hosts. Regardless of what a project entails, the feeling that you've done something that made a difference, no matter how small, is truly rewarding.

There is no better way to learn about a place, interact with the people, observe the wildlife and natural environment, experience the culture and cuisine, and be part of a destination than by volunteering. The combination of volunteering and travel—volunteer vacations—is a growing trend. Increasingly, people are choosing to incorporate volunteer activities into their vacation time, and they are enjoying the satisfaction of giving back.

Volunteer vacations need not conjure up thoughts of far-off lands and exotic activities. The reality is that one does not have to cross an ocean to engage in meaningful and important work. *Volunteer Vacations Across America* is an excellent resource for finding hundreds of opportunities to travel and volunteer within the United States. Trips range from short drives for stays of just a few days to longer excursions that might involve volunteering for several weeks or more.

I wish this book had been available when I started my career. The compilation of so many wonderful volunteer vacation opportunities, all within the United States, is extraordinary. An invaluable resource to anyone looking for information about volunteering in America, this easy-to-read guide clearly details an array of unique options in five categories: People, Communities, Wildlife, Environment, and National Treasures. *Volunteer Vacations Across America* makes it easy to identify the various types of opportunities available, including those that are free or offered as a trade. You'll learn everything you need to know to plan your trip, and you'll read informative personal stories from travelers who have taken volunteer vacations.

What better way to understand the plight of the Alaskan fur seal than to participate in a scientific research study? What better way to assist others than to work with communities to rehabilitate low-income housing so individuals in need—be they elderly or disabled veterans or people displaced due to natural disasters—can return to and stay in their homes? How better to help the next generation than by tutoring children? These are some of the exceptional opportunities you will find in this book that offer the chance to learn, grow, and change how you view the world.

Whether you're a history buff, wildlife advocate, environmentalist, or passionate supporter of human rights, and whatever your age, experience, or income, you will find an opportunity for you. Whether you prefer roughing it or playing it safe, you'll find a whole new world of exciting and unusual possibilities. I invite you to roll up your sleeves, explore, and plan a volunteer vacation.

Kristin M. Lamoureux, Director,
International Institute of Tourism Studies,
George Washington University School of Business

Acknowledgments

Volunteers are the only human beings on the face of the earth who reflect this nation's compassion, unselfish caring, patience, and just plain love for one another.

—ERMA BOMBECK

This book reflects the effort, commitment, and experiences of hundreds of volunteers. Without you, the true volunteers across America, sharing your time, energy, and passion with people throughout the United States, this book could not have been written. Your stories are educational, heartwarming, and inspirational. I learned more from speaking with you—volunteers who are literally out in the fields, towns, cities, and countryside participating in the activities documented in this book—than from any other source. I applaud and celebrate your hard work and selfless contributions.

Thank you to each and every dedicated professional working with nonprofit, for-profit, and grassroots, independent groups. The assistance and cooperation I received from the organizations and businesses highlighted in this book were invaluable. It has been immensely rewarding to interact with so many people who share the concept, vision, and enthusiasm for *Volunteer Vacations Across America*.

People, communities, wildlife, the environment, and our national treasures are in need of assistance, and it is my hope and dream that people everywhere will become more aware of the many ways in which we can all help.

Special thanks to everyone who worked with me on this book: Kermit Hummel and the staffs of Countryman Press and W. W. Norton & Company, Inc.; Lisa Hagan, Paraview Literary, Inc.; Beverly Ehrman, BEEditing; Ann-Marie Nieves, Get Red PR; and Michael Knight, Director of the Helene Wurlitzer Foundation, Taos, New Mexico.

Volunteer to conserve and protect the scenic, historic, natural, and cultural significance of the Continental Divide Trail, spanning 3,100 miles through Montana, Idaho, Wyoming, Colorado, and New Mexico.

The Beginning: Get Ready, Get Packed, Go!

We are finding that an increasing number of people are calling every day, looking for programs so that they can volunteer their services here in the United States. They are no longer as willing as they once were to incur the costs of going abroad to volunteer. Ambassadors for Children is developing more U.S. programs; the newest is to benefit two communities in New Mexico and will need many volunteers to work with at-risk youth in a very exciting program.

—VICKIE BINFORD, VICE PRESIDENT OF OPERATIONS,
AMBASSADORS FOR CHILDREN

U.S. Travel

Foreign travel is prohibitively expensive. Because of the weak dollar and rising international airfares, more and more Americans are looking to travel within the United States. With increased social awareness, people are searching for opportunities to contribute in a meaningful way: interesting places to go with something worthwhile to do when you get there. *Volunteer Vacations Across America* is designed to fulfill these requirements.

Domestic travel has the added advantage of offering road trips worth the price of gas and diverse destinations to enjoy and explore. Consider these opportunities:

- Mentor and accompany at-risk teens into the wilderness in Denver, Colorado.
- Rebuild a town with volunteers and community members in Cairo, Illinois.
- Work with servals, caracals, and binturongs in Mebane, North Carolina.
- Volunteer across America on conservancy preserves and protect lands and waters for nature and people.
- Live inside a national park and educate visitors about its historical, cultural, and geographical significance.

AMIZADE

Canyon de Chelly National Monument, Arizona, is a must-see when volunteering at the Navajo Nation.

What It Is

Welcome to *Volunteer Vacations Across America*. Prepare yourself for life-changing opportunities working with people, communities, wildlife, the environment, and national treasures in ways and places you never imagined possible. The diversity of the United States offers an enormous variety of cultures, traditions, and history. We are truly a conglomeration of people from the world over who have brought our customs with us to make America our own.

You don't have to travel abroad to find people in need and programs looking for volunteers. There are many advantages to using *Volunteer Vacations Across America* to find your perfect volunteer opportunity and to volunteering in general:

- Accessibility to locations, organizations, and programs
- Opportunity to repeat trips and continue relationships
- Ability to contribute to the welfare of fellow Americans
- Opportunity to improve the quality of life for everyone
- Identify new places you hadn't discovered before
- Return to familiar places to give back and share skills
- Learn about new and different American cultures, traditions, and pastimes

Volunteer vacations are volunteering opportunities with a travel component. They can take you anywhere across the country, including Hawaii and Alaska, and come in every price range for every budget. The volunteer experiences presented in this book are as diverse, inclusive, and unique as the United States itself. My research to find worthy and intriguing volunteer vacations has taken me into every region of the country.

Be forewarned: volunteer vacations by no means conform to the traditional concept of a vacation. With an ordinary vacation, you expect everything to be done for you; your accommodations, the views, food, and seeing the sights all become the major focus of your trip. Volunteer vacations are working vacations. You might choose to build or renovate homes, teach or tutor, translate and aid in communications, garden or farm, build hiking paths, or lead tours, among many other options. Volunteer vacations reward the traveler and the host through mutual growth, understanding, and experience. They are reciprocal—benefiting both the person who serves as well as the recipient, improving the quality of life for everyone.

The "vacation" part of volunteer vacations refers to the reality that for most people any time away from work is vacation time, and taking time off to do good for others is a carefully considered decision. These are projects, trips, and opportunities for people who are serious about helping others all over the USA and want to make a difference.

You will leave an important mark on the community you visit, take a big piece of your experience back with you, and return home a different person from the one who left.

Volunteer vacations are referred to by many different names: service trips, missions, working holidays, "voluntourism," trips with a purpose, do-good trips, and meaningful vacations.

Immersion Travel

I am the original immersion traveler. Immersion travel is the way I travel, always have, and always will. I take an active part everywhere I visit in order to learn about the unique characteristics of each particular place. Immersion travel enables you to get the most out of your travel time: connecting with the communities you visit to understand the culture, traditions, and unique characteristics. Today's travelers are not comfortable simply being consumers—you

want to participate, contribute, and give from the heart—
and this book shows you how.

In many ways, immersion travel is an attitude, a decision to get involved and to learn and absorb everything
you can from your travel experiences. Immersion travel is
for everyone, at every age and stage of life. It doesn't take
extra money or time to apply the immersion travel concept
to all of your trips and to reap benefits from them. When
arriving in a new location, be open to ways you can experience the local flavor of the community.

Volunteer vacations exemplify true immersion travel.
By the nature of the activity, traveling to a particular place
with the purpose of contributing through volunteering
requires getting involved. You connect with the people and

A content D Acres resident, Rumney, New Hampshire.

the place, contributing to and fulfilling specific tasks and needs on their turf. Volunteer vacationers repeatedly say they are amazed by the realization that after a week of total engagement in the physical, mental, and emotional interaction of teaching, talking, painting, digging, sanding, backpacking, climbing, or whatever is required, they return refreshed, revitalized, stimulated, and psyched for more.

As you will discover throughout this book, volunteer experiences affect peoples' lives, change their perceptions, inspire them to volunteer more of their time, and allow them to use their newfound knowledge to change their (and other people's) lives for the better. This can happen for you too.

Who It Is For

This book is for you if:

- You'd consider taking a vacation for the sole purpose of volunteering.
- You'd consider taking a day or two out of an already planned vacation to volunteer where you are vacationing.
- You'd consider a solo, family, or group volunteer trip.
- You have experienced a volunteer vacation and want to explore more possibilities.

Volunteer Vacations Across America provides you with everything you need to know in order to locate, select, and plan your volunteer immersion experience. We all have something to give. The resources in this book will give you the tools you need to achieve your personal goals and contribute in meaningful ways.

No matter what your age or background, *Volunteer Vacations Across America* enables you to explore opportunities to fulfill your own particular passions wherever that may lead. You are invited to engage in new adventures and live life to its fullest potential.

AMIZADE

A student volunteer is enjoying Arizona's Painted Desert outside Tuba City.

Getting Started

You want to know what you can do and how you can help, and it's all here for you. Descriptive listings will help you decide where you are going, what you want to accomplish, and how you can contribute, and provide the know-how you need to create the perfect trip.

A Personal Journal

Keeping a journal will be helpful in the planning stages for a cohesive record for all of the details you will be collecting. It will also help you compare and contrast the information you'll need now to make decisions. Begin your journal by providing the following information:

- Identify why you want to volunteer and what you would like to get out of the experience.
- Set realistic goals that can be accomplished.
- List your personal limitations and expectations.
- Consider your interests, abilities, and the skills you have to offer.
- Identify your primary requirements: location, activity, transportation, housing, privacy issues, food, and finances.

Once you have accomplished the basics, you'll be better able to assess the programs offered in the book's listings.

Volunteers leave their mark when renovating historic buildings.

If you require a private room, bath, and comfortable bed, extended backpacking and camping trips are not for you. But if you'd like to consider an overnight or weekend camping and working experience, you'll be able to find plenty of opportunities. You need to start with you and your comfort zone and what you're willing to try.

Now, let's look at the planning from another angle. You can volunteer on a regular basis or for an hour, a day, a week or two, or longer—it's up to you. There are people who return annually to their volunteer gigs. Anthony, for example, a medical research biologist, returns seasonally, on his vacation time, to count puffins' nests on an island off the coast of Maine. There are volunteers who return to the same places, and even become team leaders, and then there are those who are constantly seeking out new venues and new adventures.

Think about these questions and write down the answers in your journal:

- Do I want to volunteer in one specific task or do I need variety?
- Do I want to work with others as part of a team or on my own?
- How much time do I have to give?
- Am I looking at this as a one-time endeavor or as an ongoing commitment?
- Will I need training for what I want to do?
- Can I consider visiting the area I'm interested in and checking things out before committing to a project?

Of course, one of the major variables is whether you'll be traveling solo or with family, friends, or a group. If you are traveling with other people, be sure to include them in the planning. Knowing everyone's strengths, skills, abilities, and comfort zones is of paramount importance when planning a successful volunteer vacation. It is also important to consider the flexibility of the organization sponsoring the trip.

Let's Get Personal

We'd all like to save the world. We're not going to be able to achieve that on a one-week volunteer vacation, but we can contribute and make a significant difference in a very brief amount of time.

"The key thing is not to go into volunteering with the attitude of changing their way of life," says Rebekah Harlan, program coordinator for Amizade Global Service-Learning & Volunteer Programs. "Try not to focus on what you can do as much as what you can learn. Particularly when visiting the Navajo Nation, a unique cultural experience, it's a different mind-set of what service is. They don't necessarily need a roof built on a building as much as they need us to learn about their culture, roots, and history and take that back with us to teach our communities. Education is a service need."

It is very important to examine your own attitude toward work and mutual expectations. There are programs that offer a balanced experience, with downtime, playtime, and work-time, while other groups expect an exclusively working mentality. As the representative of one organization who opted not to be included in this book put it. "We are a work camp here. We want to stress that. We are not a vacation spot and do not wish to be associated with a vacation mind-set." That might sound harsh, but it's best to know the ground rules right up front.

Most volunteer vacations fall into one of four categories:

1. Volunteer Plus: These are volunteer opportunities that also have built-in travel, sightseeing, and recreational components.
2. Volunteer Programs: There are organizations across the country that need serious help and have developed opportunities consisting of work assignments of varying levels of difficulty. Some provide or have available housing and some do not.
3. Volunteer Internships or Service Year: These are long-term commitments, serving as a viable choice for a gap year project following graduation from high school or college but not necessarily limited to a particular age group. A service year is 10 to 12 months, but some internships are for much less than a year. "Gap year" commonly refers to the year between high school and college, or college and graduate school and full-time employment, but gap year opportunities may be available for those

considering a change of careers, or following
retirement.

4. Finally, there are volunteer opportunities you can
    arrange yourself, planning your trip around an
    activity or location, or one you can access from your
    home base or a centrally located destination.

Sponsoring organizations often provide ratings of easy,
moderate, difficult, and strenuous for the activity levels of
their trips. It's important to realistically evaluate your
physical fitness and capabilities. Always ask what the
planned and alternate activities are. Make sure you have a
clear understanding of what will be asked of you, and what
your days will be like, before signing up.

How to Evaluate and Select Programs

*When considering a trip, I read the catalog and view the
information on the Web site, and always call to speak with
the person who will actually be in charge of the trip who
can tell me more about it.*

—MARY JO, A VOLUNTEER ON MORE THAN 14 TRIPS

The volunteer vacations listed offer specific programs in
destination locations. There's a balance of free time and
work, along with immersion options to reach out to meet
people, contribute to the community, and learn more about
the area. Housing, food, and safety issues have been considered along with a detailed assessment of the volunteer
activities, requirements, and benefits

Volunteer vacations are offered by not-for-profit (NFP)
as well as profit-making organizations. One obvious way
to distinguish tax-deductible, nonprofit, mission-based
organizations is by the 501(c)(3) designation for tax pur-
poses. NFPs tend to offer packages that have all the details
figured out, which can be reviewed on the organization's
Web site.

Fees are usually charged, and they vary greatly. Some people are surprised that there is a cost to volunteering, but there are expenses associated with running an organization: maintaining an office and staff, organizing the volunteering packages, and developing relationships with the host. There are also groups, such as Earthwatch, that support scientific research.

As you will see, you have many choices. There are opportunities that range from free to trade, or from $20 a day to thousands of dollars. Compare the costs of volunteer vacation packages to find those that fit your budget. You may be able to access some opportunities on your own, while others are available only through an established group.

There are organizations that have been in business over 30 years and have long-standing reputations. But there are also smaller and newer organizations offering some very interesting opportunities that might be just right for you. When researching and evaluating sponsoring organizations, start with the people actively participating. Social exchange networks, like Facebook and Eons.com, are good ways to connect with other people who have experienced or are considering volunteer vacations.

Volunteers and organizers alike recommend participating with a flexible, can-do attitude. Things happen. People get ill, they don't do what they said they would, and travel arrangements and accommodations change, but those are things you can get past to enjoy the real essence of the trip: contributing, sharing, and experiencing a new place and new people in new ways.

Read all the printed materials available on the organization's Web site and in their catalog. Ask if they are an NFP or for-profit organization and how the fees are allocated. Inquire about tax-deduction considerations and then check with your accountant. Some trips are fully tax deductible while others may or may not qualify in part.

It takes hundreds of thousands of volunteer hours to maintain trails and parks throughout the United States.

Before registering for any volunteer vacation, speak with a representative of the organization, the group leader, and at least two people who have previously participated. Most participants connect via e-mail to plan their trips and "meet" one another. Some volunteers report dividing and sharing the load of bringing different supplies, arranging housing, and planning meals and chores months before the trip.

Questions to include on your list:

- How long has the organization been working in the area?
- Are other people in the community involved so the work continues when the volunteers leave?
- What systems are in place in case of an emergency?
- What will your day be like?
- What is the balance of volunteer activities and free time?
- Will you be able to explore your surroundings and engage in other activities?
- Will you be able to meet, talk to, and work with the people who know the area best, and form friendships with other participants who share similar interests?

Volunteer opportunities that can be arranged directly through an organization will begin with this book, or the Internet, or a phone call. Some trips will involve very little preparation, while others will necessitate attendance at a training session to educate and prepare you for what to expect.

Always ask how long the current fee is applicable. Ask about discounts. Sometimes joining an organization secures a discount that more than pays for the membership. There may be discounts for children, seniors, or groups. If you're encouraged to book ahead, due to limited space or rising costs, inquire if booking ahead guarantees you the current fee or procures a discount. Prices, dates, and Web sites quoted will vary with time and should always be checked before booking.

Organizations listed have been selected based on research, investigation, and recommendations; however, things change and you need to contact individual organizations to inquire about all of the guidelines.

Many volunteer vacations are group trips; therefore the characteristics, dynamics, and energy of each trip vary with the individuals participating. That's part of the charm and challenge. Having the group opportunity available also makes it easier to engage in activities as a single, or a solo partner. You don't need to give up doing what you'd like to do because your friends or family might not want to do it; you can enjoy it on your own with a group of like-minded people.

Guest Book

I carry a guest book with me everywhere I go and I ask almost everyone I meet to sign it. This is a great way to keep track of the people you meet in the places you go and will be a very nice memento. Some people simply sign their names or share e-mail contact information; others write a personal note. Often people will take the time to write something more thoughtful than they might ordinarily be comfortable saying. Travel guest books and journals are available on the Immersion Traveler Web Site, www.immersiontraveler.com.

How to Use This Book

Every facet of the volunteer process is covered to enable you to work through any difficulties that might arise. Having realistic expectations and a full understanding of what will take place will help you plan and take successful trips.

You will find more than two hundred opportunities in *Volunteer Vacations Across America*, organized into five sections that allow you to choose how and where you want to contribute:

1. People—Fulfilling needs and providing services in the areas of women's issues, youth, education, safety, homelessness, poverty, and human rights.
2. Communities—Working with others, in urban or rural settings, on community and economic development, construction, historic preservation, and the arts.
3. Wildlife—Studying and caring for animals, birds, and fish in their natural habitats.
4. Environment—Conserving and protecting natural resources in parks, forests, camps, farms, deserts, mountains, coastal regions, islands, and on the waterways and oceans.
5. National Treasures—Preserving federally protected areas including national parks, forests, lakeshores, waterways, and monuments, through conservation, maintenance, and stewardship

Relevant information about selecting a specific trip in any one of these categories is at the beginning of the section that covers that category. Each of the five chapters has information about choosing a volunteer vacation with category-specific considerations. You will also find information on the flexibility of programs and choices once you arrive at a destination, what your responsibilities will be, and how much free time you may have.

Each listing provides information in the following order: activity, location, name of sponsoring organization, address of the organization, telephone contacts, Web site, e-mail address, and dates and fees where applicable and available.

Suggested housing and dining accommodations are provided only if housing and meals are not part of the planned volunteer experience. It is not unusual for participants to share shopping, food costs, meal preparation, and cleanup chores. There are also organizations that provide housing without food. The particulars are covered in each listing as completely as possible, given the information available.

Counselor Jared and a Hole in the Wall Gang (Ashford, Connecticut) camper take advantage of the camp's Olympic-size pool.

Sidebars provide additional volunteer information or supplemental material for the listing, location, or experience.

"Immersion Tips" provide ways in which to expand your understanding of the culture, history, wildlife, traditions, and geography of your location.

"Immersion Excursions" suggest additional destinations within an accessible distance to broaden your immersion experience and extend your knowledge of the area.

Stories from volunteer vacationers are presented throughout the book. They offer personal insights with tidbits of wisdom and advice that could only come from people who have been there. They are not blanket endorsements, and they are not always flattering. These opinions and observations are presented for you to examine and consider.

A number of the personal stories are from residents of other countries. Volunteer vacations offer a great way to

HERITAGE CONSERVATION NETWORK

Heritage Conservation Network (HCN) workshop participants put the final touches on the Weisel Bridge restoration as they repoint the masonry arch with lime-based mortar.

get to know America. This book is intended for everyone—guests from other countries as well as people living in the United States.

When there are multiple programs sponsored by one organization, the trip descriptions are clustered together. The pertinent organization information will be found in the first listing to avoid repetition. For example, Sierra Club trips are represented in three chapters in this book: Chapter 3, "Wildlife"; Chapter 4, "Environment"; and Chapter 5, "National Treasures." In each of these chapters, the Sierra Club trips are listed one after the other. If only one trip appears in another chapter, the organization information is refreshed for that listing.

This is the first comprehensive volunteer vacation book focused solely on the United States and including volunteering possibilities for children, teens, and families. Volunteering together adds a very desirable dimension to travel, family dynamics, and building memories. Consult the Family-Friendly index to easily identify these opportunities. An additional index listing for teen trips, unaccompanied by parents, is also included.

Additional Options

Volunteer vacations are not your ordinary vacations, and the demand for them is doubling and tripling. Travelocity's annual forecast poll of active members found that 11 percent plan to volunteer during their vacations this year, and the number keeps growing. The tourism industry, recognizing this emerging market, is partnering with nonprofits to provide unusual and competitive volunteer opportunities.

CheapTickets.com, Travelocity, and Orbitz offer vacation packages for humanitarian travel and eco-friendly

YMCA TROUT LODGE & CAMP LAKEWOOD

The YMCA Trout Lodge, in Potosi, Missouri, is a great place to both volunteer and vacation.

trips. CheapTickets.com reports that they are working directly with United Way to support consumers who want to book volunteer vacations. The Travel for Good Program includes quarterly grants for longtime volunteers. More information about this program and grants can be found at http://leisure.travelocity.com/Promotions/0,,TRAVELOCITY %7C3702%7Cvacations_main,00.html.

CheapTickets.com also partners with United Way to provide consumers with volunteer opportunities through Volunteer Solutions at www.volunteersolutions.org/ct/ volunteer. Their packages consist of hotel plus airfare for two or three nights in four cities considered top volunteer vacation destinations: Albuquerque, New Mexico; New Orleans, Louisiana; Washington, DC; and Savannah, Georgia (www.cheaptickets.com/App/PerformMDLPDeals Content?deal_id=volunteer&cnt=PKH).

Travel and Visa Information for Non-Americans

All travelers to the United States need a passport valid for at least six months following the date you plan to leave your home country (www.worldstudent.com/uk/ studyabroad/usa/3d.shtml).

When it comes time for you to secure the necessary visas, documents, and passports, you will be asked about the purpose for your trip. Professionals agree that the response should be: holiday, vacation, or travel. Explanations that you'll be working or volunteering with a nonprofit or scientific endeavor, for example, tend to con-fuse the issue and raise questions about visas and neces-sary documents. Volunteer travel is considered vacation travel.

According to the U.S. State Department Web site (http:// travel.state.gov/visa/temp/types/types_1264.html), for-eign citizens must apply for a visa at a U.S. Embassy or

Consulate abroad. Citizens of certain countries may be able to travel on their passport alone without a visa on the Visa Waiver Program (VWP) if certain criteria are met. The B-1/ B-2 visa is for people traveling to the United States for fewer than 90 days, and you must have a roundtrip ticket, fly on certain air carriers, and meet additional requirements.

Plan ahead. Visa applications and/or renewing passports can take longer than you anticipate. Checking to make sure you have everything in order is simpler when there is ample time for the paperwork to be processed. Contact the U.S. Embassy or Consulate via the U.S. Department of State Web site, www.travel.state.gov; U.S. Immigration Support, www.uscis.gov/portal/site/uscis; or by calling the Visa Services public information line in Washington, DC (202-663-1225).

Keys

The majority of trips in this book are geared to adults over age 18 unless otherwise noted within the listing. There are also opportunities for families with very young to older children, teens, and seniors. It's important to read through each listing to see whether there are age-specific restrictions and to note that a family-friendly trip does not necessarily rule out singles, couples, groups, or special needs individuals.

Many of the trips that offer gap year or internship possibilities may be appropriate for someone considering a change of career, as well as recent high school or college graduates, or retirees. Trips are open to all ages unless clearly stated otherwise.

In the back of the book you will find easy-to-use indexes listing trips according to geographic locations, activities, sponsoring organizations, family-friendly trips, and trips for teens.

The Accommodations Pricing Key

	Lodging	Restaurants (per person)
$	Up to $50	Under $10
$$	$51–100	Up to $25
$$$	$101–150	Up to $50
$$$$	$151–250	Up to $75
$$$$$	Over $250	$100 or more

Listings Identification Key

 FEE-FREE: There are no fees to partake in this activity; however you will be paying travel expenses and sometimes food and housing costs. The FEE-FREE designation applies only to designated fees paid directly to the sponsoring organization and does not necessarily mean a completely free activity.

 TRADE: Services are exchanged for room and board.

 STIPEND: An allowance to be used for living expenses while participating in this activity.

 INTERNSHIP: A program that provides experience and training with supervision and instruction.

 GAP YEAR: Typically the year between high school and college; it may also refer to the year following college graduation, before further education or paid employment, and is not always limited to one age group.

 TEENS: Teen trips are specifically geared to the interests, needs, and developmental levels of young people ages 13–19.

FAQs: Frequently Asked Questions

Why do I have to pay to volunteer?

As volunteers you pay your own travel expenses. You are also paying for the sponsor's organization and management of the activity, recruiting costs, volunteer training, leadership personnel, insurance, the host's expenses and involvement, and on-site management. Volunteer vacation expenses range from covering only your own travel costs to minimal daily charges of $10 or $20, to total charges of $3,000 or more. U.S. citizens need to inquire if all or part of the program fees and travel expenses qualify as tax deductions.

What are the fees for?

Depending on the group, fees support the organization of trips, Web sites, advertising, staff, research, field expenses, housing, food, supplies, and the locations visited. Fundraising and donations also finance part of the expenses.

Can I plan my own volunteer vacation?

Absolutely. There are a lot of tips, Web sites, and resources for you to consult and use to plan your own volunteer vacation.

Are volunteer vacations only for the young?

Some trips are age specific, but the majority of volunteer vacations are for everyone. Ask for the average age on trips that you're interested in, which is often provided in the project description.

Do I need to be physically fit?

For some trips you do and others you don't. Details are provided in the listings of volunteer vacations in the next chapters.

Do volunteer vacations cost more than a standard vacation?

Volunteer vacations tend to cost far less than a standard vacation and have the added advantage of qualifying in part or wholly as a tax-deductible contribution.

Are there mostly couples on these trips?

Organized volunteer vacations are very amenable to solo travelers because it is easy for a single to join an established group. Volunteer vacations are open to all combinations of families, individuals, couples, and people with special needs. This is one area of travel where many married adults often report that they would consider and take volunteer vacations on their own.

Do I need special skills?

There's a volunteer vacation for you no matter what your skills or interests. Some trips do require particular physical conditioning or endurance. Others will train you for specific jobs, which is part of the volunteer experience. The beginning of each chapter describes what's asked of you as a volunteer for vacations in this category. The listings also describe what is expected of you. Participants often report that an added appeal of volunteer vacations is the opportunity to use skills and abilities not necessarily used in their 9-to-5 jobs.

Can a travel agent help me plan my trip?

Yes, a travel agent can suggest a trip that might be sponsored by an organization and then make the connecting travel arrangements, along with any additional sightseeing you'd like to include on either end of the volunteer vacation. Or the agent can work with you to create the experience you choose according to where you'd like to go and what you'd like to do.

Things Change

Although every entry has been researched with personal interviews and visits where possible, things change. People sell businesses, prices vary, dates shift, one project is completed and another one started. Use this book as a guide and resource for an extensive listing of volunteer opportunities, and then ask questions and make the necessary calls to learn about any revisions.

Be aware that e-mail addresses and Web sites adjust from day to day. The travel industry is a fluid business. Be sure to ask for references and speak with at least two former clients. Do not make plans or reservations based on anything you find in this book or on the Internet without completely checking out the particulars yourself. When finalizing your plans, it is highly recommended that you purchase trip-cancellation insurance, select refundable or changeable airline tickets, and obtain travel-medical insurance, which is sometimes included in the fees. Volunteers with preexisting medical conditions are also encouraged to

Fall is particularly beautiful at the YMCA Trout Lodge & Camp Lakewood in Potosi, Missouri.

investigate your personal coverage, trip coverage, and what is included in the trip fees.

Share the Info

After experiencing every volunteer vacation, included or not in this book, please log onto www.immersiontraveler .com to provide your feedback, updates for future travelers, and to share lessons learned and favorite volunteer vacation trips. By sharing what we know, we all grow, learn, and travel well!

Go!

Now go and have a great time using *Volunteer Vacations Across America* to enjoy the most fantastic total immersion volunteer vacations ever.

1

People: Make Connections and Transform Lives

Women's Issues, Youth, Education, Health, Safety, Homelessness, Poverty, and Human Rights

My teenage daughter and I joined a humanitarian mission here in the United States. I believe every student before graduating high school should participate in a mission to fully appreciate turning on a faucet for drinkable water, flushing a toilet, and knowing that others are in need.

—MARTA OCKULY, PARENT AND VOLUNTEER

When people connect with other people, they transform lives. This chapter includes listings for human needs and services to benefit children and adults. Reading the testimonials from volunteers, you can see the tremendous shift that takes place in the process of volunteering. It is very much a two-way street. The beneficiaries receive the gifts and kindnesses of those who donate their time, skills, and energy, and the volunteers benefit from experiences that change their lives forever. The connections made will last far beyond the volunteer immersion experience.

There's a wide range of volunteer opportunities available, from sharing listening skills and being supportive to climbing mountains and inspiring others to go with you. You'll find a variety of time commitments, from an hour or an occasional half-day to a longer-term or ongoing commitment.

There are also internships, service projects, and gap year positions that are available for a month or more or year-round. Read carefully through these listings because some of them are age specific.

Volunteers are needed in schools: tutoring, mentoring, distributing school supplies, and supervising recreational activities. You'll need to bring a desire to connect with other people, to set a positive example, and to share your skills and enthusiasm. There are opportunities in teaching, business, computers, and other areas where you can explore career paths. It is possible to receive special training to respond during a crisis and contribute to the relief efforts at local hospitals and shelters providing first aid, food, support, and supplies.

You'll find healthcare projects needing surgeons and other physicians and dentists along with laypeople to assist. Willingness to travel to remote, underserved areas to provide free services provides a meaningful volunteer immersion experience. Travel expenses to and from projects are the responsibility of the volunteer. Yes, it costs money to volunteer, sometimes for program fees, sometimes just for the basics like travel, personal items, and food and/or shelter. It all depends on the project and the sponsoring organization.

There are summer-camp volunteer activities with at-risk children or those with health challenges. Living in a bunkhouse with counselors and campers, accompanying the campers to activities, and helping with their daily needs are tasks requiring communication skills, compassion, flexibility, and knowledge of what you can comfortably handle. Not everyone has the patience or the emotional and physical stamina to participate directly with the campers. Perhaps you'd rather consider working in food service, office management, housekeeping, construction, or maintenance.

Adults with life-threatening diseases also need our help. Some amazing programs are highlighted in this book. Casting For Recovery provides fly-fishing retreats for women who have or have had breast cancer. You can volunteer to staff retreat weekends, teach fly fishing, or participate with a one-time or half-day commitment. The Pan-Massachusetts Bicycle Challenge raises more money for charity than any other single event in the USA, with more than five thousand riders and more than two thousand volunteer opportunities.

Bike & Build is a project that requires a combination of skills. Participants bike through different regions of the country or from coast to coast, stopping for several build days when you will help build affordable housing instead of cycling. You will benefit from cycling experience, or will need to train, but no home construction know-how is necessary.

Some projects require outdoors skills along with previous experience facilitating or guiding youth, environmental awareness, strong communication skills, and knowledge of particular geographical areas. Volunteers are needed for wilderness backpacking, canoeing, and white-water expeditions that serve low-income urban teens, 14–17 years of age.

These are all opportunities for people new to volunteering. No experience is necessary to volunteer with Great Strides, one of the therapeutic horsemanship programs. Other programs require specific skills. Certified adaptive skiing instructors are needed, from anywhere in the United States, to sign up for an exchange program to teach in Alaska with Challenge Alaska to experience a new community and location.

Volunteering with people who lack homes affords you the opportunity for learning and growth; you can explore the causes of homelessness and efforts to remedy it. Many programs have speakers and discussion groups in the evening to examine relevant issues. Follow your passion, support causes that concern you, and discover new possibilities as you become involved in social activism for human rights or the battle against hunger and poverty.

Look for ratings on the activities offered in the listings so you will understand expectations. Some programs necessitate walking for an hour, while others require hours of hiking. You also need to be aware of how you handle high altitude and elevation shifts. When in doubt, check in with your physician before booking a project at high elevations, and make sure you are physically fit for all the activities involved in the project you're considering.

Ask about accommodations and make sure you are aware of as many of the specifics as possible. Find out if housing is similar on each trip or if housing changes from year to year. The exact arrangements may not be available until just before the trip. Some organizations provide furnished dorms or other shared housing. Inquire about the ages of participants so that you are comfortable with your group and what is expected of you.

Adapting to different foods can also be challenging in different parts of the country, but most programs offer choices, including vegetarian options. Caribou and moose are available staples when volunteering in remote sections of Alaska, and it can be fun to try local specialties if you're game.

The sponsoring organizations highlighted in this chapter encourage volunteers to embrace an ethic of service, spread public awareness, and assist others. Fundraising skills are highly valued, for groups or individually. People are needed to identify and raise funds for sustainable projects or to raise or match funds to participate in or promote worthy endeavors.

The sidebars, immersion tips, and immersion excursions following the listings will help you plan your volunteer vacation and provide ways to enhance already planned trips. Traveling to someplace new for a weekend? Expand your horizons by selecting a volunteer activity that will work for you by reading about workshops, presentations, and events, checking Web postings, and signing up for monthly newsletters, if available.

Ⓢ Children with Life-Threatening Illnesses, Ashford, CT: The Hole in the Wall Gang Camp

(Ellen Buus, Volunteer Coordinator; 565 Ashford Center Rd., Ashford, CT 06278; 860-429-3444; fax 860-429-7295; www.holeinthewallgang.org; ellen.buus@holeinthewall gang.org). Volunteer to spend part of your summer at The Hole in the Wall Gang Camp, working with children with cancer and other life-threatening illnesses. Each summer, 1,000 campers (ages 7–15) from across the country and abroad attend free of charge. In addition, the camp's year-round program features weekend sessions from fall through spring, as well as a year-round outreach program for seriously ill hospitalized youngsters from New York to Boston.

Founded by actor and philanthropist Paul Newman to provide a recreational and therapeutic camping experience for children with life-threatening medical conditions, The Hole in the Wall Gang Camp, a nonprofit organization tax-exempt since 1987, also offers support to the campers' families in their communities and provides programs for healthcare professionals and social workers. Retreats are organized for campers' parents, also free of charge.

The Western-style camp, located in rural northeastern Connecticut, has log cabins, totem poles, teepees and wig-wams, stables, and a barn, as well as a lake, pool, an infirmary called the OK Corral, a theater, computer room, animal farm, and recreation center. Take a virtual tour, available on the camp's Web site, and see these facilities

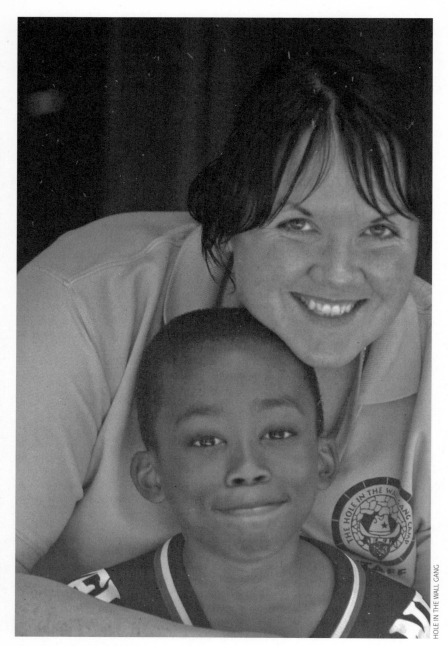

HOLE IN THE WALL GANG

Counselor Sara with a Hole in the Wall Gang camper.

and more, including a beautiful Memory Garden, a quiet space to remember friends and loved ones.

Volunteers are all ages above 19 years and are accepted on the basis of rolling admissions; applying in January or February is in your best interests. Each volunteer counselor commits to an eight-day session, which includes one day of orientation. There are nine weeklong sessions for campers, and there are 30–40 volunteer counselors per session. Two volunteers live in each of the log cabins with two staff counselors and eight to ten campers. Volunteers accompany the campers to activities and help with their daily needs. You will be given the option of a day off and will participate in a breakfast to share your thoughts and be thanked for your service.

If your summer plans do not include a trip to the Northeast, you can be a volunteer counselor at one of the other camps with similar missions located in different areas of the country. Volunteer physicians and nurses are also welcome. The application is made available on the Web site in December.

Ray's Story: The Hole in the Wall Gang Camp, Ashford, CT

Living for seven days in a summer camp cabin with terminally ill children is hard work that requires a high degree of patience, energy, and a willingness to learn about the kids. There are usually about seven or eight kids under your supervision around the clock and it's very rigorous. Everyone's up early for a polar-bear swim and to go fishing—it's all go, go, go through 9 PM. Volunteers need to be altruistically motivated. We ask that people make sure they are getting involved with our mission for all of the right reasons.

It's a beautiful, 360-acre camp with 50 very impressive, totally handicapped-accessible camp buildings

HOLE IN THE WALL G.

Counselor Jess enjoys a dip in the pool with two of the more than one thousand Hole in the Wall Gang campers who attend each year.

and activities. The climbing area looks like the arche-typal summer activity, but everything is universally accessible to every child. One girl, a paraplegic who used a wheelchair, set her goal to climb halfway to the top of the tower. She actually made it to the top and ziplined to the bottom.

Things like that happen every day. Children arrive with perceived limitations and shatter right through what they thought they could do. What I've found after volunteering over five years is that many months after camp has ended, you can ask a camper what he or she enjoyed most from the experience, and almost always it's a reference to time spent with a counselor or volunteer doing something pretty simple, one-on-one, like playing Crazy 8s on the boathouse dock. It's the human interaction and the bonds of friendship that make the experience most memorable for everyone involved.

Feeding the Hungry and Homeless in Washington, DC: Amizade (200 Robinson St., Suite 2, Pittsburgh, PA 15213; 1-888-973-4443; 304-293-6049; www.amizade.org; volunteer@amizade.org; group volunteer programs; 7-day trip, $732; 10-day trip, $1,015; 14-day trip, $1,326). Amizade Global Service-Learning and Volunteer Programs, a nonprofit organization founded in 1994 whose mission is to encourage intercultural exploration and understanding, partners with DC Central Kitchen to feed the homeless in Washington, DC. A nonprofit community corporation, incorporated in 1988, DC Kitchen has become a national model for community kitchens and operates its own programs in six states as well as in Washington, DC. The mission of the DC Kitchen is to use food to strengthen bodies, empower minds, and build communities.

In addition to working with DC Central Kitchen, Amizade volunteers participate with other partner nonprofit organizations including: So Others Might Eat, McKenna's Wagon (food distribution service), Georgetown Shelter, National Coalition for the Homeless, Capital Area Food Bank, and Street Sense (newspaper distribution). You can make a difference in the lives of the homeless and hungry by volunteering at a homeless shelter and soup kitchens. Activities include food preparation and distribution, childcare, distribution of clothing, and maintenance. You will also study the causes of homelessness and efforts

AMIZADE

Feeding the hungry and homeless in Washington, DC.

to remedy the situation through site visits, guest speakers, and discussions.

An in-depth orientation program and accommodations are provided at a conveniently located hostel. Bring bedding—a sleeping bag or pillows, sheets and blankets. You will have access to a kitchen and bathrooms. Included in the cost of the volunteer vacation are food and lodging; local transportation; educational, cultural, and recreational activities; and a site director. Program details, a list of cultural and recreational attractions, and a packing list are available on Amizade's Web site.

An Amizade Group Facilitator's Story, Washington, DC

A group from a private high school in Detroit came to Washington, DC, on their spring break to experience a week of public service with the Amizade program. Initially nervous and uncomfortable, the kids learned a lot about themselves and each other as they lived and worked with the homeless for a week. They joined street people out selling newspapers and had the experience of being looked down upon and disregarded. The 10 kids and 8 men made a potluck dinner together one night.

Each homeless man told his own story about how important it was never to let himself take that drug or drink alcohol. They talked about how careful the kids needed to be, about how to spend their money and to

Volunteers serve meals and deliver supplies.

study hard, advice that was so sensibly presented with everyone speaking the same language. That these people were homeless was a hugely eye-opening experience for the students and their teacher.

Immersion Tips

A trip to Washington, DC, is a great time to visit your congressman or senator. If you're traveling with children, this can be an important living-history excursion to connect with the people who represent you in the House and the Senate, and to make your voice heard. Contact information for all senators is available at www.senate.gov/general/contact_information/senators_cfm.cfm?. It is simple to sort by the Senator's name, your state, and party. To identify your congressperson in the U.S. House of Representatives and to acquire contact information, visit www.writerep .house.gov/writerep/welcome.shtml. Use a scrolling alphabetical list of states, enter your zip code, and you will be given all the information you need to line up a Washington visit. It's recommended to call ahead to secure appointments.

Tutoring Children, Promoting Learning, Tuba City, AZ: Amizade (200 Robinson St., Suite 2, Pittsburgh, PA 15213; 1-888-973-4443; 304-293-6049; www.amizade.org; volunteer@amizade.org; group volunteer programs; 7-day trip, $849; 10-day trip, $1,121; 14-day trip, $1,463). Spend your vacation tutoring children of the Navajo Nation in Tuba City, Arizona. Work with the teachers and help promote learning activities, develop a school-wide, weeklong art program, and assist in the library, computer lab, reading rooms, and physical education classes. Amizade, a nonprofit organization founded in 1994, encourages intercultural exploration and understanding through volunteer service.

Native art in the Navajo Nation adorns adobe buildings.

The Navajo Nation is the largest reservation in the U.S., and its members face the challenge of preserving their cultural identity in a changing world. Education is a priority, and Amizade partners with the Tuba City Boarding School to promote lifelong learning, success, personal growth, and a sense of self-worth. The school works with parents, community members, and volunteers who all want to provide the children of Tuba City with the best possible chance to grow into responsible and productive adults. Learn more about the Navajo Nation at www.navajo.org.

Amizade encourages its volunteers to embrace an "ethic of service," which means that the entire immersion experience is one of service to fellow human beings. In addition to completing your service commitments, it is hoped that you will engage in the community and connect with community members, volunteering to help in other capacities as well.

Part of the volunteer experience is exploring your surroundings.

The program is staffed by experienced and motivated people, and you are encouraged to get to know the staff members as well as your host community. You will partici-pate in an orientation program upon your arrival in Tuba City. Group living is an important component of all Amizade programs, and you are asked to approach group living, working, and spending leisure time together in a flexible, open, and constructive manner, with respect for your fellow volunteers.

Housing is at Grey Hills Academy, a boarding high school, with either single or double dormitory-style rooms, communal living room and bathroom, and small kitchenette. The staff will provide a light breakfast, and lunch will be served in the school cafeteria or at your volunteer project. Dinners vary, and there are diners, restaurant, and fast-food options available in Tuba City, as well as a local grocery store.

Included in the cost of the volunteer vacation are food and lodging; educational, cultural, and recreational activities; and a local site director. You will also participate in community activities and have opportunities to observe the Navajo Nation's traditions.

Amizade recommends flying into the Phoenix or Flagstaff airports. Volunteers are responsible for transportation to Tuba City and during the program. Check the online handbook, www.amizade.org/HandBooks/Navajo NationHandbook.pdf, for travel information, a packing list, and other trip details.

Educational, Social and Community Service in Cities Across the Country: City Year

(287 Columbus Ave., Boston, MA 02116; 617-927-2500 or 617-927-2510; www.cityyear.org; joinus@cityyear.org; applications accepted until Nov. 30, Feb. 15, Apr. 15, and May 31 for programs beginning with the school year—late Aug. or early Sept. depending on location). City Year, founded in 1988, is a member of AmeriCorps, a federally funded network of national service programs in education.

If you are between the ages of 17 and 24, you can commit 1,700 hours of service over a 10-month period working in 17 locations around the U.S., including Chicago, Cleveland, Detroit, Los Angeles, New York, Seattle, and Washington, DC. Service is full-time, as a tutor or mentor in schools, running after-school programs, leading and developing youth leadership programs, and organizing vacation camps for children and their communities.

A living stipend is given, the amount determined by the location, with a $4,725 AmeriCorps education award upon

As mentors and role models, City Year corps members make a difference in children's lives by raising their self-esteem.

completion of a full term of service. Basic healthcare coverage is included, and you will begin to earn vacation, personal, and sick days from the start of your service. More information about the program and application process can be found online at www.cityyear.org/faq.aspx.

Megan's Story, City Year, Chicago, IL

I'm serving in my second year with City Year in Chicago with the Young Heroes, our leadership development program that teaches middle-school students about their ability to make a difference in their communities. I really believe in the unique curriculum of this program.

The first year for sixth-graders is half curriculum-based and half service, with their actually getting out

and doing physical service, cleaning up a park or planting trees. It varies, and the students play a big part in
feedback sessions to select projects they feel are relevant. The second year they learn about the culture, philosophy, and mission of developing leadership skills. In
their third year they are able and ready to lead others
by participating and planning large-scale service and
programming events.

I grew up in many different places and at age 21
didn't have many options because I hadn't completed
high school. City Year enabled me to prepare for my
GEDs, and I aspire to continue for my bachelor's degree.
I'm close enough in age to really relate to the 150
middle-school Young Heroes, share the problems of
being a high-school dropout, and inspire them to not
make the same mistakes. I want to be successful, and I
want all of them to achieve their full potential, to face

City Year corps members help children learn to read.

challenges, and to know that they can achieve their
goals and dreams. That's what I'm doing every day. Once
you get really involved and committed, it's hard to stop.

**At-Risk Youth, Santa Fe, NM: Ambassadors For
Children** (40 Virginia Ave., Indianapolis, IN 46204; 317-
536-0250; 1-866-338-3468; fax 317-536-0258; www
.ambassadorsforchildren.org; contact@ambassadorsfor
children.org; costs range from $949 to $1,199, for quad to
single rooms; $500 deposit due upon booking, balance
90 days prior to departure). Ambassadors for Children
(AFC) is a nonprofit organization that serves children
through short-term humanitarian service trips. It provides
volunteers with hands-on interaction with disadvantaged
children, balanced by sightseeing excursions and immersion in the community served.

Founded in 1998, AFC has sponsored hundreds of
humanitarian trips benefiting thousands of children and
has donated about $5 million in aid. Volunteers work in
schools, supervise recreational activities, assist in construction projects, help with medical and dental assess-
ments, and distribute school supplies and other requested
items. AFC also identifies and raises funds for sustainable projects.

Join a five-day trip to Santa Fe, New Mexico, and work
with at-risk youth on conservation projects while learning
about Native American traditions. Santa Fe, the oldest capital city in the country, has a diverse population and culture. It is also a beautiful setting and a popular tourist
destination. Visiting and working side by side with Native
Americans offers travelers a different perspective. Be prepared to work on outdoor conservation projects and other
moderately strenuous physical tasks.

The cost of the trip includes transfers to volunteer
sites and tours of Santa Fe, Bandelier National Monument,
Spence Hot Springs, Chimayó, and Taos; breakfast, orienta-

tion and closing dinners; projects and activities with New Mexican youth; and the services of an AFC trip leader. Accommodations are at the Ghost Ranch, which is an education and retreat center located in an adobe-style building within walking distance of Santa Fe's main square.

Jennifer Rosen, Director of New Programming, Ambassadors for Children

The work we are doing in Chimayó and Española, New Mexico, is awe-inspiring. It benefits everyone—the workers, the recipients, the communities. Chimayó has one of the highest poverty levels and lowest standards of living in the country. Española has the highest use of heroin in the United States. New Mexico also has the highest diabetes rate in the entire world.

This is a unique project integrating conservation work with teaching the population about its heritage. We are partners with the Native American School in Santa Fe, New Mexico, and the Bandelier National Park Mountain Center. Our goal is to get at-risk youth out of the house and into nature. Generations of both Spanish and Native American farmers have lost their land, and without the ability to farm they suffer depression and disorientation. We can help change their future through positive experience. Participants dig foundations, conserve landscapes, build traditional Puebloan structures, and take great pride in their culture and accomplishments.

We also want to promote education to counteract the existing problem of distrust in their current, poor educational system. Native Americans were traditionally sent to boarding schools to learn new ways and assimilate, creating the distrust in the system. We are learning that when you are working side by side with an individual from another culture and socioeconomic bracket, on a mission with a heart and a vision, it results in the most beautiful form of mutual exchange and personal growth.

Family Volunteerism

Doing Good Together (5141 16th Ave. South, Minneapolis, MN 55417; 612-822-6502; doinggoodtogether.org; mail@doinggoodtogether.org). Doing Good Together (DGT), a nonprofit organization founded in 2003, encourages family volunteerism and supports and educates parents and caregivers who want to teach children the value, importance, and rewards of helping others. It is a local and national resource that focuses on families with young children. You can sign up for a newsletter and listing of volunteer activities, and find out how to initiate and participate in programs for families through school, work, or faith-based groups. DGT can help you plan volunteer projects and events and provide materials to enhance your experience. Visit the Web site for a list of workshops, presentations, and other resources, and to sign up for the free monthly newsletter.

Providing Youth with Access to Rivers and Canyons of the Colorado Plateau, Southwestern U.S.: Grand Canyon Youth (P.O. Box 23376, Flagstaff, AZ 86002; 928-773-7921; fax 928-774-8941; www.gcyouth .org; info@gcyouth.org). Grand Canyon Youth (GCY), a nonprofit organization founded in 1998, provides river trips for youth of diverse backgrounds and opportunities for personal growth, teamwork, and experiential education. Program components include a pre-trip educational project, the earning of a portion of the trip cost, a community service requirement, and alumni involvement.

Become a GCY volunteer and help with trip preparation, equipment and educational material, office and clerical duties, chaperoning service projects, staffing information tables, and working on special projects. Each trip has a volunteer Trip Coordinator to assist with pre-trip planning and both on-river and post-trip activities. There are two training sessions offered each winter for volunteer Trip Coordinators, and many coordinators return year after year.

Requirements include previous experience facilitating or guiding youth, white-water rafting, supervising youth for an extended time in a remote setting, good communication skills, an understanding of experiential education, knowledge of the Colorado Plateau, and the ability to commit to Trip Coordinator responsibilities. Your volunteer

Give Back Getaways

The Ritz-Carlton hotel chain is offering Give Back Getaways. Hotel guests are given the opportunity to give back to the community by spending half a day in a humanitarian or environmental project unique to each destination, and will work alongside Ritz-Carlton staff. Most programs cost $50 to $100 to cover transportation and a donation to the partnering group.

The goal is to spread public awareness and encourage volunteerism. Guests at Coconut Grove, Florida, can volunteer at the Good Hope Equestrian Riding Center. Guests in Dallas, Texas, can work at World Without Hunger, and guests in Atlanta, Georgia, can help by Sorting Food for Families in Need. In Bachelor Gulch, Colorado, you can help the Snowboard Outreach Society, and in Sarasota, Florida, you can work at the Big Cat Sanctuary. In Phoenix, Arizona, you can help Preserve the Sonoran Desert, and in Washington, DC, you can help by Preserving Our Monuments, Memorials, and Parks. Go to corporate.ritzcarlton.com/en/About/GiveBack Getaways.htm for a complete list of destinations and opportunities.

commitment is all the payment GCY asks, and in return you are rewarded with experiencing, with the trip participants, an exciting and educational river trip. Applications are available online.

Teaching Assistant, Hilo, HI: Institute for Cultural Ecology

(P.O. Box 991, Hilo, HI 96721; 808-557-1743; fax 866-252-8060; www.cultural-ecology .com; ecology@mail.com; 4 weeks, $1,895; 6 weeks, $2,600; 8 weeks, $2,970; 12 weeks, $3,850). David Adams, the founder of the Institute for Cultural Ecology, conceived the idea in 1998, based on his own student experiences, that students could gain new perspectives and give back through an immersion experience in the field, exposed to native cultures and the environment.

Spend a month or longer volunteering as a teaching assistant working with elementary/junior high school students, or in an innovative preschool. This works as a gap year program or student internship, or if you are considering a career or life change. Volunteers are matched with internships in a variety of fields, including education, business, communications, marine sciences, graphic design, and social service.

Combine traveling to Hawaii with positively impacting children's lives and supporting quality education. Hawaii is making efforts to improve its school system, and you can help. Teaching assistants become part of the community and experience Hawaiian values and customs firsthand. Positions are available year-round, and the minimum length of commitment is four weeks.

Housing is in an apartment or a university dorm. The program cost includes internship setup, housing, in-country contact person, airport pickup, and guidebook. You are responsible for airfare, food, and in-country transportation. A résumé must accompany the application form available on the I.C.E. Web site.

Immersion Excursion: Lava Glows at Night

Hilo is the largest city on the east coast of the Big Island, Hawaii, with beautiful beaches, many cultural attractions, and a wonderful market with arts and crafts, local produce, fish, flowers, and more. Puna, known for its hot springs and marine life, is located south of Hilo. North of the city, the Hamakua coast leads to the Waipio Valley and Waimea. A short distance away is Volcanoes National Park. Inquire at the Kilauea Visitor Center about the lava-flow activity and conditions along the 11-mile Crater Rim Drive and the Chain of Craters Road, which descends 3,700 feet in 20 miles. There are also day hikes and wilderness hikes on more than 150 miles of trails, or you can choose to bike the volcanoes on designated routes. There are two drive-in campgrounds, which are free with proof of payment of park entrance fees, available on a first-come first-served basis. Go to the Hawaii Volcanoes National Park Web site at www.nps.gov for more information. Be sure to take sufficient food and supplies with you.

Communities for People with Disabilities, Multiple Locations in North America: Camphill Communities in North America: Volunteer in one of ten Camphill Communities in North America for people with special needs. Find the complete listing in Chapter Two, "Communities."

Organic Farming, Locations Across the Country: WWOOF USA (P.O. Box 1098, Philmont, NY 12565; 831-425-FARM; www.wwoofusa.org; info@wwoofusa.org; single membership, $20; dual membership, $30). World Wide Opportunities on Organic Farms-USA (WWOOF-USA) is part of a worldwide effort (started in the United Kingdom in 1971) to link volunteers with organic farmers, promote an educational exchange, and build a global community conscious of ecological farming practices. WWOOF-USA is an independent project of the Ecological Farming Association, a nonprofit organization that began in 1981 and works to promote ecologically and economically sound agriculture.

WWOOF produces a directory that lists more than 700 organic farmers across the United States, including some in Hawaii, Alaska, and the U.S. Virgin Islands, who would like to host volunteers. Volunteers usually work for half a day (4–6 hours) in exchange for room and board. Arrangements are made between member farmers and volunteers, who must also become members. Contact the farmer before your visit to discuss the details of your stay, accommodations, food, length of commitment, and what your responsibilities will be.

Some farms will host volunteers for just a few days, while others require longer stays of one to three months. The directory, with descriptions of every WWOOF farm, which crops are grown, and what kinds of projects are being offered, will be sent to you when you join. You will also receive an online member login and password to the Web site directory. WWOOFers learn about organic vegetables, flowers, fruit and nuts, wine grapes, medicinal herbs, mushrooms, native plants, and biocontrol gardens. WWOOFers can also volunteer for construction projects, beekeeping, land restoration, animal husbandry, cheese making, dairy operations, and more.

When you contact a farmer, ask about bringing children; while they cannot work as volunteers, they are often welcome on the farm. Volunteers must be 18 years or older, or be accompanied by a guardian. Some farms accept younger children and find appropriate work for everyone.

Eric's Story, Big Dipper Eco-Farm, Kingsley, MI

We host volunteer learning and growing vacations from May through October 31. People can visit for an hour, a day, or a week or longer, and all ages are welcome from five years old and up. Organic farming novices work with the seasoned farmhands one-on-one. Farm tasks include weeding, hoeing, pulling carrots, transplanting seedlings, picking, and packing. The volunteers who stay with us get together to cook and eat. We can handle about four people at a time in the house, but bigger groups come with camping gear, camper, or an RV; we have a trailer hookup.

We work hard and play even harder. It's important to pass along sustainable agriculture know-how to future generations. Come stay with us and learn to farm organically from a guy who's doing it without pesticides or conventional chemicals; it's farming the way it was done before 1945. We've been producing ecologically grown heirloom tomatoes, potatoes, onions, carrots, 40 different culinary/medicinal herbs, Asian salad greens, zucchini, snap beans, cucumbers, pickles, fruit, flowers, and potted plants on a 40-acre Upper Michigan family farm for more than 25 years.

Ending Hunger and Poverty, Perryville, AK; Rutland, MA; Los Altos Hills, CA: Heifer International (1 World Ave., Little Rock, AR 72202; 1-800-422-0474; Learning Center Volunteer Manager, 501-889-5124; www.heifer.org; lcvol@heifer.org). A heifer is a female calf that has not had its first calf. Given to hungry families who agree to "pass on the gift" and donate female offspring to other families, heifers are a source of continued nutrition and income and much more than just short-term relief.

Heifer International, a nonprofit organization, works to end world hunger and poverty by providing sustainable gifts of livestock and agricultural training to people struggling daily for food and income. Since 1944, it has helped more than 9.2 million families in 125 countries move toward self-reliance.

You can volunteer in the United States at Heifer International's Learning Centers. The Learning Center programs explore issues of world hunger and poverty while challenging visitors to examine their own habits, consumption patterns, and beliefs on the path to becoming more responsible global citizens. Become a residential volunteer (ages 18 and older) and help facilitate the educational programs that teach and promote sustainable solutions.

At the Heifer Ranch, in Perryville, Arkansas, and Overlook Farm, in Rutland, Massachusetts, you will also help with farm operations and livestock, host drop-in guests, and assist with administrative tasks. It's a hands-on opportunity that connects people working together to end hunger and poverty. Volunteers come from all over the country and abroad; they range from high school and college graduates to retirees and seniors. Preference is given to volunteers who have needed skills. Different volunteer positions and learning-center locations have different minimum time commitments—to be a residential volunteer and eligible for housing, you must serve a minimum of 40 hours a week and the designated length of time for that position.

Heifer Learning Center at Hidden Villa, in Los Altos Hills, California, 39 miles south of San Francisco, will soon be Heifer International's newest Learning Center. Day volunteers will be needed to facilitate the Heifer Global Village programs and provide behind-the-scenes support.

Zoe's Story, Heifer International, Little Rock, AR

This may sound a bit hokey, but four years ago, at age 33, I had an epiphany that it was time for me to make a change. I quit my job, gave up my home, and after I finished a year with Americorps I asked for a sign of what to do next. Within a day, I received three signs. A friend called to tell me that she had just finished volunteering

Zoe and the goat kids enjoy lunch.

at Heifer International and said that I should look into it. Someone else handed me an article she thought I should read, about Heifer International. And then it hit me that every Christmas my dad received the Heifer International catalog and each member of my family selected an animal to give to a needy person. My favorite donations were honeybees and goats.

Here I am, living in Little Rock, Arkansas, at Heifer International, milking goats, composting, and making my own cheeses and candles. I've had a lot to learn. I had no idea that over a billion people are starving and we have enough grain in the world for every person to have 3,500 calories a day.

I had two weeks of training to work with visiting school groups. We teach middle and high school

Heifer volunteers learn through teaching service how to properly milk a goat.

students inside a mock global village, where their task is to figure out how to feed everyone. Some groups bargain, share, and trade for a communal meal while others try to tough it out on their own. The big question is, if there's enough for everyone, why don't all people have enough to eat?

Retreat and Education Center, Abiquiu and Santa Fe, NM: The Ghost Ranch (Abiquiu location: HC 77 Box 11, Abiquiu, NM 87510; 1-877-804-4678; 505-685-4333; fax 505-685-4519. Santa Fe location: 401 Old Taos Hwy., Santa Fe, NM 87501; 1-800-821-5145; fax 505-986-1917; Human Resources Office, 505-685-4333 ext. 157; www.ghost ranch.org; leew@ghostranch.org). The Ghost Ranch facilities in both Abiquiu and Santa Fe host conferences, meetings, retreats, and workshops, and offer a wide variety of seminars and events. There are also museums of anthropology and paleontology at the Abiquiu location. The artist Georgia O'Keeffe lived in Abiquiu for many years, and there are tours of the landscape she loved and painted.

Programs for volunteers are offered in both locations. Past openings at the Ghost Ranch in Santa Fe have included building maintenance, front-desk reception, half-time maintenance work, and plumbing. The Ghost Ranch in Abiquiu uses volunteers for front-desk reception, computers, school activities, the gift shop, and the Education and Visitor Center. These are considered long-term positions and housing is provided.

You may also be interested in joining the Abiquiu Service Corps. Volunteers work about five hours a day during the summer and pay one-half the housing fee, which includes meals. Campers pay one-half the tent/trailer fee and receive one free meal per day. Work includes light maintenance and construction, food service, housekeeping, library, offices, and museums.

Henry's Story, the Ghost Ranch, Abiquiu, New Mexico

I was a member of the very first Peace Corps group and then went on to work with the Corps for my entire career. Retired now, my wife and I live in Florida and spend our summers here at the Ghost Ranch in Abiquiu. It doesn't get much better than that. The area is rich with history, the views are spectacular, and we've made good friends among the many returning volunteers. My wife does quality control in the kitchen, meaning that her job is to make sure everything tastes good, and I work in the museum. It's my own special place, and I meet people throughout the day from all over the United States and beyond. I love it.

Henry, a professional with a 40-year career with the Peace Corps, was a member of its very first group of volunteers.

Mentor Urban Youth/Wilderness Program, Multiple Locations: Big City Mountaineers (1667 Vine St., Denver, CO 80206; 303-271-9200; fax 303-271-9201; www.bigcity mountaineers.org; info@bigcitymountaineers.org; volunteer manager, Brie Brower, at brie@bigcitymountaineers .org or 303-271-9200, ext. 409; 8 days, $100). Big City Mountaineers (BCM), a nonprofit organization founded in 1990, conducts wilderness outings for at-risk teens. With a nationally unique program design of five adult volunteers working with five teens, you will have the opportunity to mentor youth and positively impact their lives in the areas of self-esteem, environmental awareness, interpersonal relationships, and age/ethnic diversity.

Volunteers are needed for trips like a five-day wilderness backpacking expedition and a weeklong canoeing experience. BCM partners with youth organizations that

Leading the Way Program

Global Explorers (www.globalexplorers.org; david@globalexplorers.org) offers educational programs for middle and high school students and educators emphasizing the world as classroom in science, culture, leadership, and service. Their Leading the Way program, in partnership with blind climber Erik Weihenmayer, sponsors hiking and white-water rafting expeditions for blind and sighted students to the Colorado River and into the Grand Canyon. Check their Web site for current offerings.

serve low-income urban teens, 14–17 years of age. Adult team leaders are from the youth organization and BCM.

You can make a difference in the lives of at-risk youth if you are 21 years of age or older (exceptions are made on a case-by-case basis for qualified persons over 18) and reside within 200 miles of Denver, Oakland, Portland, or Seattle for backpacking trips, and within the states of Illinois, Wisconsin, or Minnesota, for paddling trips.

The volunteer fee covers food, lodging, and a portion of trip expenses; you are responsible for your own transportation to and from the trip site. You need to be physically fit (trips average 5–8 miles daily, gaining as much as 2,000 feet in elevation) and prepared to work with youth who may be low in self-esteem and need support and encouragement as they leave their environment for the first time. You also need to be able to handle difficult situations in a positive way, and be a role model for the teens.

Wheelchair and Handcycle Racing; Multiple Locations in AK: Challenge Alaska (3350 Commercial Dr., Suite 208, Anchorage, AK 99501; 907-344-7399; fax 907-344-7349; www.challengealaska.org; www.sadlersakchallenge.org; heather@challengealaska.org or ian@ushf.org, $400). Challenge Alaska, founded in 1980, is a nonprofit organization that improves the lives of people with disabilities, including

IAN LAWLESS

Racers are on the attack with Denali in the background during stage three of Sadler's Alaska Challenge.

physically and mentally challenged children and adults, through sports, recreation, and education. The Sadler's Alaska Challenge attracts athletes from all over the world and showcases different parts of Alaska on a safe, scenic, and competitive race course. Volunteers have the opportunity to learn more about the amazing abilities of athletes with physical disabilities as well as see the beauty of Alaska.

Join the support crew and note your skills and experience on the volunteer application available on the race Web site. Bike-mechanic and first-aid experience is helpful. Your fee covers all camping/lodging costs and food for eight days, plus vehicle and ferry fees.

In addition to the annual Sadler's Alaska Challenge in July, Challenge Alaska has opportunities for volunteers throughout the year. The Challenge Alaska Ski and Snowboard School needs teachers, and the Therapeutic Recreation Programs in Anchorage and the Mat-Su Valley

IAN LAWLESS

Racers and volunteer crew members relax at Lake Lucille in Wasilla, Alaska.

need volunteers year-round to help with sports and recreational activities, including soccer, snowshoeing, hiking, camping, fishing, rafting, cooking, and reading.

Assist with building maintenance, office duties, or program administration, or become a mentor, reading tutor, or buddy to someone who needs assistance in everyday life, such as going to the gym, a book club, or other activity. Volunteers are also needed for special events and fundraisers, which include the annual Charity Auction in February, Snowblast in March, and the Extreme Ski & Snowboard Film (October), in addition to the Sadler's Alaska Challenge.

Instructor Exchange Program, Adaptive Skiing: Challenge Alaska (3350 Commercial Dr., Suite 208, Anchorage, AK 99501; 907-783-2925; fax 907-783-3207; www.challengealaska.org; ski.challenge@alaska.net). Challenge Alaska Adaptive Ski and Snowboard School offers an Instructor Exchange Program that provides the opportunity for adaptive-ski instructors across the country to experience teaching in Alaska. Adaptive skiing uses special equipment to enable skiers with disabilities to participate in skiing. The goal of this program is to share knowledge and enhance the adaptive ski program at Mt. Alyeska, Girdwood, Alaska.

This is a great opportunity to ski in Alaska, learn from Challenge Alaska's program, and teach Challenge Alaska about yours. Your cost is your airfare and food. Challenge Alaska provides housing in a slopeside building with full kitchen and showers, lift tickets for the duration of your stay, and free skiing to equal the time you are teaching, clinics, and interaction with locals who will show you around the mountain and town.

A PSIA Adaptive certified Level 1 is required, along with a recommendation from your ski-school director. You will give lessons and help with program delivery half of your time. Call or e-mail with questions or to discuss details.

LOU BEAUDRY

Challenge Alaska ski instructor Tom Beatty and student Greg Peck hit the slopes at Mt. Alyeska, Alaska.

Mt. Alyeska has 2,500 vertical feet of terrain, an average annual snowfall of 631 inches mid-mountain, and 742 inches of snow at the summit. There are 2,000 vertical feet available for night skiing, and the most spring daylight hours anywhere in the country. The season begins in mid-November and extends through mid-April, depending on conditions. There are nine lifts and 68 runs, only 40 miles south of Anchorage and 90 miles north of Seward.

Immersion Excursion: Kenai Fjords National Park

While in the area of Seward and Anchorage, be sure to plan a full one-day boat excursion in the Kenai Fjords National Park (Alaska Heritage Tours Reservations, 509 W. 4th Ave., Anchorage, AK 99501; 1-877-777-2805; 907-265-4501; fax 907-777-2888; www.kenaifjords.com; info@alaskaheritage tours.com; 6-hour tours include lunch, onboard wildlife guide, and free parking; $129–139 adults, $64.50–69.50 children). There are a number of different tour companies to select from and many different discounts available. You'll see spectacular fjords, glaciers, whales, sea otters, sea lions, harbor seals, and an occasional black bear. People of all ages gasp and giggle as the puffins float by. Their antics are charming and epitomize the Alaskan experience, particularly when they seem to be waving at a bald eagle overhead or an osprey passing by. The Kenai Fjords are a highlight of any Alaska trip and perfect for visitors of all ages and nationalities.

Work with Youth, Warwick, NY: Camp AmeriKids
(AmeriCares Foundation, 88 Hamilton Ave., Stamford, CT 06902; 1-800-486- HELP; www.campamerikids.org; camp@americares.org). Volunteer at Camp AmeriKids and make a positive impact on children infected with or affected by HIV/AIDS. The camp is located in Warwick, New York, and serves youth from the tristate area. You can help provide a traditional camp experience.

Camp AmeriKids is looking for cabin counselors ages 18 or older, Wellness Team members who are licensed social workers and psychologists (or have other relevant experience), operations assistants to ensure that everything runs smoothly, and program staff to lead camp activities. The entire staff attends an orientation prior to the arrival of the campers, and many volunteers and campers return year after year. New volunteers must submit three references in addition to the application.

When Help Is Needed in a Hurry

Diversity World Traveler (10404 Santa Cresta Ave., Las Vegas, NV 89129; 702-821-1555; 1-888-747-8811; fax 702-233-9605; www.diversityworldtraveler.com; jcohen@diversityworldtraveler.com). Whether you or a member of your travel party has special needs considerations, or a special requirement arises during your trip—a wheelchair, transport, or handicapped-accessible lodgings—Diversity World Traveler (DWT) can provide what is necessary. This service may also be used while planning a trip or selecting a destination.

LEIGH LEIBEL

Americares' AmeriKids are happy campers.

The camper-to-counselor ratio is approximately 2:1, and counselors spend each day accompanying their cabin group to all activities, meals, and special events. If you are a social worker or psychologist volunteering as part of the Wellness Team, you will work to help alleviate any emotional stress and manage behavioral issues that arise.

Program Staff applicants must have expertise and/or teaching experience in one or more of the following areas: sports, arts and crafts, drama, dance, video production, spoken word (poetry), lifeguarding, and singing/music. The medical staff provides 24-hour medical support for the entire camp community. Some seasonal positions are awarded small stipends at the completion of the camp season.

Mary's Story, Camp AmeriKids, Warwick, NY

I work with major gifts and donations for the AmeriCares Foundation. Before coming here, I had been an assistant director with a number of different summer camps. I knew I wanted to work with Camp AmeriKids and applied and interviewed to be a camp counselor during my vacation time. Some of my co-workers, friends and family were concerned that with my demanding job and extensive hours, I'd need much more of a rest on my vacation.

Working with the Frogs, the oldest camp group of 14- to 16-year-old girls, I laughed so much my cheeks hurt. I love the camp staff and feed off their energy, which is through the roof all day long. There's a lot of love for the kids, and they thrive on it. We're up and singing morning, noon, and night.

And that is what a great vacation is all about, leaving work and typical routines to fulfill something inside

LEIGH LEIBEL

"Cat" camper on the prowl at Camp AmeriKids

you that you don't get to pay much attention to in your
regular life. I come back to work after a week with
AmeriKids much happier than from a typical vacation.

Adults with Special Needs, Mid-Atlantic, Southern, and Northeastern States: Sprout

(893 Amsterdam Ave., New York, NY 10025; 1-888-222-
9575; 212-222-9575; fax 212-222-9768; www.gosprout
.org; Leadership@GoSprout.org). Share your vacation by
leading small groups of adults with mild to moderate
mental retardation on 3- to 7-day trips to Boston, Niagara
Falls, Lake George, the Catskills, Cape Cod, Virginia Beach,
Washington, DC, and other destinations. There are typically three group leaders, age 21 or older, for 10 participants. Your responsibilities include overseeing the safety
of the participants and making sure everyone has a good
time. You may volunteer anywhere from one week to several months.

Sprout, a private nonprofit organization founded in 1979,
has been offering vacations to adults with developmental
disabilities for 25 years. You will travel by 15-passenger
vans, stay in hotels, dine in restaurants, and take part in
activities and sightseeing excursions. Between trips, you
are welcome to stay at the International Youth Hostel in
which the Sprout office is located. You may also have the
opportunity to lead activities in the evenings and on weekends in New York City.

Trip leaders will be trained in group dynamics and
need to be caring, sensitive, friendly, and responsible.
You will be briefed about Sprout's philosophy and trip
logistics, and have access to a 24-hour support system
for questions or emergencies that may arise. All trip
expenses, including meals and accommodations, are
covered, plus a daily stipend. There are no fees or
program costs for the volunteers.

Vacations for Adults with Developmental Disabilities, Multiple Destinations: People and Places (P.O. Box 184, South Wales, NY 14139; 716-937-1813, 716-496-8826; fax 716-937-1814, 716-496-8829; www.people-and-places.org; vacations@people-and-places.org). People and Places is a nonprofit organization that provides small-group travel for adults with developmental disabilities. Since 1975, People and Places has offered year-round vacation experiences to thousands of participants with special needs. Groups of six to eight vacationers, supervised by human services professionals, explore Coastal New England, the Old West, Historic Cities, Folk Traditions, Spectacular National Parks, Warm Retreats, the Pacific West, Country Music, All Florida, Cruises, Outdoor Adventures, Healthy Retreats, Earth-Friendly Resorts, and more.

As a volunteer tour guide, you can help people enjoy safe, educational, and exciting travel opportunities with the satisfaction of seeing the vacationers practice learned skills, discover new interests, and enlarge their world. If you love travel and helping others, this is a great opportunity to see the world at no expense to you. People and Places needs responsible, dependable, positive, caring, and friendly volunteers who have experience with people with special needs. You need to have good judgment, leadership skills, and excellent references. Contact People and Places for a current vacation catalog, tour-guide application, and personal interview.

Development and Environmental Internships, San Francisco Bay Area, CA: Bay Area Wilderness Training (c/o Earth Island Institute, 300 Broadway, Suite 23, San Francisco, CA 94133; 415-788-3666, ext. 122; fax 415-788-7324; www.bawt.org). Bay Area Wilderness Training (BAWT) creates opportunities for at-risk

BAY AREA WILDERNESS TRAIN

Climber/fundraiser Rick Rondeau stands atop Mt. Whitney, the tallest peak (14,505 feet) in the lower 48.

and underprivileged youth in the San Francisco Bay area to get outdoors, explore the wilderness, and experience nature. BAWT offers six-month internships in four areas: Development, Program, Marketing, and Climbing for Kids.

As an intern at BAWT, you will learn about environmental projects sponsored by Earth Island Institute, a non-profit, membership organization founded in 1982 that offers support to groups and people who care about social and environmental issues. When possible, you will be assigned a specific project depending on the current needs of the organization.

There are two different Development Internships available—a grant-writing development internship and a major-donor development internship. Experience with Microsoft Word, Excel, graphic design, and Web development are plusses.

The Program Intern works with the Program Manager, CEO, BAWT volunteers, course participants, and Program and Marketing committees. Responsibilities include providing registration support, preparation, and organization for BAWT courses, managing gear reservations, and assisting at a new BAWT gear library.

The Marketing Intern's responsibilities may include helping to formulate BAWT marketing and outreach materials, working with volunteers, organizing BAWT's marketing committees, and other tasks.

The Climbing for Kids Intern will work with the Climbing for Kids Coordinator, committee, and Co-Executive Directors on various initiatives ensuring the continued success of these events.

Interns receive a $200-per-month travel and living stipend, tuition-free courses, an Earth Island Institute membership, and free outdoor equipment rentals. Fall internships begin on September 30 (apply by September 15), spring internships start on January 30 (apply by January 15), and summer internships begin on June 1 (apply by May 15). To apply, send a cover letter, résumé, and three references to the e-mail address of the appropriate staff person, available on the BAWT Web site.

At-Risk and Underprivileged Youth, San Francisco Bay Area, CA and Multiple Climbing Locations: Climbing for Kids, Bay Area Wilderness Training (300 Broadway, Suite 28, San Francisco, CA 94133; 415-788-3666, ext. 150; fax 415-788-7324; www.climbingforkids.org; climbingfor kids@bawt.org; $3,500 donation). Help inner-city youth experience a wilderness adventure that will change the way

BAY AREA WILDERNESS TRAIN

This team raised more than $15,000 for BAWT.

they see themselves and their environment. Climbing for Kids is a fundraising event sponsored by Bay Area Wilderness Training (BAWT), an organization that creates opportunities for at-risk and underprivileged youth in the San Francisco Bay area to get outdoors, explore the wilderness, and experience nature.

You choose a peak to climb: Mt. Whitney, the highest peak in the contiguous 48 states; Mt. Shasta, standing 8,000 feet higher than its surroundings; Mt. Hood, the second most climbed peak in the world; Mt. Rainier, with its huge glaciers; or Grand Teton, known as one of the 50 most classic climbs in North America. Register online and create a profile, including your clothing size, as you will receive $1,500 worth of gear to use during your climb.

Next you set up an online fundraising page, as you need to raise $3,500; you'll be sent fundraising hints, ideas, and techniques and be instructed on how to set up your page with photos, stories, and information about Climbing for Kids. You may also send e-mail messages, track funds raised, and thank your donors.

All donations made on behalf of a climber by someone other than the climber are tax deductible. If you make a donation on your own behalf, the tax-deductible contribution is the amount of your donation minus the value of the goods and services you receive. BAWT also accepts corporate matching gifts. For every thousand dollars you raise, about 17 kids will benefit from a wilderness adventure. You can impact the lives of more than 50 kids by participating in this fundraising event.

You need to be in good physical condition but no previous climbing experience is required; there is free pre-trip training provided by Bay Area Wilderness Training. All trips are led by professional mountaineering guides. A month before your trip, you will receive your new climbing gear, including a backpack, sleeping bag, shell jacket and pants, trekking poles, and more. Visit the Web site to check out the current schedule of hikes, training sessions, and personal pages of climbers.

Shannon's Story, Bay Area Wilderness Training, San Francisco, CA

> I was really into rock climbing and then began spending most of my free weekends mountaineering. A friend told me about BAWT, and it sounded like just the right opportunity for me to combine my passion for helping people and my passion for the outdoors. I love climbing and I wanted a way to give back to the community.

BAY AREA WILDERNESS TRAINING

Climber and fundraiser Shannon Lucas and guide Jonathan Willy are all smiles on their way down from a successful summit day.

I spoke with the director about it, since I hadn't been above a few thousand feet. He gave me good advice on how to proceed.

My first climb was Mt. Whitney. There wasn't a lot of snow, so it was more like a slow, grueling hike. The second climb was Mt. Rainier, considered a mountaineer's mountain. Climbers in training for Mt. Everest train on Rainier and Denali. It was quite an experience being part of a rope team when there is avalanche potential.

BAWT provides free wilderness training to all area leaders of nonprofit youth organizations and maintains a free gear library to provide at-risk children with the supplies and outdoor experience they wouldn't otherwise have. More than five thousand children have benefited from the gear library alone.

One Volunteer Opportunity at a Time

One Brick (www.onebrick.org). One Brick, headquartered in San Francisco, California, is an all-volunteer, nonprofit organization founded in 2001, whose mission is to enable people to get involved by creating a social and flexible volunteer environment. There are chapters in San Francisco, New York City, Chicago, Washington, DC, and Minneapolis–St. Paul. When you plan your next trip to any of these five cities, check the One Brick Web site for volunteer opportunities and events during your stay. Each volunteer event is followed by a gathering at a local restaurant or café so that participants can relax and get to know one another. Events benefit children, the environment, food banks, schools, inner-city neighborhoods, and other worthy causes.

Environmental Children's Camp, Anchorage, AK: Volunteers for Alaska: Volunteer at a camp for children ages 4–16, from all economic, social, and cultural backgrounds. Located on 740 acres of wilderness, the camp focuses on the environment and educational experiences. Read the complete listing in Chapter 4, "Environment."

Tutoring Children, Tuba City and Cameron, AZ: Elderhostel (11 Ave. de Lafayette, Boston, MA 02111; 1-877-426-8056; fax 1-877-426-2166; Elderhostel registration agent, 1-800-454-5768; www.elderhostel.org; registration@elderhostel.org; 6 nights, $635 per person, adults age 55 and older). Volunteer to tutor children on the Navajo Reservation at Eagle's Nest School (grades 3–5) in Tuba City, Arizona, and Gray Mountain Elementary School (grades K–6) in Cameron, Arizona. You will work alongside teachers and interact with parents. Included are a field trip to a traditional hogan and evening programs on Navajo culture.

You will also have free time to explore your surroundings. Within two hours' drive of Cameron are the Sinagua ruins at Wupatki National Monument, Walnut Canyon National Monument, Grand Canyon National Park, Sunset Crater National Monument, Kachina Peaks Wilderness Area, Lowell Observatory, Museum of Northern Arizona, and Northern Arizona University. Northern Arizona University is one of the largest sponsors of Elderhostel (www.nau.edu/elderhostel) offering programs throughout the Southwest since 1983.

This program is rated activity level two, which means you need to be able to handle your own luggage, climb a few stairs, stand for up to an hour, get on and off a motor coach, and walk a few blocks, inside and outdoors. Elderhostel activity ratings range from levels one to six, the latter being the most strenuous. Project sites are at 4,200 feet elevation, so check with your physician if you have heart or

The Cameron Trading Post

In 1911, a suspension bridge was built across the Little Colorado River Gorge at Cameron, an isolated outpost on the Navajo Reservation. In 1915, local traders opened the Cameron Trading Post, where Navajo and Hopi Indians bartered their handmade goods for food. Today, the Trading Post provides an opportunity to learn about Navajo culture through its art, silver and turquoise jewelry, rugs, pottery, baskets, and paintings. Items crafted by many other southwestern tribes are also on display and for sale. Cameron is also a great base camp for excursions to Grand Canyon's South Rim, Lake Powell, Sedona, Monument Valley, the Petrified Forest, and Zion National Park.

lung issues. Accommodations are at the Cameron Inn, and all meals are included. Contact the inn for rates of additional nights before or after your trip (1-800-842-7293).

Human Rights, Civil Liberties, and Healthcare, New York, NY, and the West Coast: Doctors of the World–USA (80 Maiden Lane, New York, NY 10038; 212-226-9890; fax 212-226-7026; www.dowusa.org; info@dowusa.org; Lisa Jimenez, Human Rights Clinic Program Associate, Lisa .Jimenez@dowusa.org or 212-584-4866). Doctors of the World–USA (DOW), a New York–based nonprofit organization founded in 1990, mobilizes health-care professionals to promote and protect basic human rights and civil liberties in the U.S. and abroad. DOW collaborates with affiliates where health is endangered by violations of rights and liberties. American volunteers provide care and services while training community residents to support the DOW mission.

In 1993, DOW founded the Human Rights Clinic (HRC) in New York City to help survivors of torture and other human rights abuses who apply for asylum in the United States. DOW volunteers, physicians, and mental-health professionals offer clinical, medical, and psychological exams to survivors and document their torture and abuse. The HRC provides extensive training and support to volunteers, who then join a network of professionals operating in 10 states; the HRC has helped over 2,000 people from more than a hundred countries.

DOW needs licensed physicians and mental-health professionals to volunteer for Human Rights Clinics in New York City and on the West Coast. You would conduct interviews, clinical exams, and documentation of torture for those seeking asylum. An affidavit from a DOW-trained professional raises the chances of asylum seekers from about 25 percent to over 80 percent.

⑤ Retreats for Women Who Have or Have Had Breast Cancer, Locations Across the USA: Casting for Recovery (P.O. Box 1123, 3738 Main St., Manchester, VT 05254; 1-888-553-3500; 802-362-9181; fax 802-362-99182; www.castingforrecovery.org; info@castingfor recovery.org). Casting For Recovery (CFR) provides fly-fishing retreats for women who have or have had breast cancer. These no-cost retreats are offered at various locations across the country and promote and support both mental and physical healing. Currently scheduled retreats are listed on the CFR Web site by region: Mid-Atlantic/ Southeast, Midwest/South, Northeast, West Coast/ Southwest/Rockies. CFR, a national nonprofit organization founded in 1996, offers support and education to women whose lives have been affected by breast cancer.

CFR needs female volunteers over the age of 21 to work as weekend retreat staff; other volunteer positions as River Helper and Greeter only require a half-day commitment. Retreat staff attend the entire retreat (midday Friday through late Sunday), and your cost would be your transportation to and from the retreat location. CFR is looking for Retreat Leaders who would be responsible for the management of the retreat according to CFR guidelines. Requirements are attendance at a training session and previous experience instructing at a retreat.

Professional psychotherapists with experience leading group sessions are also needed for retreat weekends. Medical professionals knowledgeable about breast cancer, treatment, and complications work closely with the psychosocial facilitator, presenting informational sessions and leading warm-up exercises before casting practice.

If you have previous experience as a fly-fishing instructor, you can lead or assist with fly-fishing demonstrations and classroom sessions, and be an instruction guide for catch-and-release fishing. You need to have excellent communication skills for these volunteer positions. Hospitality volunteers offer general support for participants and staff.

⑤ Reconstructive Surgery for Disadvantaged Children, San Diego, CA: Fresh Start Surgical Gifts (2011 Palomar Airport Rd., Suite 206, Carlsbad, CA 92011; 1-888-551-1033; 760-944-7774; fax 760-944-1729; www.freshstart.org; mimi@freshstart.org). Volunteer to spend a weekend providing reconstructive plastic surgery to children with physical deformities. The services, including dental and speech therapy, are free, and are all performed in San Diego. Surgery Weekends are offered seven times a year at a local surgery center. Fresh Start is a nonprofit organization that has been organizing Surgery Weekends in San Diego since 1991.

Surgeons, dentists, orthodontists, nurses, medical technicians, and support staff are needed to provide disadvantaged children with high-quality medical services. Nonmedical volunteers are also needed to help with patients and assist with office chores. In one Surgery Weekend, 10–15 major surgeries will be performed along with minor surgeries, laser treatments, patient evaluations, and speech services. Dental support staff provide dental-health education as well.

More than 575 volunteers participate in this program every year, and there is nothing as rewarding as using a vacation weekend to help children in need. The surgeries and support services enable children to communicate effectively and develop self-esteem, as well as correct craniofacial disorders. Medical and nonmedical volunteer applications are available on the Fresh Start Web site.

Ⓢ Vision and Dental Care, Rural Communities: Remote Area Medical Volunteer Corps (Remote
Area Medical, 1834 Beech St., Knoxville, TN 37920; 865-579-1530; www.ramusa.org; ram@ramusa.org). Ophthalmologists, optometrists, and dentists can volunteer their services in rural communities and provide vision and dental care for people in underserved areas of the United States. The Remote Area Medical (RAM) Volunteer Corps, founded in 1985, is a nonprofit organization providing free health care to people in remote areas of the United States and the world.

The Rural America program provides eye exams and eyeglasses, which make an immediate difference in people's lives, enabling them to read, to drive safely, to perform at their jobs (or find jobs if they are unemployed), and to participate more fully in all activities and improve their quality of life. Serious dental problems can often be treated in a single visit. The program provides emergency extractions, restorations, cleanings, and other treatments.

A recent expedition to Knoxville, Tennessee, brought 1,343 free services to people in need, with 504 pairs of eyeglasses provided, 1,066 teeth extracted, and 567 fillings completed. The total value of the services of 276 volunteers was $235,497. There are ongoing programs in Tennessee, Virginia, and Kentucky, where out-of-state medical licenses and certificates are acceptable.

Volunteers participate in expeditions at their own expense; medical supplies, medicines, facilities, and vehicles are donated. The most frequent RAM expeditions provide dental, vision, and women's health services in the rural communities of the Appalachian region. Each month, RAM volunteers spend a weekend providing services free of charge to communities that have asked for help.

There are also openings for dental hygienists, dental technicians, nurses, EMTs, CNAs, opticians, optical lab technicians, and other licensed professionals. If you have a skill that would be useful to RAM patients, volunteer applications are on the RAM Web site. Medical and nursing students may also volunteer, with school sponsorship and supervision by a licensed practitioner.

Medical Support Services, Locations Across the Country: Medical Reserve Corps (Office of the Civilian Volunteer Medical Reserve Corps, Office of the Surgeon General, U.S. Department of Health and Human Services, 5600 Fishers Lane, Room 18C-14, Rockville, MD 20857; 301-443-4951; fax 301-480-1163; www.medical reservecorps.gov; MRCcontact@hhs.gov). If you are a practicing or retired medical professional (doctor, nurse, emergency medical technician, pharmacist, nurses' assistant, dentist, public health professional, and others), consider volunteering with the Medical Reserve Corps (MRC).

MRC partners with Citizen Corps (www.citizencorps .gov), a national network of volunteers dedicated to hometown security. It is part of the USA Freedom Corps (www .usafreedomcorps.gov), which promotes volunteerism and service. Although MRC units are locally based, MRC volunteers support communities in need nationwide.

After the hurricanes in the Southeast in 2004, more than 30 MRC units contributed to the relief efforts at local hospitals and shelters and provided first aid to the injured. During the 2005 hurricane season, MRC members provided support for the American Red Cross and the U.S. Department of Health and Human Services, staffing shelters, community health centers, and clinics in the Gulf Coast region.

The MRC Web site has an interactive map to search units by region or state. The MRC provides the opportunity to share your skills, belong to a group of dedicated, like-minded people, and qualify for free emergency-response and public-health training.

Volunteers may also participate in public-health initiatives such as flu vaccination clinics, diabetes screenings, and injury-prevention programs. Being trained and prepared to step in when first responders are overwhelmed by the immediate needs during an emergency is another very important part of the MRC volunteer experience. It is possible to make a minimal time commitment or contribute only during times of crisis.

Workamper Program, Eastern Ozarks, MO: YMCA Trout Lodge & Camp Lakewood (13528 State Hwy. AA, Potosi, MO 63664; 573-438-2154; direct line from St. Louis, 314-241-9622; fax to Trout Lodge, 573-438-5752; fax to Camp Lakewood, 573-438-3913; www.ymcaoftheozarks .org; jaclay@ymcastlouis.org). Volunteer at one of the largest YMCA family and conference centers in the country, a branch of the YMCA of Greater St. Louis, the fifth-largest YMCA in the U.S. The Volunteer Workamper Program requires a minimum commitment of 6 weeks, with a maximum stay of 12 weeks. You are required to provide 25 hours of service per week.

The Workamper Program runs from March 1 through November 30. Volunteers must have a camper or live-in RV. You will be provided with three meals per day, per person, as well as water, electricity, and septic hookups. You will have the opportunity to meet staff and families who live and work on the property, and enjoy access to many recreational facilities and activities.

Responsibilities vary, and your skills will be matched to appropriate tasks. You may work in general maintenance, grounds or lodge maintenance, as a food service worker, with conference services, in housekeeping, or as a counselor, craft instructor, naturalist, nurse, or tour leader.

Trout Lodge, in Missouri's Eastern Ozarks, is on a 360-acre lake surrounded by 5,200 acres of forest. Camp Lakewood, adjacent to Trout Lodge, is a residential camp for ages 6–17 and an outdoor education center when camp is not in session.

The traditional art of spinning is learned and practiced under the trees at the YMCA Trout Lodge & Camp Lakewood, Missouri.

YMCA TROUT LODGE & CAMP LAKEWOOD

Alpine swings are not only for kids.

Bob's Story, YMCA Trout Lodge, Potosi, MO

My wife, Elizabeth, and I believe it's better to give than to receive. We're from New Hampshire, but we're full-time RVers. I run the fishing boats out on the lake with families who come for day trips or overnights, or with campers for a week at a time. I also repair fishing rods and kids' bicycles.

One of the most interesting parts of being here is meeting the international students, ages 18–22. We

have anywhere from 40 to 60 of these kids working
for extended periods of time from eight months to
two years.

What I started to realize for myself is that it's fine
to do the physical work but what I have found as a volunteer is that I feel like an ambassador to kids from
around the world. Every day is different and from the
smiles and thank-you notes I receive, I know I'm making
a positive contribution that's very heartwarming and
satisfying for me too.

**Annual Bike-a-thon, Across Massachusetts: Pan-
Massachusetts Challenge** (77 Fourth Ave., Needham, MA
02494; 781-449-5300; fax 781-449-5301; www.pmc.org;
panmass@pmc.org; $500–$4,200 donation). The Pan-
Massachusetts Challenge (PMC) raises more money for charity than any other single event in the country. Since 1980 it
has contributed over $204 million to cancer research and
treatment at the Dana-Farber Cancer Institute through the
Jimmy Fund. The annual Bike-a-thon travels through 46
towns across Massachusetts, with over 5,000 riders and
over 2,000 volunteers. There are seven routes for cyclists
varying in ability and time commitment; each cyclist raises
between $500 and $4,200, depending on the age of the participant and the route.

You can be part of this amazing effort either as a cyclist
or a volunteer. Volunteers map the route, construct food
and water stops, provide medical attention, and ensure
event safety. Volunteer crews are run by the Volunteer Head
Staff who work throughout the year as well as on PMC weekend. Riders come from 36 states and eight countries and
range in age from 15 to 83. Some are cancer survivors. All
monies raised go directly to the Jimmy Fund.

Volunteers choose a site in Massachusetts and a job:
bike mechanic, medical team, sign crew, transportation,
information, food, massage therapy, photography,

communications, family fun, logistics, luggage, parking, information, registration, site beautification, technical support, route guidance, and security, among others. Whatever your skills and interests, you can donate your time and make a difference while enjoying a great weekend and meeting new people.

As a cyclist you will find fundraising tools, tips, forms, logos, letters and more on the PMC Web site. You will also find training information, advice, and resources, and more information on the event, area hotels, and how to register.

Service Projects for High School Students, Multiple Locations: Landmark Volunteers: One- and two-week spring and summer programs for students entering 10th, 11th, or 12th grades. Volunteers may elect to work in a national park, or with disadvantaged youth, at a summer camp for children with serious illnesses, at an adaptive sports center, with wildlife, at historic sites, or contribute to sustainable agriculture and green projects. The complete listing can be found in Chapter 4, "Environment."

Therapeutic Horsemanship, Damascus, MD: Great Strides (26771 Howard Chapel Dr., Damascus, MD 20872; 301-253-1166; www.greatstrides.org; Info@GreatStrides.org; volunteer coordinator Laura Favin, Laura@GreatStrides.org). The Great Strides mission is to promote healing and growth in partnership with horses. Great Strides offers equine-facilitated psychotherapy, therapeutic horsemanship, and equine-facilitated learning. The staff includes licensed mental-health professionals, certified therapeutic riding instructors, and skilled horse handlers. The Volunteer Paddock, on the Great Strides Web site, has information about opportunities to help; no horse experience is necessary. Great Strides is a nonprofit organization, tax-exempt since 2000.

You can make a difference in the lives of Great Strides clients, be part of the healing environment, and gain hands-on experience working with and around horses. You can help with barn work, lessons, horse care, and grounds work. Training sessions are provided on the first Saturday of the month and include a review of paperwork, a confidentiality agreement, volunteer policies, volunteer openings, the mission and background of Great Strides, horse safety, and a farm tour.

Volunteers are also needed at Great Strides events such as community fairs, ride-a-thons, fundraising events, and open houses. Contact the volunteer coordinator to see what you can do and what fits your time frame and travel plans.

Therapeutic Horsemanship, Waimanalo, HI: Therapeutic Horsemanship of Hawaii (P.O. Box 138, Waimanalo, HI 96795; 808-259-7107; 808-342-9036; www.thhwaimanalo.org; info@thhwaimanalo.org). Therapeutic Horsemanship of Hawaii (THH), a nonprofit organization tax-exempt since 1982, improves minds and bodies using horses as a tool. All activities are under the supervision of a Therapeutic Riding Instructor certified by the North American Riding for the Handicapped Association (NARHA), whose mission is to change lives by promoting excellence in equine-assisted activities.

THH can use both experienced and inexperienced volunteers to help with daily feeding, getting the horses from the paddocks before lessons, grooming and saddling horses when the rider is unable or needs assistance, leading the horse to the arena or during the lesson if the rider is unable to use a lead line, side walking if the rider needs more support, assisting with lesson activities, unsaddling and grooming if the rider needs help, and returning the horse to the paddock. Additional duties include grounds maintenance, mucking the paddock, checking and filling water buckets, combing manes and tails, caring for riding equipment, and cleaning up the barn.

Download the Volunteer Manual on the THH Web site for more detailed information about the program, the

Consider the United Way

Volunteer Opportunities: Hawaii Island United Way (Kalakaua Place, 142 Kinoole St., Suite A, Hilo, HI 962721; 808-935-6393; P.O. Box 3318, Kailua-Kona, HI 96745; 808-326-7400; www.hawaiiunitedway.org; hiuwdarla@hawaiiantel.net). There are many ways to help through United Way while visiting Hawaii. You can work at special events, volunteer in an office setting, work for the United Way campaign, or serve on a committee. You can also find a volunteer activity through Volunteer Hawaii, a service provided by the United Way. Click on the link for the events calendar on the Volunteer Hawaii Web site (www.volunteerhawaii.org) for date-specific volunteer opportunities and orientations. Browse current openings, or search for an opportunity by keyword or location. Wherever you'll be traveling, consider contacting the local United Way to find out about volunteering opportunities at local events.

volunteers' responsibilities, horse care and behavior, safety procedures, and dealing with riders. You can learn more about horses from the instructors and more experienced volunteers by participating in a Community Horsemanship class on Saturday afternoon. Riding lessons are available to volunteers at a discount.

Rabbi Josh's United Way Story, Waimanalo, Hawaii

I had planned a sabbatical from my professional job as a rabbi, and the program fell through at the very last minute. I found two great opportunities on the United Way Web site in Hawaii, one working with special needs children and therapeutic horseback riding, the other with the Wild Dolphin Foundation.

I've often wondered what it would be like to be a marine biologist, and dolphins have always fascinated me. To help, even in a tiny way, with wild dolphins is great; to swim with them, profound. I had the feeling of being connected with something much larger than myself—nature, animals—and being on the ocean is complete serenity. I saw humpback whales, monk seals, and sea turtles, and I left with a better understanding of ocean ecology.

My congregation is very oriented around environmental issues. My experiences provided me with skills I didn't have before and a deeper understanding of the roles we all play. In my regular life, people focus on me as a rabbi. On the boat, it was an interesting dynamic. No one had any idea who I was washing snorkel masks. It was very humbling. My experiences have influenced my sermons, conversations, and actions with my congregation. I have a heightened awareness of the work we all need to do to make our waters safe.

Immersion Tips: A Historical Memorial

Visit Pearl Harbor and the U.S.S. *Arizona* Memorial (open daily 7:30 AM to 5 PM except Thanksgiving, Christmas, and New Year's; free tickets are issued on a first-come first-served basis at the Visitor Center and are often unavailable after noon) honoring the battleship's 1,177 crew members who died in the attack on Pearl Harbor on December 7, 1941, and where World War II began for the United States. The site is managed by the National Park Service and the U.S. Department of the Interior (www.nps.gov/usar) and includes two theaters, a museum, bookstore, and exhibits about the attack. The guided tour includes a documentary film, a boat trip, and a self-guided exploration of the memorial. Strict security measures are enforced, and all backpacks, bags, purses, fanny packs, etc., are prohibited. You may bring a camera or camcorder.

Tutor, Mentor, and Teach, Worthington and Austin, MN, and Appalachia, West Virginia: Global Volunteers (375 E. Little Canada Rd., St. Paul, MN 55117; 1-800-487-1074;

651-407-6100; fax 651-482-0915; www.globalvolunteers
.org; email@globalvolunteers.org; 1-week program, $995
with discounts for Internet users, returning volunteers, and
students). Make connections and transform lives by teaching children of newly arrived immigrants to speak English
in a rural midwestern community. There are opportunities,
in Worthington and Austin, Minnesota, to help children and
adults communicate effectively, encouraging understanding and trust. Global Volunteers is a private, nonprofit
organization, tax-exempt since 1985, engaging short-term
volunteers in partnership with local communities.

Renovate homes or tutor children in the Appalachian
coal-mining towns of West Virginia. Assist with labor and
education projects and learn construction skills while helping to provide affordable housing for low-income families.
You can mentor local youth, help students study for their
GEDs, and assist with an after-school program.

There will be free time after your workday to enjoy
cultural activities in your host community, explore your
surroundings, and engage in other leisure activities.
Lodging may be in cabins or dormitories. You will have an
experienced team leader and extensive preparation material, with on-site orientation sessions and team-building
exercises.

The current service projects dates are on the Web site,
along with an online application. You will need to send a
deposit to receive a volunteer manual, and then complete
information forms and send personal references before
your application is processed. The service program fee is
tax deductible.

**Leadership Development, Southwest AZ: Leaders
Today** (225 Carlton St., Toronto, Ontario, Canada M5A
2L2; 416-964-8942; fax 416-964-2199; www.metowe.com;
erinblanding@metowe.com; 2 weeks, $1,995 per person).

Participate in a personal discovery and leadership development program, for ages 13–21, at the Arizona Wind-Song Leadership Center at the Arizona/Mexico border. Volunteer placements may include building a school, volunteering at an orphanage or hospice, or teaching English. You will also benefit from leadership training and cultural experiences, and explore issues of poverty, inequality, and immigration policies. Leaders Today is a for-profit international youth-leadership organization; founded in 1999, it is dedicated to supporting the work of Free the Children.

The Arizona Wind-Song Leadership Center, located on a private ranch, hosts up to 18 people and consists of several houses, each with kitchen facilities and air-conditioning. You can walk though a labyrinth inspired by traditional Native American design, and reflect on each day's activities at lookout points. The fee covers accommodations, food, volunteer placements, training materials, and donations to local communities. Airfare to and from Tucson, Arizona, is not included.

An Idea Exchange

Idealist (www.idealist.org) is an interactive site where you can find volunteer opportunities, create a personal profile, and sign up to receive daily alerts about new opportunities that match your interests. To search for volunteer opportunities, fill in as many fields as possible on the online questionnaire to narrow your search. Use keywords and choose from a list of areas of focus, including children and youth, economic development, disaster relief, environment and ecology, farming and agriculture, health and medicine, job training, and many others. Advanced options allow you to specify skills, time availability, ages of participants, and whether appropriate for individuals, children, teens, seniors, or families. Resources include a career center, a community action center, a section for kids and teens, a mid-career transitions center, and links for teachers and organizations.

Building Affordable Housing from Coast to Coast: Bike & Build (6109 Ridge Ave., Building #2; P.O. Box 35033, Philadelphia, PA 19128; 267-331-8488; fax 661-752-9806; www.bikeandbuild.org; info@bikeandbuild.org; $4,000 donation). Bike & Build is an independent nonprofit organization, founded in 2002, that offers cross-country bicycle trips for young adults (ages 18–25) to benefit affordable-housing groups. Each participant is responsible for raising a $4,000 contribution. Following the initial $1,000, you will receive a brand-new road bike to keep after successfully completing the trip. Bike & Build has contributed over one million dollars to affordable housing projects.

Bike & Build trips include: Central U.S., Northern U.S., Providence to Seattle, Providence to San Francisco, Southern U.S., North Carolina to San Diego, and Boston to

Dan Oates biked 4,000 miles from Long Island, New York, to Nooksak, Washington, stopping along the way to work on affordable housing projects.

Santa Barbara. Housing is provided along the way in churches, synagogues, YMCAs, and campgrounds. Each trip has several build days when you will help build an affordable house instead of cycling. No construction experience is necessary. After you reach your destination, Bike & Build will host a reception for your group and arrange for two additional nights' accommodations. You are responsible for arranging your transportation home.

Becca's Story, Bike & Build, Philadelphia, PA

> I didn't exactly plan it this way, but experiencing biking cross-country and working on building projects, helping people improve their homes, this feeling grew in me that I had a power and a purpose and a way to continue the work in my regular life. I talk to other people considering participating in the cross-country project. I contribute to the newsletter and fundraising efforts. We all work together to make really great things happen and I'm happy to contribute my part. It complements my life.

Youth Enrichment, Hilton-Winn Farm, ME: Volunteers For Peace (1034 Tiffany Rd., Belmont, VT 05730; 802-259-2759; fax 802-259-2922; www.vfp.org; vfp@vfp.org; 2-week program, ages 18+, $300). Volunteers For Peace (VFP), a nonprofit corporation, was formed in 1982 with the goal of "promoting peaceful relations among nations." Since then VFP has moved from organizing local to national service programs. Projects across America are in partnership with various nonprofit, environmental, and community action groups.

You can volunteer to work at this VFP-sponsored program, the Youth Enrichment Center at Hilton-Winn Farm, a nonprofit corporation, tax-exempt since 2003, whose mission is to provide children with a country farm experience through environmental education, and to encourage

growth in communi-
cation, teamwork,
tolerance, and
esteem-building.

Manual work
includes gardening,
animal care, barn
work, farm chores,
and trail mainte-
nance, as well as
working with chil-
dren on outdoor
group activities. If
you like working

The Youth Enrichment Center at Hilton-Winn Farm, Cape
Neddick, Maine, provides a country farm experience for
children.

with children and working hard outdoors, this could be
something you'd greatly enjoy. Accommodations will be in
the farmhouse with beds and linens provided. Leisure
activities include night hikes, ocean visits, and barbecues.

The Hilton-Winn Farm dates back to the 1700s. There
have been extensive renovations. Both the house and the
barn, along with the surrounding fields and forests, are
being preserved, creating a place for children to learn
where their food comes from and to understand their connection to the natural world.

**Reintegration into Society after Prison: Volunteers
For Peace** (1034 Tiffany Rd., Belmont, VT 05730; 802-259-
2759; fax 802-259-2922; www.vfp.org; vfp@vfp.org; ages
24+; 3-month program fee, $300). Dismas House, in
Rutland, Vermont, is a transitional housing opportunity for
men and women who need to rebuild their lives and be
reintegrated into the community. It is a drug-, alcohol-, and
violence-free community that allows recently released prisoners to reconcile with the outside world before living
independently. Volunteers accompany the co-directors on
visits to the prison to observe the interview screening

Service

> Service to others is the payment you make for your space here on earth.
>
> —Muhammad Ali

process and become familiar with their assigned residents. The paroled prisoners and volunteers live together, sharing the same responsibilities as part of a communal household.

VOLUNTEERS FOR PEACE

Volunteers For Peace work together in Rutland, Vermont, to ease the transition from prison into the mainstream community.

Volunteers work five to six hours a day outside traditional working hours that may include weekends and evenings. Dinners are eaten together at the house from Monday through Friday, and you are also expected to attend the weekly evening meeting. Responsibilities include computer and office work, participation in fundraising, student recruitment, speaking engagements, working with food and clothing donations, and participation in house group activities.

Accommodations will be a shared room in a large Victorian house in Rutland, a small city (population 17,500) in the Green Mountains. Group activities and sightseeing are offered, and there are many leisure activities available nearby, including skiing, hiking, camping, and biking. For information about the Rutland region in central Vermont, visit the Rutland Chamber of Commerce Web site at www.rutlandvermont.com.

Ending Childhood Hunger: Share Our Strength (1730 M St., Suite 700, Washington, DC 20036; 1-800-969-4767; 202-393-2925; fax 202-347-5868; www.strength.org; info@strength.org). Share Our Strength, a nonprofit since 1985, believes no child in America should grow up hungry. With the culinary and food-service industry as a primary partner, Share Our Strength raises funds and provides support to nonprofits across the country that are dedicated to ending childhood hunger. In 1988, Share Our Strength founded the largest culinary benefit in the U.S., Taste of the Nation, which now takes place in 55 cities across the country and raises awareness of hunger as well as significant funds.

Share Our Strength programs such as Great American Dine Out, Great American Bake Sale, Operation Frontline, and A Tasteful Pursuit have made a real difference. Motorcycle-riding chefs can take part in the annual Chefs-on-Bikes fundraiser for food professionals throughout the mid-Atlantic area. Sign up on the Web site and you will be notified when the Chefs on Bikes are ready to ride.

Join Up!

Join the Manhattan-based Culinary Corps (www.culinarycorps.org) sponsored by Share Our Strength, which organizes outreach programs for culinary students and professionals. Often called "the Peace Corps for cooks," Culinary Corps recently focused its efforts on rebuilding the culinary resources of New Orleans. Join a team and use your kitchen skills to reach out and help others.

Culinary Corps team members travel to farmers' markets, school gardens, crisis kitchens, and restaurants to donate their skills, talents, and time. Sample itineraries and volunteer information, including costs and upcoming trips, are available.

2

Communities: Volunteer in Rural or Urban Areas

Community and Economic Development, Construction, Historic Preservation, and the Arts

Together we can save a nation by building homes, with homes we build families, and with families we build communities.

—KATHLEEN PRICE, FOUNDER AND DIRECTOR, MISSION OF LOVE

A decision to devote your vacation to volunteering in rural or urban areas, contributing to social and economic development by means of construction projects, historic preservation efforts, and promotion of the arts, affirms the possibility that every person is able to make a difference and help create and support healthy communities.

There are tens of thousands of opportunities available to experience, firsthand, the joy and satisfaction of working with a group of people toward a common goal. Volunteer opportunities are available in both thriving and forgotten communities in every region of the United States.

You need to decide how and where you can contribute and make a difference.

Years after Hurricanes Katrina and Rita, there are still appeals for help in the areas devastated by the torrential rains, wind, and flooding. Volunteers are needed in New Orleans and other areas to donate their time, energy, and construction skills, and in return receive free housing from the community and gratitude for life. The needs are ongoing and so is the response. Your decision to help means hard work from morning until night, often in extreme heat, surrounded by others who have made the same decision.

Volunteers repeatedly express their surprise at their own strength and capabilities beyond their normal day jobs, discovering and developing new skills that they take back home with them. One person new to volunteering has recommended helping out on local building projects, to get a sense of what you're comfortable doing, before planning a major trip. There are jobs for everyone; just make sure you know what is expected of you on the trip you are planning.

Choosing to visit and serve in a community culturally different from your own requires flexibility, tolerance, acceptance, and willingness to compromise. The Sioux YMCA sponsors outreach programs and community camps with the mission of helping people and communities to help themselves, fight poverty, improve their living conditions, and make a better life for their children. You can set an example with your positive attitude, leadership skills, healthy lifestyle choices, entrepreneurship, fitness, advanced education, and career choices.

There are opportunities to learn how to rehabilitate historic buildings, or build a new community through a fusion of architecture, environment, and sustainability. Volunteers are needed in communities across the country to build safe and affordable housing, and to help preserve cultural and architectural heritages. Living and working with local people, connecting, sharing, and learning about the history and culture of the places you visit add up to an immersion experience you will never forget.

Perhaps you'd like to volunteer working with and getting to know people who have developmental and other disabilities. Volunteers are needed to offer support and services that may include cooking, sharing meals, and organizing activities. Good communication skills, a background in working with people with special needs, a can-do attitude, and pleasant personality are all highly valued.

Learning about and contributing to the arts by volunteering with a community theater and working cooperatively with others benefits everyone involved. Volunteers are needed to promote, organize, and assist in every detail of theater operations, and are considered part of the theater family.

Organizations such as VISTA help communities fight poverty, improve health services, and encourage economic development. Volunteering can lead you to find the focus of your ambitions, goals, and future professional opportunities where you can gain and develop career skills through specific volunteer programs and internships.

There are opportunities to literally go to work on the railroad with The Friends of the Cumbres & Toltec Scenic Railroad, maintaining and preserving the historic, steam-era railroad. You can paint, repair, and polish an important piece of American culture and history and indulge a passion for American narrow-gauge rails.

There are foundations and community groups across the country, such as the Theodore Roosevelt Medora Foundation, that benefit from ongoing beautification projects, site maintenance, lawn care, visitor center staffing, and gift shop sales. Volunteering to rebuild and strengthen communities is about placing yourself in different situations and getting to know, understand, and learn about people by experiencing life as they do.

As with any volunteer vacation, make certain you know what to expect and what will be expected of you; ask

questions of both the sponsoring organization and participants who have volunteered with the program. While living
in the community you serve, you may be dealing with the
same problems, issues, and hardships the residents face.
Special considerations include knowing your comfort zone
and how far from it you are willing to travel.

**⑤Rebuilding New Orleans: Common Ground
Relief** (P.O. Box 6128, New Orleans, LA 70174; 504-
304-9097; volunteer opportunities, 504-218-6613; www
.commongroundrelief.org; commongroundvolunteers@gmail
.com). Join a grassroots effort to support the residents of
New Orleans as they rebuild their neighborhoods. Common
Ground Relief is looking for volunteers skilled in drywall
hanging, carpentry, painting, legal aid, social work, media
and public relations, computer technology, cooking, gardening, wetlands restoration, and bioremediation. Both
short- and long-term volunteers are needed.

Common Ground Relief, a nonprofit organization tax-
exempt since 2007, works with other community-based
nonprofits to prioritize the needs of the community and
identify the issues that have held up reconstruction. Lack
of communication has been a large problem, with many
residents in need unaware of the help available to them.
Meetings with residents, representatives from nonprofit
organizations, and government officials are ongoing, in
order to coordinate relief efforts and ensure that the concerns are addressed.

Go to the Project Areas section on Common Ground
Relief's Web site and indicate your preference(s) when registering. There are travel directions, a map, and answers to
frequently asked questions as well as a packing list. Download an application or request one by e-mailing the volunteer coordinator, and allow one week for a response after
submitting your application. Communal housing is provided for all volunteers.

HERITAGE CONSERVATION NETWORK

Heritage Conservation on-site work discussion.

Ⓢ Community Projects, Pine Ridge Reservation, SD: Mission of Love (Kathleen Price, Director and Founder, Mission of Love Foundation, Hemlock Court, Youngstown, OH 44515; www.missionoflove.org; Amission oflove@sbcglobal.net).

Mission of Love (MOL) is a nonprofit humanitarian relief organization, tax-exempt since 1995, that supports indigenous efforts on a grassroots level. MOL responds to needs identified as important by indigenous peoples involving education, health, homes, and other programs. It supports initiatives for medical and educational facilities, nutritional programs, and child survival programs.

Volunteer your vacation time on a trip to the Pine Ridge Reservation, located in the southwest corner of South Dakota and into North Dakota, near the Nebraska border, and home to the Oglala Lakota. With an estimated population of 40,000, its needs are immense. It is the eighth-largest reservation in the U.S., and most of its land lies within two of the poorest counties. Unemployment is high, and about half the population lives below the federal poverty level. Residents have one of the shortest life expectancies of any group in the Western hemisphere, and the infant mortality rate is five times the national average.

Donate your time and skills to assist with the building of homes, schools, and other much-needed facilities. Along with helping to rebuild the community and improve living conditions, you will learn about the history of indigenous peoples and experience their culture and traditions.

Marta's Building Story

When Kathy Price first told me about Pine Ridge Reservation, she described it as America's own third-world country, with the lowest per-capita income in the United States. I remember hearing the story that

President Clinton was shocked when he toured the reservation. There are many disparities between life on the reservation and the rest of America. Unemployment far exceeds that in other communities, and the eye-opening, shocking poverty is horrible, with people living in burned-out shells of trailers. The prices in the stores are astronomically high compared to groceries off the reservation, but the people have no transportation to shop elsewhere. They've had many struggles, and I knew, as a volunteer, I had to deal with these issues too while I was there.

For over a hundred years, the Lakota people have had a lot of tragedy, poverty, and a great deal of need. Our mission was to help create a traditional building that would be a central place where children and elders could gather to share meals and learn about their own culture. The reservation had contacted Mission of Love with their request, and Kathy Price went to the reservation to speak with the elders. The elders and young people in the community joined together with the MOL volunteers building something the people felt was most important to accomplish. We worked and ate together, shared, and learned about the culture of the Lakota Indians in a true bonding experience.

About 25 volunteers arrived from all over the country. What's really amazing is you never know who is going to come, but somehow there's all the right talent to get the work done. I put varnish on things and helped build windows, tasks I had never done in normal life. The volunteers do what they need to do and somehow magic happens.

We paid for our transportation and motel, and purchased food together to keep expenses down. The workweek was very long—five days with two days off for sightseeing and cultural activities. I worked really hard from early in the morning until late at night, but the days off were very relaxing and enjoyable. I've participated in six missions, and they are transformational. I go to help contribute to the well-being of women, children, and families and have returned a changed person from every trip. I have become an advocate, and feel a sense of responsibility toward helping them. I leave feeling so much love and appreciation for how others deal with struggles and how blessed I really am.

Leonard Little Finger's Dream, Pine Ridge Reservation, SD

Lakota Circle Village, Inc. (P.O. Box 47, Oglala, SD 57764; 605-867-5626; www.lakotacirclevillage.org; leonard@lakotacirclevillage.org).

I encourage people to come here to spend time learning about my culture, spirituality, history, and language. I'm a retired healthcare administrator in Indian health services. My dream is to build a school and community center to educate our future generations in the Lakota language.

Kathy Price has been involved in building homes on Pine Ridge Reservation with volunteer workers. I told her this is what I want to do, and she said, "I will help you." She set a date and arrived with three semi-loads of building materials, said a little prayer, and they started from the ground, laying cement to build the foundation. Five days later we had a building up: the shell, the walls, roof, ceiling, windows, and doors. The local people were amazed at how a building of this size, 80 feet long by 60 feet wide, could go up in five days.

It's a domino effect, with local people seeing what could be done and working with Kathy on other projects, donating their time here too. Groups have since returned to complete the flooring, wiring, and painting. Kathy has the ability to root out materials, supplies, discounts, and donations.

We've received discounted kitchen appliances, discontinued flooring, and a solid cherry wood conference table and chairs from a synagogue in Ohio. It's been a cooperative effort. Kathy is willing to go places where no one else is looking to help.

Restoring and Preserving Historic Buildings, Cairo, IL; Virginia City, MT; and Other Locations: Heritage Conservation Network (1557 North St., Boulder, CO 80304; 303-444-0128; fax 303-444-0128; www.heritage conservation.net; info@heritageconservation.net; program costs range from $450 to $1,200 per week depending on location and amenities; local residents may attend at very low or no cost). Historic preservation saves architectural heritage and preserves the important role these buildings still play in their communities. Heritage Conservation Network (HCN), a nonprofit organization tax-exempt since 2002, supports community-driven projects by bringing professionals, volunteers, and community members together in a hands-on workshop to provide expertise and labor at little cost.

The process begins with a request for assistance from a community. HCN helps figure out what needs to be done, the skills involved, and recruits people to bring the project to completion. Volunteer workshop participants pay a fee that covers accommodations and some meals, field trips, instruction, and insurance. HCN seeks grants and corporate funding to pay for materials and for a building-conservation specialist who teaches and guides volunteers as they work at each historic site.

Lodging is usually at a bed-and-breakfast or a small local hotel. You will learn new skills and gain hands-on experience using them, participate in field trips, and take home a sense of satisfaction that will stay with you forever. No building experience is necessary and there are tasks for all levels.

Each one- or two-week adventure begins with a get-together to meet fellow volunteers, a site orientation, and description of the project. Techniques will be demonstrated before you begin work each day, and you may choose activities depending on your interests and experience. There will be a half- or full-day excursion to local historic sites, and if you choose a two-week adventure, the weekend is free for sightseeing.

Cairo, Illinois
Help rehabilitate abandoned shotgun-style houses in Cairo, Illinois, to provide quality affordable housing in an economically depressed region. HCN is partnering with Southern Illinois University and local residents in this historic city, an important steamboat port in the 19th century that was strategically valuable during the Civil War, with wonderful examples of 19th- and early 20th-century architecture. For information about this trip, go directly to www.heritageconservation.net/ws-cairo.htm.

Virginia City, Montana
Join HCN in Virginia City, Montana, to learn advanced techniques in the conservation of log structures. You can help preserve the Susan Marr House, a 19th-century vernacular wood-frame house, in this Old West Victorian mining town located high in the Rocky Mountains.

Shotgun-style house, Cairo, Illinois

Main Street USA needed major repairs in Virginia City, Montana.

The exterior of the Ellendale Opera House

Ellendale, North Dakota

Future workshops will include the opportunity to restore the Ellendale Opera House, listed as one of the most endangered historic properties in North Dakota. Built in 1908, it was the largest opera house between Minneapolis and Seattle, with traveling performers who attracted audiences from surrounding areas.

Santa Monica, California

You can help save the sole surviving shotgun-style structure in Santa Monica, California. This type of building housed the city's working class and this one remaining example has been placed in storage, awaiting a new life in its new location as a preservation resource center.

Participants in all HCN workshops are as enthusiastic about the people they meet and work with as they are about the project and the skills learned. Team effort, cooperation, and seeing a project through from beginning to end are highlights of each adventure.

HERITAGE CONSERVATION NETWORK

The balcony collapsed into the Ellendale Opera House, Ellendale, North Dakota.

The Perfect Match

Volunteer Match: Where Volunteering Begins (717 California St., 2nd Fl., San Francisco, CA 94108; 415-241-6868; www.VolunteerMatch.org; support@volunteermatch.org). A great way to contribute time and energy when visiting a new place is to use an online service such as Volunteer Match. They match hundreds of nonprofit programs with thousands of people looking to help, and you can review their online lists for potential ideas.

Volunteer Match is dedicated to helping everyone find a great place to volunteer. All you need to do is visit the search page and enter a city or zip code. Find an opportunity that interests you and click on the title for more information, and then click on "I want to help." After you register as a Volunteer Match member, an automatic message will be sent to the organization notifying them of your interest.

Preserving Affordable Housing, Multiple Locations Across the County: Rebuilding Together (National Headquarters, 1536 16th St. N.W., Washington, DC 20036; 1-800-473-4229; fax 202-483-9081; www.rebuildingtogether.org). Rebuilding Together, a non-profit organization established in 1988, has a network of affiliates across the country whose mission is to preserve affordable housing for low-income homeowners. These projects bring volunteers and the community together to rehabilitate existing housing so that the elderly, the disabled (including returning veterans), families with children, and those directly affected by natural disasters will be able to return to and stay in their own homes. With the rising costs of living and diminishing availability of services, safe and affordable housing is out of the reach of those who need it most. There is no charge to the low-income homeowners.

Each year in April, Rebuilding Together sponsors a National Rebuilding Day. After a year of planning, a nationwide group of volunteers repairs and restores houses and nonprofit facilities.

In addition to this major event, the organization's affiliates work together to offer emergency services and promote green building values in order to conserve energy and reduce consumption. It is involved in disaster recovery and reconstruction (one goal is rebuilding one thousand homes on the Gulf Coast) and meeting the needs of veterans from present and past wars.

Volunteer to help rehabilitate homes by contacting an affiliate in your area or one that you will be visiting. There is an easy search feature on the organization's home page that allows you to choose by state, and an interactive map of the country shows the affiliates grouped by region. Once you decide where you want to volunteer, or choose a destination close to where you will be on an already planned vacation, contact the affiliate organization to inquire about ongoing or upcoming projects.

Rebuilding Together is the largest volunteer home-rehabilitation organization in the nation. It is supported by private industry, donations, and volunteers, has 232 affiliates in 46 states, and assists in over 1,800 communities.

Sandy's Family Story, El Paso, TX

My husband and I wanted very much to teach our children about giving to others in ways that they could understand. We felt it was very important to help them develop a sense of philanthropy through doing simple things that they could build on as they got older. When the girls were very young, we filled recycled toilet paper rolls with prizes they had received and collected from local restaurants and arcades, along with assorted candies wrapped up as festive little gifts, and delivered them to children in the hospital.

Now that they are ages 11 and 14, they initiate different projects themselves. When we go camping, we clean up things that animals shouldn't eat. When we travel, we look for ways to become involved or learn something special about the community. Small acts of charity are not only financial; they begin with compassion, time, spirit, awareness, attention, and taking action.

Community Theater, Honolulu, HI: Institute for Cultural Ecology (P.O. Box 991, Hilo, HI 96721; 808-557-1743; fax 866-252-8060; www.cultural-ecology.com; ecology@mail.com; 4 weeks, $1,895; 6 weeks, $2,600; 8 weeks, $2,970; 12 weeks, $3,850). An Institute for Cultural Ecology (I.C.E.) internship is a perfect gap year volunteer project, or opportunity, as a student, to earn academic credit. It is also a great way to explore a new career option, or for retirees who want to get involved and learn new skills.

Before your internship, you will receive a guidebook and be assigned a contact person who will help you prepare for your experience. That person will brief you on your location, pick you up at the airport upon your arrival in Hawaii, help you plan your immersion experience with things to do and see, and check in with you twice a week.

The Hawaii Performing Arts Company has staged continuous, year-round productions since 1969. The 150-seat theater hosts a variety of performances from recent Broadway, Off-Broadway, and regional theater productions. Volunteers interested in learning about the various aspects of theater and becoming involved in management, organization, creative direction, and design will be assigned work according to their interests and skills. Past intern projects have included assisting the technical director, constructing sets, and helping with costume design and stage props.

The theater is a short bus ride away from intern accommodations at the East-West Center dormitory at the University of Hawaii at Manoa and 20 minutes from downtown Honolulu. Placements are available year-round but need to coincide with the production schedule. Interns are expected to contribute a minimum of 25–30 hours a week to the theater. The program cost includes internship set-up, housing, contact person, airport pickup, and guidebook. You are responsible for airfare, food, and island transportation. The application form is available on the I.C.E. Web site, and needs to be accompanied by a résumé or acceptable equivalent.

Youth and Community Support, Dupree, SD: Cheyenne River Reservation Sioux YMCA (General Convention of Sioux YMCAs, P.O. Box 218, B St., Dupree, SD 57623; 605-365-5232; fax 605-365-5230; siouxymca.org; crandall@

siouxymca.org). The General Convention of Sioux YMCAs offers youth, recreational, and camping programs to youth and families living in small villages spread over the 4,500-square-mile Cheyenne River Sioux Reservation. Based in a log cabin in Dupree, the Sioux YMCA has outreach programs and community camps in several of the villages served.

Volunteer at the Sioux YMCA between September and May, with a six- to eight-week commitment. You need to be age 19 or older, able to lift 35 pounds, have a valid driver's license and a good driving record, and agree to a tobacco-, alcohol-, and drug-free lifestyle during your service period. A written application and an interview are required. Special summer positions may be arranged.

Program areas include teen leadership, entrepreneurship, health, fitness, and learning/education support. The Lakota Achievers Program stresses staying in school, advanced education, career options, and decision-making, and includes trips on and off the reservation. Healthy Steps promotes wellness for youth and adults and stresses physical and mental heath. You might help participants keep a record of their progress, offer nutritional cooking classes, lead physical activities, and reinforce efforts to live a healthy lifestyle.

The Arts and Crafts Program sells hand-made jewelry and crafts and sponsors art camp and classes in beadwork, sewing, and entrepreneurship. There is also a photography project, an after-school program, and sports clinics. The YMCA works with tribal organizations including Youth Diabetes Prevention, Four Bands Community Fund, Tribal Ventures, local schools and churches, community centers, and community health representatives.

Volunteers share a three-bedroom, one-bathroom house with heat, air-conditioning, and a DSL line. Most cell phones do not work in the area, and a calling card is necessary for long-distance phone service. The house is within walking distance of a grocery store, post office, and laundry.

You will have the opportunity to learn about a different way of life, and that each Native People has its own history, traditions, culture, and current-day issues. Visit and/or volunteer at cultural events such as powwows and explore your surroundings; the Black Hills, Bear Butte, Devil's Tower, and the Badlands are within driving distance.

Educating Future Generations

Amizade offers Global Service-Learning courses in partnership with West Virginia University (www.amizade.org/service_learning/courses/index.html; volunteer@amizade.org; college credits and prices vary). Experiences focus on the complexities of interactions when visiting, working, and living with a cultural group different from one's own. Class offerings differ from year to year; one recent course was "Journey with Indigenous Cultures: Psychological Issues and Self Awareness" in Crownpoint, New Mexico, Navajo Nation. Another program, "Social Documentary and Civil Rights," a two-week summer course in Alabama, Georgia, and Pennsylvania, introduces students to key aspects of the U.S. civil rights movement and the role community organizers have played in the movement. On the Web site, click on "Find a Course" to see the complete list of programs currently offered, with specific information about each.

Service Projects, Juneau, AK: Wilderness Ventures (P.O. Box 2768, Jackson, WY 83001; 1-800-533-2281; 307-733-2122; fax 307-739-1934; www.wilder nessventures.com; info@wildernessventures.com; 3-week trip for teens, 9th–12th grades; tuition, $4,090). Teens are grouped by age and will earn 50–65 community-service hours while experiencing a fabulous summer volunteer vacation. Service projects vary from year to year and have included volunteering at a local tribal house, building trails, restoring native totem poles and a historic carousel, and constructing fencing.

Orientation takes place in Juneau, followed by your first volunteer experience at a salmon hatchery, learning about the fish that is so important to the Alaskan people and economy. Included in the trip will be a hike near the Mendenhall glacier, rafting the Mendenhall River and the Yukon's Blanchard River, and hiking and working on scenic trails in Alaska state parks.

Learning about the history and culture of the places you visit is an important part of the experience. You meet and work with the locals on community projects. No experience is required, and trip leaders will teach you about wilderness travel: minimum-impact camping, backcountry cooking, and navigation skills. A passport is needed to cross the Canadian border to raft the Blanchard River. Trip dates, online application, map, frequently asked questions, a day-to-day itinerary, a list of what to bring, and a trip journal are all available online.

Alejandro's Story, New York City, NY

I started volunteering in the second grade. The teacher asked who could stay after school to help change over the bulletin boards. I loved school and I enjoyed staying later and longer to help out. In the third grade I started visiting senior centers with my grandmother and her dog, Duncan. They had been trained as a therapy team and visited people who needed to talk and who enjoyed petting the dog. I talked to people while they were waiting for a turn with Duncan. That led to my visiting the center on my own to read out loud to small groups and my tutoring people in English whose first language, like mine, is Spanish. That led to my reading and writing letters for others who couldn't express

themselves in English. Now that I'm in high school, I
volunteer wherever I can as much as I can, for biking
events and fundraisers. I was so excited when I found
out that I can reach beyond my neighborhood and visit
places all over the United States doing what I love to
do—it's called volunteer vacations.

**Service Projects, NM, AZ, and CO: Wilderness
Ventures** (P.O. Box 2768, Jackson, WY 83001;
1-800-533-2281; 307-733-2122; fax 307-739-1934; www
.wildernessventures.com; info@wildernessventures.com;
16-day trip for teens, 9th–12th grades; tuition, $3,190).
Earn 60 hours of community service by volunteering at a
local elementary Navajo immersion school, help restore
a traditional sweat lodge, renovate a Navajo house, and
assist a local medicine woman. Learn about the customs
and traditions of the Native Americans, visit their pueblos,
and work on a Navajo farm.

This volunteer vacation will begin in Albuquerque, New
Mexico, where you will meet the other trip members, learn
how to set up your tents, and make dinner at the campsite
before heading to Fort Defiance, Arizona, the next morning.
Over the next several days you will work on various projects and get to know the Navajo community.

After traveling through the Navajo Reservation you
will head to Lake Powell, hike Horseshoe Bend on the
Colorado River, and be introduced to canyoneering by
experienced guides. After you explore the Slot Canyons,
there will be trips to Monument Valley, the Painted Desert,
and Anasazi ruins.

In Canyon de Chelly you will work on a local farm repairing fences, planting crops, and helping construct shade
huts. During your time off you can explore the cliff houses
and spend your evenings around the campfire. After your
work is completed you will head to Durango, Colorado, to
enjoy a day of white-water rafting on the Animas River,

E. BLAU

Create your own volunteer opportunities. Reading to children in the Taos, New Mexico, Head Start program is a great way to give back while on vacation.

through the Smelter, Sawmill, Santa Rita, and Pinball rapids, followed by the final banquet in historic Santa Fe. Certificates of Service will be awarded. Contact Wilderness Adventures for trip dates, maps, frequently asked questions, a packing list, trip journal, and application.

Summer Theater, Danville, KY: Pioneer Playhouse (Holly Henson, Artistic Director; Pioneer Playhouse, 840 Stanford Rd., Danville, KY 40422; 859-236-2747; www.pioneerplayhouse.com; pioneer@mis.net). The Pioneer Playhouse, founded in 1950, is the oldest outdoor theater in Kentucky. The hand-built theater serves a pre-dinner show outdoors and has live performances Tuesday through Saturday every summer. The Playhouse needs volunteers for 12 weeks from early June through mid-August, but shorter stays are negotiable. Individuals, couples, or groups can help with ushering, costumes, concessions, and backstage work.

Volunteers live on the property in cabins, or if you own a motor home, without charge in the adjacent campground. You will have your own room, bathrooms are com-

The Pioneer Playhouse, founded in 1950, is the oldest outdoor theater in Kentucky.

PIONEER PLAYHOUSE ARCHIVES

From the main stage of the Pioneer Playhouse, the manager presents a review of what's to come.

munal, and meals are provided except on Sundays. You need to be available to work four hours a day, with Sundays and Mondays off.

There are five plays staged in 10 weeks, so there is plenty of work and you will gain a lot of theater experience in addition to meeting and living with new people and donating your time and skills to a nonprofit organization with a limited budget and staff. Volunteers are considered part of the resident summer company, enjoying the "theater family" experience that develops over the course of the summer.

Danville is a 45-minute drive from Lexington and a two-hour drive from both Louisville and Cincinnati. The current play schedule, travel directions, history of the theater, and press can be found on the Pioneer Playhouse Web site. For information about the area, contact the Danville–Boyle County Convention & Visitors Bureau at 1-800-755-0076 or www.danville-ky.com.

Donna's Story, Pioneer Playhouse, Danville, KY

I met Colonel Hensen, founder of Pioneer Playhouse, when he was riding on his bike. We had a nice conversation, and I told him about my years volunteering as a campground host in Alaska. Hensen said to me, "Forget about Alaska and come here and volunteer with us." I decided I liked the Danville area; I have a very good friend there and drive down in my motor home every year arriving May 22 and leaving August 20 to go back to Arizona.

An aerial view of the Pioneer Playhouse in Danville, Kentucky.

PIONEER PLAYHOUSE ARCHIVES

When I started volunteering here five years ago, I cleaned the living areas for the actors and actresses, did laundry and ironing, and put flyers and posters up around town. I became good friends with the wardrobe mistress and found my place mending, doing alterations, and making sure those clothes fit. I love getting to know all of the people and having the satisfaction of seeing them look really good onstage and knowing I had something to do with that. I'm 76 and plan to be back next year.

Pioneer Playhouse stars from the past and the present.

PIONEER PLAYHOUSE ARCHIVES

Ⓢ Post-Hurricane Rebuilding, LA, MS: Relief Spark

(P.O. Box 10562, Jefferson, LA 70181; 504-377-7854; fax 1-866-415-9218; www.reliefspark.org; volunteer@relief spark.org). Relief Spark is a community-based, nonprofit organization that provides disaster relief for people and pets. Teams from Relief Spark have been working with volunteers since September 2005, helping families who lost homes in the flooding of Louisiana and Mississippi.

Volunteers rotate to a variety of jobs according to experience and skills. Housing is in the Uptown district of New Orleans, within walking distance of a grocery store, shops, and restaurants. Meals are southern style. Relief Spark can house 100 volunteers per week and introduce you to people from all over the country. Saturday is Arts and Culture Day and often includes trips to the zoo, aquarium, parks and playgrounds, festivals, movies, theater, museums, and art performances.

You may choose to work with any of the organizations in Relief Spark's network, including Animal Rescue and Care, Environmentally Safe Lawn Care, House Gutting, Rebuilding, Neighborhood Service, and Tutoring. There is a registration form on the Relief Spark Web site, and one of Relief Spark's coordinators will contact you within 24–36 hours.

Immersion Excursion: Breaux Bridge Crawfish Festival
(P.O. Box 25, Breaux Bridge, LA 70517; 337-332-6655; fax 337-332-5917; www.bbcrawfest.com; entry fees vary). Celebrate in the crawfish capital of the world by attending the annual Breaux Bridge Crawfish Festival held annually in May. Since 1960, the festival has offered hungry visitors the best of Louisiana cuisine along with authentic Cajun, Zydeco, and Swamp Pop music. More than 30 bands perform during the three-day event, which also includes dance contests, music workshops, cooking, accordion-making demonstrations, and, of course, crawfish. Enjoy crawfish

prepared every imaginable way: boiled or fried, in pie, jam-balaya, boudin, bisque, étouffée, and crawdogs. Satisfy your Cajun cravings with shrimp, crab, gumbo, red beans and rice, and other favorites. Root for your favorite in the crawfish race, shop for handcrafted and novelty items, enjoy midway rides and games, and watch the parade honoring the Crawfish Queen, King, Junior Royalty, and Ecrevettes. If you have the stomach for it, enter the crawfish-eating contest. The volunteer Breaux Bridge Crawfish Festival Association (BBCFA) oversees the festival, named one of the top 10 food festivals by *USA Today,* and promotes the crawfish industry and Cajun culture. The BBCFA has contributed over $300,000 to civic organizations and city improvements, including scholarships and grants to local schools.

Janeen's Story on Volunteering at a Food Festival, New Bern, NC

> Volunteering is great fun and very rewarding; however, I tell newbies to be prepared for a fiasco. Something always goes wrong—the food doesn't arrive, and it rains during dry season so there isn't a tent, But it's also wonderful that you bring together a bunch of strangers and everyone knows what to do and everything just kind of falls in place and works out amazingly well. Now that's a great achievement.

Strengthen Communities, Regional Centers in CO, CA, MD, IA: AmeriCorps NCCC (1201 New York Ave., NW, Washington, DC 20525; 202-606-5000; www.ameri corps.org; questions@americorps.org). AmeriCorps NCCC (National Civilian Community Corps) is a full-time residential program for men and women ages 18–24, and would be a perfect gap year opportunity to volunteer in a national service program. Volunteers are based at one of four campuses: Denver, Colorado; Sacramento, California; Perry Point, Maryland; and Vinton, Iowa.

AmeriCorps NCCC team members work to strengthen communities and develop leaders through community service, in partnership with nonprofit and community organizations and state and local agencies. A 10-month commitment is required to be a member of a 10- to 12-person team assigned to projects in the region served by your campus. Training in CPR, first aid, public safety, and other skills is included.

You may work with community organizations both faith-based and secular, national nonprofits, schools, cities and towns, national and state parks, and Native American tribes. Projects last from six to eight weeks and may include tutoring students, constructing and renovating low-income housing, responding to natural disasters, cleaning up streams, and helping develop emergency plans.

Upon completion of your service you are eligible for an AmeriCorps Education Award of $4,725, which can be used to pay for higher education, educational training, or to repay qualified student loans. You have seven years after service to claim your award.

Fight Poverty Nationwide: AmeriCorps VISTA

(Volunteers in Service to America, 1201 New York Ave., NW, Washington, DC 20525; 1-800-942-2677; 202-606-5000; www.americorps.org; questions@americorps.org). AmeriCorps VISTA is a national service program that has been fighting poverty for more than 40 years. In 1963 President John F. Kennedy suggested creating a national service corps to address the needs of both rural and urban poverty areas. Two years later President Lyndon Johnson declared "War on Poverty" and welcomed the first group of 20 VISTA volunteers.

By the end of the first year there were more than 2,000 members working in the Appalachian region,

Summer Service

NCCC Summer of Service is a residential program open to youth, ages 14–17, living near Denver, Colorado; New Orleans, Louisiana; and Sacramento, California. Volunteers serve alongside and under the supervision of year-round AmeriCorps members. For more information call 202-606-7514.

migrant worker camps in California, and in the poorest neighborhoods in Hartford, Connecticut. Today VISTA has 6,500 members who serve in 1,200 projects nationwide. There are 37 million Americans who live in poverty.

VISTA members do not provide direct services. As a VISTA worker you will help build the organizational, administrative, and financial support that is necessary to fight poverty, improve health services, encourage economic development, and assist low-income communities. Projects include creating an illiteracy awareness campaign, recruiting mentors and tutors, coordinating transitional housing, organizing shelter and job opportunities, and setting up programs to help people obtain affordable health insurance.

Only in New York

What better way to get to know a community than to visit it with people who live there? **Big Apple Greeter** (visitor information, visitrequest@bigapplegreeter.org; 212-669-8159; volunteer contact, volunteerdepartment@bigapplegreeter.org; 212-669-7308) is made up of more than 300 New Yorkers from all walks of life and offering diverse skills and languages who serve as volunteer guides to the city they live in, know, and love. Tours are offered daily, between 9 AM and 3 PM, in any of the five boroughs, beginning in Manhattan, and using public transportation.

This is a great opportunity for recent college graduates to gain career skills, or for experienced adults, including retirees, to apply their skills and knowledge to new challenges while gaining the satisfaction of helping those most in need. During your year of service you will receive a small living allowance, healthcare, and other benefits. Upon completion of your commitment you will receive an education award worth $4,725, or $1,200 in cash.

Youth Immersion Building Homes, Multiple Locations Across the Country: Habitat for Humanity (121 Habitat St., Americus, GA 31709; 1-800-422-4828; www.habitat.org; publicinfo@habitat.org; Youth Immersion information, 1-800-HABITAT, ext. 7552 or yi@habitat.org; 1-week Youth Immersion for ages 16–25, $500). Habitat for Humanity, a nonprofit, ecumenical Christian housing ministry founded in 1976, is dedicated to providing decent, affordable homes for those in need. Habitat builds and rehabilitates homes with the help of partner families, then sells the homes to those families at no profit and financed by low-cost loans. The monthly mortgage payments are used to build more homes.

The Youth Immersion program provides a one-week experience for volunteers between the ages of 16 and 25. Participants partner with local affiliates to help build homes and learn about social issues, substandard housing, diversity, civic leadership, and the causes and consequences of poverty. Accommodations may include local churches or volunteer houses, arranged by the local affiliate.

You do not need any building experience and will be provided with a safety briefing, tools, and supervision. The program fee covers meals, lodging, activities, transportation, and medical insurance for the week of your trip, and an affiliate donation. Transportation to and from the project site is not included in the program fee. There are scholarships available for qualified applicants.

Gulf Coast Recovery Effort, AL, LA, MS, TX: Habitat for Humanity (121 Habitat St., Americus, GA 31709; 1-800-422-4828; www.habitat.org; publicinfo@habitat.org). Help is still needed in the areas affected by Hurricanes Katrina and Rita and other natural disasters. The best way to volunteer is to contact one of the local Habitat affiliates working along the Gulf Coast. You will find a list of current volunteer activities in Alabama, Louisiana, Mississippi, and Texas on the Web site and contact information for the coordinating affiliate.

Accommodations range from modified Habitat homes, local churches, or other similar lodging arranged by the affiliate for a nominal fee and/or donation, to camps with dormitory-style housing, RV parks, and nearby motels that offer discounts to volunteers. Some facilities provide two or more meals a day.

Habitat for Humanity's hurricane-response program helps low-income families affected by Hurricanes Katrina and Rita build affordable, permanent housing. Construction of the first house began just six weeks after Hurricane Katrina devastated the area. To date, more than 1,300 homes have been built or are under construction. Before the hurricanes, 57 Habitat homes were constructed each year in the region—since the storms, 52 homes per month have begun construction. One thousand volunteers are needed each week.

The time commitment varies, with volunteers usually arriving on Sunday or Monday and working either Monday to Friday or Tuesday through Saturday. In New Orleans, it is possible for your teenaged children to join you; ages 14–15 can participate in non-construction-related activities, and ages 16–17 can help at the build site but are not permitted to use power tools or work at heights above 12 feet. All youth must be accompanied by a parent or have adult supervision.

Habitat for Humanity of the Mississippi Gulf Coast (228-314-0011; www.hfhmgc.org; volunteer@hfhmgc.org) in

Biloxi provides accommodations in Habitat Village, a former high-school football stadium owned by the Salvation Army. There are four bunkhouses and a lounge area with computers, wireless Internet, a dining area for volunteers, TV, pool table, games, and art supplies. The bunkhouses have bunk beds, bathrooms and showers, heat, and air-conditioning. Three meals a day are provided Tuesday through Friday, as well as dinner Monday night following orientation. There is a $100 registration fee.

Amy's Story, New Orleans, LA, and Cedar Rapids, IA

A Do-It-Yourself Volunteer Vacation

After our house flooded during Hurricane Katrina, a volunteer group from Pennsylvania appeared on our front porch. They had driven 25 hours in their church van, knocked on our door, and said, "How can we help you?" I was inspired by that and wanted to return the kindness to others in New Orleans. I asked friends and neighbors if they wanted to get involved. We became an official group of concerned citizens providing meals for those in need.

When I heard about the flooding in Cedar Rapids, I posted a message on www.corridorrecovery.org/VolunteerSignup.asp:

CEDAR RAPIDS: Cooking, Serving Meals, Supplies
ADDRESS: Cedar Rapids Area
TYPE OF WORK: Light Duty

We are a group of volunteers from New Orleans planning to travel July 31–August 4. We need help August 1–4 cooking, cleaning, and serving meals to needy families. We also welcome any food supplies, cups, napkins, drinks etc. Lastly we need lodging for volunteers. We will serve 1,500 meals during that time.

CONTACT INFO: Amy
EMAIL: neworleanscooks@yahoo.com
www.corridorrecovery.org/VolunteerSignup.asp

People donated food, supplies, gas, gift cards, and
housing; it was amazing. We ended up with 15 people
with New Orleans connections and 220 volunteers in
Cedar Rapids. We served 1,500 meals and delivered an
additional 1,500 meals. We made the whole thing happen in three weeks and raised enough money to adopt
a family, giving them $2,500 to fix their home, and
another $1,000 in gift cards were handed out. People
who were supposed to be away on vacation changed
their plans to work with us. You don't have to be an
official nonprofit to go out and do good things.

Tourism and Recreation, Medora, ND: Theodore Roosevelt Medora Foundation (P.O. Box 198, 301 5th St., Medora, ND 58645; 1-800-633-6721; 701-623-4444; fax 701-623-4494; volunteer coordinator, 701-223-4800; www.medora.com; volunteer@medora.com). Take your volunteer vacation at North Dakota's number-one vacation destination. Home to Theodore Roosevelt National Park, Medora has a lot to offer, including theater, a heritage center, museums, horseback riding in the Badlands, biking, hiking, and other recreational opportunities. The Theodore Roosevelt Medora Foundation (TRMF) is a public nonprofit organization (since 1987) that operates lodging, entertainment, recreation, and services in the Badlands.

TRMF has three different volunteer categories, with pre-season volunteer opportunities in May, in-season opportunities from May to September, and end-of-season opportunities from August to September. Over 300 volunteers work with a full-time staff and seasonal employees. In the spring you can help with cleanup, preparing the grounds

and the facilities for the influx of visitors. During high season you can work in a variety of locations including the
Information Center, Chuckwagon Buffet, Harold Schafer
Visitor Center, Pitchfork Fondue—where steaks are skewered
on sticks and cooked over a campfire—and the Medora
Musical in the Burning Hills Amphitheater. The end-of-the-
season volunteers step in after college workers head back to
school, replacing them in a variety of jobs including retail,
grounds, maintenance, and catering.

Contact TRMF for current start and end dates. There is
no cost to volunteers, and TRMF considers room and board
their gift to the volunteers that share their time with them.

The Conservationist President

Theodore Roosevelt first visited the Dakota Territory in 1883, when he was just 24
years old. He had come to hunt bison, but the herds that once thrived there were
largely gone, hunted or killed by disease. When he learned more about the endangered wildlife and habitats, he grew more and more concerned with conservation,
and as president he established the first 51 bird reserves, four game preserves, 150
National Forests, and the National Forest Service. He also signed into law legislation
creating five National Parks and 18 National Monuments. The 26th president of the
United States, he is thought of as the "Conservationist President." The Theodore
Roosevelt National Park in North Dakota memorializes his contributions to the
preservation of our country's natural resources.

Sheryl's Story, Theodore Roosevelt National Park, Medora, ND

I arrived at the Theodore Roosevelt National Park at
twilight. The Visitors Center was closed and I thought I
was alone as I looked out over the magnificent view
and wondered where I'd have dinner and if I'd find a

place to stay nearby. At first I thought the sound I
heard was the wind until I realized, no, there was a dis-
tinct chewing sound, along with a brushing back and
forth, followed by heavy breathing. An American bison
ate his dinner within a few feet of me. What I thought
was a garbage bin or perhaps a storage shed was a living, breathing animal—enormous, strong, and imposing.
I didn't move; he didn't stop eating. I enjoyed his pres-
ence so close by, the angle of his neck as he grazed,
the bend in his legs, the strength in his shoulders, and
the scritch-scratch of his mane against a log fence. It
was one of those times I wished I'd had my camera
handy, but it was more important to relax, reflect, and
enjoy the moment.

**Building and Renovation, Rock Point Navajo Nation,
AZ: Global Citizens Network** (130 North Howell St., St.
Paul, MN 55104; 1-800-644-9292; 651-644-0960; fax 651-
646-6176; www.globalcitizens.org; info@globalcitizens.org;
8-day trip, $975). Global Citizens Network (GCN) is a non-
profit organization, tax-exempt since 1992, that provides
opportunities for volunteers to interact in communities in
the United States and around the world with the purpose of
developing local solutions to global problems.

For this trip, volunteers arrive in Albuquerque and
travel together to Rock Point to meet community members
and participate in community events. GCN projects in Rock
Point include renovation, painting, and constructing patios
and fences and take place Monday through Thursday;
Friday may be a day off to explore the area. Accommodations are in the Chapter House, where you sleep on the
floor in the community room; you may bring an air mat-
tress or sleeping bag or pad. There is a kitchen and a bathroom on site, and meals are prepared together and shared,
often with community members.

Clare and Jake hold a baby goat at a livestock farm they visited on the Navajo Nation reservation.

There will be opportunities to explore the nearby sights at Canyon de Chelly and Monument Valley, get to know the host community, and enjoy the activities the locals enjoy— horseback riding, rodeos, hiking, and sporting events. Many volunteers choose to extend their stays in Arizona and New Mexico either before or after their volunteer commitment.

The Navajo Nation is located on 25,000 square miles in New Mexico, Arizona, and Utah. Rock Point, with a population of about 2,600 (and unemployment at 60 to 70 percent) is in the Four Corners region of Arizona, about a five-hour drive from Albuquerque, New Mexico. There is a Chapter House (the seat of the local government), the Rock Point

Community School, a gas station/convenience store, a post office, laundromat, senior center, and three churches.

The program cost includes on-site accommodations and meals, roundtrip transportation between Albuquerque and Rock Point, training materials, T-shirt, a portion of the team leader's expenses, and a donation to the project. Airfare and costs of activities off-site are additional. Ask about discounts for returning participants and early sign-up for the trip. All trip-related fees are tax deductible. Children ages 8–15 and groups are welcome on this trip.

Building a Community, Preserving a Heritage, La Push, WA: Global Citizens Network (130 North Howell St., St. Paul, MN 55104; 1-800-644-9292; 651-644-0960; fax 651-646-6176; www.globalcitizens.org; info@globalcitizens .org; 8-day trip, $975). Be part of a volunteer team in La Push, on the Pacific coast of the Olympic Peninsula,

Clare, age 11, learns about medicinal plants while on a walk with a Navajo Nation elder.

about four and a half hours from Seattle, Washington. La Push is the home of the Quileute Tribe (www.quileutenation.org) who for centuries fished and hunted sea mammals. Their unique language, with clicked sounds and epiglottal stops, is one of only five languages in the world without nasal sounds and one of the few languages unrelated to any other. Only a few elders still speak the Quileute language, and with the decline of the fishing industry, the Quileute Nation struggles to maintain its culture and traditions.

The Quileute Tribal Counsel and Global Citizens Network (GCN), work together with the community to preserve the Quileute heritage. Projects may include building a home for the Self Help Drumming Group, an amphitheater to showcase cultural traditions, and a museum to house tribal artifacts. Past projects have included building observation decks, clearing trails, and recording elders' stories.

Team members meet in Seattle and are transported to La Push to meet with local residents and participate in some of their events. From Monday through Thursday, volunteers work with community members on various projects, with Friday possibly free to hike along the Olympic National Park beaches, visit the hot springs, and explore your surroundings.

Volunteers stay in a community building, sleeping on the floor in one room—bring air mattresses, sleeping bag, or pad—with kitchen and bathroom facilities located on site. Some families opt to camp, and sometimes rooms are available at the tribe-owned resort. Meals are communal and often shared with community members.

Many volunteers choose to extend their stays in Washington to visit other outdoor and cultural sites. The program cost includes on-site accommodations and meals, roundtrip transportation between Seattle and La Push, training materials, a donation to the project, and a portion of the team leader's expenses. Airfare and off-site activities are additional and the participant's responsibility.

Kathy's Story, Quileute Nation, La Push, WA

Typically, during spring break, my husband, two children ages 11 and 13, and I go to Florida to see the grandmothers. This time I wanted to expose them to a different culture and people who live differently from the way we live. A spring-break family volunteer vacation sounded interesting.

It wasn't smooth sailing. My son didn't have the best attitude and didn't particularly want to work over vacation. My daughter had hoped for something more exotic, like riding on an elephant. My husband had problems with the cost. He's a very generous person who doesn't mind giving to charity, but this trip was going to cost us more than we usually spent on spring vacation.

We were part of a group. There were the four of us, another couple, two single adults who didn't know each other before, and our team leader. We felt it was so unorganized when we arrived. Nobody seemed to know why we were there. Things came together slowly, and the trip was more than memorable.

We got a lot more out of it than we gave. We worked minimally and felt we could have contributed more. People of all ages enjoyed sharing themselves and their culture with us. My daughter met a young girl who gave her a tour of her farm and hugged her like a best friend. We spent evenings talking about what to expect and our purpose for being there. We visited a school in the Navajo Nation and enjoyed learning new words in the Navajo language. The trip was a ton of cultural exchange.

Karen's Story, La Push, WA

Our trip to La Push was a good experience that pushed us out of our comfort zone. We met 14- and 16-year-olds going to Alcoholics Anonymous. We spent time with Don Black, a Native American who, along with his wife, provides food and clothing to children in need. Chris Morganrock taught us Native American sacred stories. We enjoyed a cultural evening in a hogan with Tara Chee, who shared information with us about traditional Native American ceremonies and introduced us to her uncle, a highly respected medicine man.

We met people who talked very openly about the problems they were facing. We felt like part of their community at the end of the trip, and I know I never felt like a tourist. Since that trip, I'm more sympathetic to others' hardships, more culturally tolerant, and more culturally aware.

Building and Restoration Projects, Lucky Fork, Owsley County, KY: Global Citizens Network (130 North Howell St., St. Paul, MN 55104; 1-800-644-9292; 651-644-0960; fax 651-646-6176; www.globalcitizens.org; info@globalcitizens.org; 8-day trip, $975). Owsley County, located in the Eastern Coal Field region of Kentucky, is the poorest county in the state.

GCN is working with the nonprofit Faith Hill Community Center to restore a log church, log house, and log hospital built in the 1930s in Lucky Fork, Kentucky, and to assist families in the county. You can help repair buildings and sidewalks, plant gardens, raise money for a new community center, and preserve historic landmarks, among other restoration projects.

Volunteers are also needed to help with grant writing and setting up PowerPoint presentations. Your team will meet at the airport in Lexington and travel by van to Lucky Fork to meet community members and work with them on projects from Monday through Thursday, with time Friday to explore the area.

Team members will stay at the Manse, a community building, and at the hospital, with meals prepared together at the church kitchen or outside on grills and shared with community members. There are hiking trails and swimming holes nearby, and your hosts will share their wood crafting, cooking, canning, drying, freezing, and baking skills with you.

Airfare to Kentucky is not included in the fees. Discounts are available for returning participants, early registration, children ages 8–15, and for groups. Trip expenses are tax deductible.

Two Women, One Trip, Two Experiences

Ann C.'s Story

I read an article on adventure volunteer trips, called for more information, received a brochure, and looked at the trips online. Everything sounded so good. I contacted one or two people familiar with the organization's trips but they had not been on the trip I planned to take.

What appealed to me most in the description of the trip were the words: Come meet people in the community. Visit children, teach them your skills, and then you'll learn skills back from them. A dental hygienist was in our group and she never met a child. All we saw was each other, painting and cleaning.

I signed up and flew into Lexington, Kentucky, where I was met by a driver with a van for the few hours' drive. There were 13 women in our group, including the leader and assistant. When we arrived, no one seemed to know we were coming. We had to clean the cabin we'd be living in from top to bottom. It all

seemed very disorganized, and there was clearly fric-
tion between the community and the community liai-
son over disbursement of funds.

I had signed up to work on a local project, building
a bath house, which we were under the impression was
for the community but was just for this church, and the
bath house was on the property. We laid the cinder-
blocks, wrapped wire, cemented, and painted—heavy-
duty labor. I definitely learned new skills. I know how
to insert rat wire between the logs and then cement
over it.

I met two women on the trip who will be my
friends forever. One actually lives in the same
Connecticut town I do, and the other is in Tennessee.
These are people I could relate to, who weren't afraid
to sweat, get dirty, and work hard. We joked and had a
good time.

There was only one day when we visited the local
community thrift shop to drop off the lunch boxes
and backpacks we had been asked to bring with us as
gifts for children. It was so frustrating that we had
brought food and school supplies with us from all
over the country and we were told to drop everything
off in a pile to be picked up at the end of the week
for distribution.

I went on this volunteer adventure with an open
heart; things have gone well for me and I wanted to
give back. I thought I was going to get a feeling of ful-
fillment from the experience. If anything, I felt taken.
With the airfare and additional costs, it was not inex-
pensive, and I'm not sure the money is reaching the
intended people.

I'm not saying I wouldn't do a trip like this again—I will, but first I will seek a lot of input from people who have been on the program I want to attend, and not just accept the information provided by the organization. I'd also like to speak with someone at the site I'll be visiting. We were given evaluation sheets to fill out and I told them how I felt, as did some other people. I never heard back from them.

Anne P.'s Story

The last ten years of my mother's life, she went on many volunteer trips with GCN. She traveled alone, with friends, grandchildren, or other family members. She loved every trip and every place she went. Unfortunately, I never took a trip with her. After she died, my sister and I went on the La Push, Washington, trip in honor of my mother. My sister-in-law was the group leader, and my niece came along.

The year after the La Push trip, my sister and I went to Lucky Fork, Kentucky, again with my sister-in-law. My sister and I went back to Kentucky together on three additional trips and took our mother's 90-year-old friend who used to be one of her favorite travel companions. I later went on a fourth trip to Lucky Fork myself as a group leader. My involvement all started out as a personal family thing.

When I left La Push, I wanted to go back, but I went to Kentucky. When I went to Kentucky, I wanted to go back and I did. I love the experience of a new place, and I have loved going back to a familiar place and learning more and watching how things have changed.

Many of my friends have very specific expectations for volunteer vacations, wanting to work on a specific project and feel good about what they accomplished. When I go on a volunteer vacation, I don't have big expectations, other than that I will be immersed in a community somewhat different from my own, and that I will learn things that are new and meet people I hope to connect with. I also know, because of these trips, I go to places I would not normally see on my own.

 ### Communities for People with Disabilities, PA, NY, MN, CA: Camphill in North America

(P.O. Box 221, Soquel, CA 95073; 831-476-5492; fax 831-476-0690; www.camphill.org; info@camphill.org). Volunteer at a Camphill Community and work with and get to know people with developmental and other disabilities. You can offer support in a household community; responsibilities may include cooking and sharing meals and other household tasks, working on a farm or in a garden or workshop, engaging in household and community evening activities, and organizing and celebrating community events.

Full-time volunteers are called co-workers and receive full room and board, medical insurance, a small stipend, and time off. Camphill prefers a one-year volunteer commitment, but there are seasonal opportunities in some rural, farming communities. Most volunteers have graduated from high school or have some college experience. It is a perfect gap year experience or break between college and graduate school or for a sabbatical or retirement experience.

Camphill was established in North America in 1959 and has been a tax-exempt organization since 1997. Each of the Camphill communities is different. Check out the current opportunities in each of the communities listed on their Web site. There are more than 100 Camphill communities around the world that are connected to their surrounding communities and culture.

   If you join AmeriCorps and meet eligibility require-ments, you will receive an AmeriCorps Education Award of $4,725 following one year of service.

Railroad Maintenance and Preservation, CO, NM: Friends of the Cumbres & Toltec Scenic Railroad (6005 Osuna Rd., NE, Albuquerque, NM 87109; 505-880-1311; fax 505-856-7543; www.cumbrestoltec.org; info@cumbrestoltec .org). Volunteers help maintain the structures and rolling stock of the best-preserved steam-era railroad in North America. The Cumbres & Toltec Scenic (C&TS) Railroad, built in 1880 and owned by the states of Colorado and New Mexico, covers 64 miles of the former Denver and Rio Grande narrow-gauge rail system.

FRIENDS OF THE CUMBRES & TOLTEC SCENIC RAILROAD

A volunteer with the Friends of the Cumbres & Toltec Scenic Railroad, Albuquerque, New Mexico, paints the lettering on a vintage tank car.

The railroad, designated a National Historic Site, has more than one hundred historic freight and maintenance-of-way cars. The Friends of the C&TS, a nonprofit organization tax-exempt since 1989, is the official museum support group for the railroad and provides the volunteer force to repair the historic items. The C&TS attracts visitors from around the world, and you can help enhance their experience and preserve an important piece of American history. The Society of International Railway Travelers called the C&TS one of the best 20 railway experiences in the world.

The Friends of C&TS conduct six one-week work sessions each year during the spring and summer at different locations along the railroad. Projects vary, with painting and lettering rolling stock an annual necessity. You need to be a current member of the Friends of the C&TS to volunteer. Download registration forms, sign-up instructions, skills inventory, list of planned jobs, and work and safety rules on the Web site. There is a $25 registration fee and a $30 charge for lunches for each one-week session. You are responsible for your own travel, food, and lodging, which are tax-deductible contributions. There is a complete list of accommodations on the Web site.

Immersion Excursion: Ride the Rails

The Trails and Rails Partnership Program (www.nps .gov/Trails&Rails) is a joint venture between the National Park Service and Amtrak. If you love riding the rails and connecting with people and American history, this may be the volunteer opportunity for you. Amtrak personnel join volunteer vacationers to educate train riders across the country. Lists of the growing number of participating parks on the National Park Service Web site have connecting links where you will find contact information for volunteer opportunities. Select the section of the country you'd most like to visit, or go from place to place. The Sunset Limited runs between Del Rio and Alpine, Texas, and operates from

Geotourism Defined and Explained

The Center for Sustainable Destinations (CSD) is part of the Research, Conservation, and Exploration division of National Geographic Mission Programs (1145 17th St. NW, Washington, DC 20036; 202-828-8045; www.nationalgeo-graphic.com/travel/sustainable/about_csd.html; sustourism@ngs.org). Its mission is geotourism, defined as tourism that sustains or enhances the geographical character of a place and takes into account a location's environment, culture, aesthetics, heritage, and the well-being of the people who live there. Sustainable tourism conserves resources, encourages good stewardship, and respects culture and traditions. Geotourism adds to sustainability with the emphasis on geographic character, a "sense of place" that recognizes a location's unique characteristics and intensifies the experiences of both visitors and residents.

the Amistad National Recreation Area. Or there's the Missouri Service Trails & Rails, based at the Jefferson National Expansion Memorial, which operates from St. Louis, Missouri, to Springfield, Illinois. This is true immersion travel. Different routes offer different programming, such as musical selections, or volunteer rangers dressed in living history attire educating passengers and adding to your knowledge of your destination. Railroads have been an important part of American history, and Trails and Rails continues this tradition by connecting railroads to national parks.

Western Quaker Workcamp, Pine Ridge, SD: American Friends Service Committee (2852 W. Gamez Rd., Benson, AZ 85602; 520-907-6321; www.afsc.org; project coordinator Mike Gray, 520-907-6321; mgray@afsc.org or afsc-imym-jsp@att.net; cost varies depending on the community and project). Intermountain Yearly Meeting (IMYM) of the Religious Society of Friends and three regions of the American Friends Service Committee (AFSC) started this project to provide volunteer opportunities and intercultural experiences. For over a decade, volunteers have worked with the Oglala Lakota community in North Dakota to remodel a community center and build and repair housing across the reservation.

Following Hurricanes Katrina and Rita, groups worked south of Houma, Louisiana, with the Biloxi-Chitimacha people in the bayous, repairing roofing, siding, and home interiors. Dates for specific projects were not definite at publication time, but trips tend to be planned for either spring break or summer vacation and can be customized for a group. Fees cover food, lodging, and travel by van from the closest big-city airport to the community. The American Friends Service committee is a nonprofit organization, tax-exempt since 1950.

Architecture and Ecology, Mayer, AZ: Arcosanti (HC74, P.O. Box 4136, Mayer, AZ 86333; 928-632-7135; fax 928-632-6229; workshops 928-632-6233; www.arcosanti.org; workshop@arcosanti.org; 5-week workshop, $1,350; 1- and 2-week programs and 13-week internships also available). Arcosanti, a project of the Cosanti Foundation, a nonprofit corporation since 1993, is an experimental urban laboratory 70 miles north of Phoenix, Arizona. Arcosanti focuses on ways to improve urban conditions and lessen our negative impact on the earth. Designed by Italian architect Paolo Soleri, it is an example of his concept of arcology, a fusion of architecture and ecology.

The workshops offered at Arcosanti teach the philosophy of arcology, building techniques, architecture, design, agriculture, planning, community, and more. Students of all ages and different backgrounds come from around the world to participate. The one-week program introduces the concepts of Paolo Soleri and arcology, design development, construction history, local ecology, and future plans. Tours of the site and buildings and a half-day hike through the natural area surrounding the site are also included.

Students may opt to stay for a second week, which includes a trip to Phoenix and a stay at Cosanti, Soleri's original studio, and the opportunity to engage in other work projects. The Cosanti trip includes a visit to Taliesin West, architect Frank Lloyd Wright's famous residence and offices. For those who sign up for the five-week workshop, weeks three, four, and five are the hands-on, intensive portions of the experience. Volunteers work in construction, facilities maintenance, agriculture, archives, landscaping, or other areas. Those who successfully complete the five-week workshop also have the opportunity to stay on or return to the Arcosanti community as a volunteer or employee resident, which includes housing on site.

Previous experience or knowledge of construction or architecture is not necessary. You must be 18 years or older to apply, or be accompanied by a parent or guardian. Tuition, accommodations, and meals are included in workshop fees. Financial assistance is available for some applicants. Participants are housed in dormitory-style accommodations with minimal heating and no air-conditioning. Contact the workshop coordinator for more information, and current workshop dates, or register online.

Matteo's Story, Arcosanti, Mayer, AZ

Paolo Soleri made a presentation in Milan that I found very interesting. A few months later I quit my job with a telecommunications company (my background is in international law) to see Arcosanti myself. I arrived for a five-week workshop, and like many others, decided to stay longer and longer until it became my permanent home. I spent most of the first weeks in construction, working with my hands for the first time in my life.

The main reason I am here is to be able to work side by side with fantastic people. Paolo Soleri himself, at 90, is active and involved with those who come to

create their own prototypes. Here, people way ahead
of their time can take charge of a piece of land and
develop the property to indicate a way for the rest of
the world to see hope for the future. The experience is
unique: the creation of sustainable architecture in the
high Arizona desert with beautiful landscapes in an
international community.

**Reintegration into Society after Prison, Rutland, VT:
Volunteers For Peace:** Help recently released prisoners
adjust to transitional housing and reconcile with the community before living independently. Read the complete listing in Chapter 1, "People."

**Community Projects, San Francisco and San Mateo
County, CA: The Volunteer Center** (1675 California St.,
San Francisco, CA 94109; main office, 415-982-8999; San
Mateo County, 650-235-3550; fax 415-982-0890; www.the
volunteercenter.net; info@thevolunteercenter.net). The
Volunteer Center, a private nonprofit organization estab-
lished in 1946 and tax-exempt since 1953, serving San
Francisco and San Mateo County, is a network of nonprofit,
public, business organizations, and private citizens united
by a common goal—to improve local communities.

Each year, Volunteer Services connects 15,000 volunteers to almost 1,000 nonprofit agencies, schools, and government organizations. You can search hundreds of local

Belief

I have inherited a belief in community, the promise that a gathering of the spirit can
both create and change culture. In the desert, change is nurtured even in stone by
wind, by water, through time.

—Terry Tempest Williams

Volunteering for People with Disabilities

The Transitional Volunteer Program (TVP) was established by the Volunteer Center (www.thevolunteercenter.net) in 1974 to place people with mental, physical, and environmental challenges in structured volunteer positions with San Francisco nonprofit organizations. TVP supports transitional volunteers by working with nonprofit managers and mental-health professionals to ensure a good experience for the volunteer, who benefits from new opportunities, increased self-esteem, and stronger connections with the community. Contact TVP at 415-982-8999 or tvp@thevolunteercenter.net.

volunteer opportunities throughout the Bay Area, including one-day events, and contact the organizations you want to work with directly on the Volunteer Center's Web site.

Log in and register to set up an individual account and receive e-mail notification of volunteer openings; then search one-time opportunities that fit your travel schedule. Click on the event that interests you to read a description of the activity, and find the sponsoring agency, available dates and time commitment, whether the opportunity is for individuals, family, or groups (with age guidelines), and contact information.

Opportunities include beach cleanups, restoration projects, clothing sales, being part of a cooking team, hosting special events, working with native plants, and even kayaking to raise awareness of pollution in the San Francisco Bay.

Support the Arts, Jackson, WY: Jackson Hole Film Festival (P.O. Box 1095, Jackson, WY 83001; 307-733-8144; fax 307-733-8145; www.jacksonholefilm festival.org; tmark@jacksonholefilminstitute.org). Spend a week in Jackson Hole, Wyoming, and support a competitive film festival dedicated to advancing the art of independent film. The Jackson Hole Film Festival (JHFF), a nonprofit organization established in 2003, includes screenings, forum discussions, evening events, and opportunities for festival attendees to interact with film industry professionals.

Volunteers play an important role in making the festival happen each year. You can register on the JHFF Web site and choose which activities interest you, in order to create your own volunteer schedule and sign up for available shifts. Volunteer for over 12 hours and receive a cinema pass for five days or volunteer for 6–11 hours for four tickets of your choice. All volunteers receive a JHFF T-shirt, entrance to opening- and closing-night films on a space-available basis, food and beverages at the volunteer lounge, and an invitation to the post-festival volunteer barbecue. The Web site has maps, travel information, restaurants, and hotels.

Immersion Tips: In and Around Jackson

The combination of JHFF activities and recreational opportunities in and around Jackson makes this a perfect immersion travel volunteer vacation. With nearby mountain biking, hiking, climbing, camping, white-water rafting, golf, horseback riding, and breathtaking scenery, you will find plenty to do and enjoy. Aspen Travel, www.aspentravel .com, is the official travel agent for the JHFF. For information on Jackson, visit the Jackson Hole Chamber of Commerce Web site at www.jacksonholechamber.com.

Discover Iowa: RAGBRAI–*Register*'s Annual Great Bicycle Ride Across Iowa (P.O. Box 622, Des Moines, IA 50303; 1-800-474-3342; www.ragbrai.org; info@ragbrai.org; entry fee for weeklong rider, $125; entry fee for nonrider, $35). RAGBRAI is sponsored by the Des Moines *Register* and is the longest, largest, and oldest bicycle touring event in the world. It is a celebration of Iowa and a way to help all Iowans. After expenses, proceeds are given to nonprofit organizations and causes in Iowa, focusing on families and children, literacy, community enrichment programs, and supporting statewide programs. Contributions are also made to the communities that host the RAGBRAI riders.

The first ride, in 1973, was initiated by two columnists from the *Register* who invited friends to ride with them. The annual seven-day ride takes place the last week of July and averages 472 miles. Beginning along the western border of the Missouri River and ending along the eastern border of the Mississippi River, the exact route changes, with the eight overnight host towns announced in January.

The host towns open their campgrounds to riders at no charge; you will need to pack a tent and camping equipment, which will be transported by truck along with your clothing and personal items. The fee includes daily luggage transportation, emergency medical services, a "sag wagon" to pick up or assist riders, camping areas, maps and route markers, bike shops along the route to service your bike, a free entry for a bike raffle, and access to long-

Abe Lincoln greeted riders as they passed through Nevada, Iowa, along the Lincoln Highway.

DES MOINES REGISTER

Riders cycle out of Bennett, Iowa, on their way to the Mississippi River.

term parking and bike-shipping stations. Charter services are available to transport you from the end town back to your starting point.

You need not be an Iowan to participate in this annual event that attracts participants from all 50 states and many foreign countries. What a great way to contribute and experience a state, its communities, and the people who live there!

Josh's Story, RAGBRAI, Coralville, IA

Each year there are five or six designated overnight towns along the Ragbrai route. In 2001 and 2006, Coralville hosted overnights. I served on the executive committee as president of the Coralville

Convention and Visitors Bureau. It was amazing how the entire community, 2,000 people, came together to host 15,000 people from every state and around the world.

For six solid months we met every week, planning with friends and neighbors and culminating in an overnight opportunity to show off what Iowa is known for: Midwest ethics, hospitality, and pride. It was just great meeting people in the community I never would have met otherwise.

Finally I said the riders are having way too much fun. I loved being a volunteer planner, but it was time for me to participate, and I started to train. My first ride was in 2007. Ragbrai is Iowa's own little Tour de France for amateurs. Every 5 to 7 miles we biked through another small Iowa town with the entire community out on the road cheering us on, spraying us down with water hoses, and feeding us chunks of peach and apple pies.

 Historical Transitions, Washburn, ND: Lewis & Clark Fort Mandan Foundation (P.O. Box 607, Washburn, ND 58577; 701-462-8535; fax 701-462-8535; www.fortmandan.com; info@fortmandan.org; volunteer coordinator, 1-877-462-8535 or mprice@fortmandan.org). The Lewis & Clark Fort Mandan Foundation, a nonprofit organization tax-exempt since 1995, focuses on historical transitions beginning with the Lewis & Clark Expedition at Fort Mandan, through the fur trade, the riverboat era, and pioneer settlement of the region. The foundation's goal is to illuminate and preserve the unique stories of the people and places and ensure historical accuracy.

The Volunteer Program includes an extended-stay option for couples or individuals for either an eight-day or one-month stay, from May 1 to October 31. Training is provided on site, and you will receive an RV site with full hookups, discounts at the gift shop and local attractions, and other perks.

Volunteer opportunities may include helping with mailings, filing, copying, and answering phones, mail, and e-mail. Groundskeeping positions include light gardening, watering, washing picnic tables, and sweeping picnic shelters. Docents answer questions about exhibits, escort tour groups, and help with historical programs. You can greet visitors, staff the information desk, assist with crowd control, maintain the brochure rack, or work in the gift shop.

There are also short-term opportunities and special events listed on a calendar on the Web site. If you'd like to apply, fill out the Volunteer Request Form or call the volunteer coordinator with any questions.

Creating Healthy Communities

Points of Light Foundation and **HandsOn Network** have merged to become **Points of Light Institute** (www.pointsoflight.org). This new organization believes that each person is able to make a difference and contribute to creating healthy communities. The HandsOn Network is the largest volunteer and citizen-action network in the country. HandsOn Action Centers enable you to search for volunteer opportunities in your local community or in communities across America. If you are interested in using your skills to help people or causes that are important to you, want to meet people who share your interests, and learn how to get involved, visit www.handsonnetwork.org, go to "Action Centers," and click on a state to find an affiliate. Volunteer opportunities will be listed by city and organization with a key that provides links to directory (including contact) information, Web sites, online volunteer matching, and volunteer management training.

Ⓢ Conservation and Preservation, Alexandria, VA: Alexandria Archaeology Museum and The Friends of Alexandria Archaeology (105 N. Union Street, #327 Alexandria, VA 22314; 703-838-4399; fax 703-838-6491; oha.alexandriava.gov; archeology@alexandriava.gov).

Volunteer with the Alexandria Archaeology Museum and contribute to the conservation and preservation of historic Alexandria. The Friends of Alexandria Archaeology is a non-profit organization whose mission began in 1986 with a small group of volunteers who wanted to find ways to support Alexandria Archaeology, expand volunteer opportunities, and raise public awareness of archaeology. There are many ways to volunteer, from working in an office answering phones, helping with mailings, and photocopying, to excavating, washing, marking, and cataloging artifacts.

Current opportunities are listed on the Web site and may include helping with an Oral History Project, collecting personal oral histories of longtime residents. If you have skills writing, interviewing, working with video, indexing, or transcribing, you can note your interests on the volunteer application. You may also be able to work on the Alexandria Freedman Project, researching the history of slaves during the Civil War and finding living relatives of escaped slaves and black soldiers.

Excavation takes place year-round, but most digging is scheduled between May and September, so plan your vacation to coincide with a current dig, such as the Shuter's Hill Site in Old Town Alexandria, the former site of an 18th-century mansion and a Civil War fort. The site has been active since 1995 as archeologists locate and document remains from the earlier structures. A field orientation is available to new volunteers once a year, and there is a waiting list for volunteers who want to dig.

Researchers are needed to trace the history of properties and to find out about the people who lived on the archaeological sites. Volunteers with skills and previous experience in scale drawing and artifact photography, graphics and layout, or exhibit design should indicate their availability on the application. Volunteers also help with educational and public programs at Family Dig Days and at special events.

Archaeology and Natural History Preserve, Lubbock, TX: Lubbock Lake Landmark (Museum of Texas Tech University, 3301 Fourth St., P.O. Box 43191, Lubbock TX 79409; 806-742-2490; volunteer coordinator, 806-742-1116; fax 806-742-1136; www.depts.ttu.edu; lubbock.lake@ttu.edu). Volunteer with an international crew at the Lubbock Lake Landmark, a field laboratory and archaeological and natural history preserve. The Museum of Texas Tech University conducts research of and education about the preserve, located in the Lubbock Lake Landmark State Historical Park.

The Lubbock Lake Landmark site is a field laboratory for soils, geology, and radiocarbon dating studies. You can work with professional staff on surveys, geoarchaeological prospecting, and mapping and participate in excavations to uncover extinct species. You'll acquire experience in field methodologies and field recording technology, conservation of materials, and laboratory work.

The 300-acre Lubbock Lake site is a National Historic and State Archaeological Landmark. The site contains deposits relating to cultures that existed in the area over the last 12,000 years. The extinct animals hunted by the native peoples include the bison, short-face bear, and giant armadillo. The museum offers programs, seminars, interpretive guided tours, and presentations for visitors.

As part of Texas Tech University, the Museum of Texas Tech University is a nonprofit institution and an education resource, tax-exempt since 1955. Its goal is to support the academic and intellectual mission of Texas Tech University and collect, research, and distribute information about the natural and cultural heritage of local and related regions.

Volunteer Facts

Here are some interesting facts from www.networkforgood.org
- Over 109 million Americans volunteer annually
- On average, volunteers contribute 3.5 hours per week
- Fifty-nine percent of teenagers volunteer an average of 3.5 hours per week, representing 13 million teens contributing 2.4 billion hours

Concord Community Camp, Concord, NH: Volunteers For Peace (1034 Tiffany Rd., Belmont, VT 05730; 802-259-2759; fax 802-259-2922; www.vfp.org; vfp@vfp.org: 2-week program, $300). Join international volunteers, ages 18–30, in Concord, New Hampshire, at the Audubon Society's children's nature camp. Help with camp activities including games, crafts, stories, environmental education, and outdoor adventures. The camp's theme is peace in the tradition of Gandhi and Martin Luther King.

You will also participate in landscaping and maintenance work at the Unitarian Universalist Church where you will be living during your two-week stay. Evening workshops are offered by New Hampshire artists on peace poetry, peace drumming, and peace songs, and there are open discussions about peace issues. The program includes time for leisure activities: canoeing, hiking, yoga, swimming, and more.

Your fee covers room and board; living arrangements are cooperative with volunteers sharing food preparation, work projects, and recreational activities. You can copy an application from the Web site and submit it with a short statement of motivation that applies to the project. Placements are usually made within five days of receipt of your application, and if accepted, you will receive an information packet with details of the project.

Volunteers For Peace, founded in 1982, is a nonprofit membership organization that promotes International Voluntary Service as a means of intercultural education and community service. VFP organizes service projects in the USA where people from diverse backgrounds work together to meet needs and overcome violence and environmental decay.

Service and Whales, Maui, HI: Sierra Club: Live and contribute in the Honokowai Valley on Maui for a 10-day trip to a large archaeological site, protected by Maui Cultural Lands, Inc. and used as an educational center for learning about ancient Hawaiian culture. Read the complete listing in Chapter 3, "Wildlife."

Habitat Restoration Weekends, Southwestern U.S.: Sky Island Alliance (P.O. Box 41165, Tucson, AZ 85717; 520-624-7080, volunteer coordinator, ext. 23; fax 520-791-7709; www.skyislandalliance.org; info@skyisland alliance.org; volunteer coordinator, sarah@skyisland alliance.org). Sky Island Alliance, founded in 1991, is a nonprofit grassroots organization dedicated to the protection and restoration of native species and habitats in the Sky Island region of the southwestern United States and northwestern Mexico.

Sky Island has education and outreach programs that involve the public in preservation and conservation efforts. The alliance works directly with volunteers, scientists, landowners, public officials, and government agencies to establish protected areas, restore landscapes to health, and promote public appreciation of the region's biological diversity.

You can help restore the ecology of the Sky Island region by volunteering to document the impact of illegal roads on public lands, collect data on wide-ranging species in wildlife corridors, and restore habitat for endangered species. Sky Island Alliance's Road Closures and Habitat

SKY ISLAND ALLIANCE

Sky Island Alliance, Tucson, Arizona, posts weekend opportunities for volunteers to enjoy the great outdoors doing conservation work and camping out.

Restoration Weekends are physically demanding and include placing barriers and signs to block user-created roads, breaking up the road surface, and planting native vegetation.

You do not need experience, and there are jobs for all fitness levels. Field weekends are scheduled year-round; you can choose a day trip out of Tucson or a weekend camping and working. Fill out and submit a volunteer interest form on the Sky Island Alliance Web site or contact the volunteer coordinator for more information and current schedule.

The "islands" are actually forested mountain ranges with desert and grassland plains between them. They represent the most diverse ecosystems in the world, with a mixture of tropical and temperate climate zones. The Sky Island region supports over half the bird species in North America, 29 bat species, 3,000+ plant species, and 104 mammal species. Southeast Arizona has about a quarter of the 40 Sky Islands within its borders, including the

Chiricahua, Dragoon, Pinaleno, and Tumacacori mountain ranges.

Immersion Excursion: Stalactites and Stalagmites

Kartchner Caverns State Park (P.O. Box 1849, Benson, AZ 85602; reservations, 520-586-2283; azstateparks.com/ Parks/KACA; park open daily 7 AM to 6 PM except Christmas Day; tours every 20 minutes from 8:40 AM to 4:40 PM; day-use fees for AZ parks range from $3 to $10; reservation fee of $3 included in tour fee; park entrance fee $5 per car up to two adults, or free with tour reservation; Rotunda/Throne Room tour open year-round, fee $9.95 ages 7–13, $18.95 ages 14 and up, free for children 6 and younger; Big Room tour open Oct. 1–Apr. 15, fee $12.95 ages 7–13, $22.95 ages 14 and up). Kartchner Caverns is a limestone wet cave in southeastern Arizona, discovered in 1974. Walk along a 1.2-mile barrier-free path to see the stalactites and stalag-mites, helectites, and minerals found only in these cav-erns—many of the formations have been growing for tens of thousands of years. There are exhibits, regional displays, and educational information about the caverns in the park's Discovery Center. The tours begin with an electric tram ride from the Discovery Center, and you enter through a 420-foot tunnel sealed by airtight doors that preserve the cave's interior climate of 68 degrees with 98 percent humidity. The first space after the last airlock is the Rotunda Room, a 200-foot-long, 120-foot-wide cavern with an arched, 45-foot-high ceiling. The Rotunda/Throne Room tour and the Big Room tour are 1/2 mile and 1 1/2 hours each. Reservations for tours need to be made in advance, as more than 200,000 visitors tour the caverns each year. Kartchner Caverns State Park is 40 miles east of Tucson.

3

Wildlife: Work with Mammals, Birds, and Fish
Animals, Natural Habitats, and Scientific Research

Volunteers with a passion for animals and animal rights will find a wide array of fascinating and rewarding activities in this chapter, from sampling wildlife in New York City to helping care for gibbons in Santa Clara, California. Perhaps you'd like to study moose and wolves as part of a research project on the predator-prey system, in a remote wilderness setting on Isle Royale, Michigan, or volunteer with Rerun, an organization with chapters in New Jersey, New York, and Kentucky that arranges adoptions of thoroughbred racehorses.

Travel across America and you'll find opportunities to work with animals, protect their natural habitats, and contribute to scientific research. Begin your selection process by asking yourself what you want to get out of the experience. There are opportunities to be directly and actively involved with animals, or to contribute with the hard work it takes to support them. There are organizations where all staff members are volunteer, and others where the volunteers support a core team.

Volunteering to protect and support wildlife may cover maintenance chores, data collection, and educating the public, working both independently and with others. Volunteering is work, providing care and attention to the animals and their needs, and the vast majority of volunteers enjoy it very much.

Protecting wildlife and natural habitats through observation, and by contributing to scientific studies, may require extensive hiking or sitting for hours in an observations blind. For some studies, volunteers may be trained in the specific protocol and methodology of data collection. In other instances the emphasis is on rescue, rehabilitation, and release efforts.

There are both boat- and land-based volunteer opportunities. On the sea, volunteers are trained to work with tourists, spot wildlife, and record identifying data. There's also the opportunity for hands-on experience aboard a research vessel monitoring ecosystem changes and collecting environmental data.

You will find refuges dedicated to providing permanent and appropriate homes for abused or unwanted animals both exotic and familiar. Animal care is hard, often strenuous work, and may involve preparing meals and feeding, and cleaning, repairing, and constructing animal enclosures.

Qualified volunteers may be trained to assist in the rescue, care, rehabilitation, and release of sick, injured, and orphaned native wildlife. Tasks such as transporting injured birds, mammals, and reptiles; repairing cages; and helping with grounds maintenance and gardening are likely. Assisting with fundraising might include event planning, sending invitations, selling tickets, working booths, parking, and other tasks.

If you choose to become involved in education efforts, many organizations provide training for outreach presentations to service clubs, schools, and other groups. Some projects are devoted to protecting one species, while others are concerned with a variety of animals.

There are opportunities for families with young children to help out with dogs and cats, birds, rabbits, horses, and potbellied pigs, and the possibility, for committed adults, to learn how to socialize wolves.

Match your interests and available time with the specific chores you will be responsible for and the required time commitment. Ask about the average workday, downtime to relax, and the activities enjoyed by previous volunteers.

Inquire about what kind of housing is available. Some programs provide campsites, RV hookups, trailers, apartments, dormitories, or hotel or bed-and-breakfast accommodations. Others do not offer accommodations, so you'd need to provide your own. Often local housing suggestions are provided.

Consider the location of the project and do further research about the area and opportunities for side trips, sightseeing, recreation, and ways to get involved in the community.

Each and every opportunity in this chapter has something phenomenal to offer. And so do you. Which volunteer vacation with wildlife will spark your interest? What do you think you'll enjoy most? Personalized stories from people who have participated in these activities will help you in making your own decisions.

New York City Wildlife, New York, NY, and Environs: Earthwatch Institute (Earthwatch Institute, 3 Clock Tower Place, Suite 100, P.O. Box 75, Maynard, MA 01754; 1-800-776-0188; 978-461-0081; fax 978-461-2332; www.earth watch.org; info@earthwatch.org; 9 days, contribution of $1,746). Earthwatch, founded in 1971, is an international, nonprofit organization that offers volunteers the opportunity to join research teams and actively contribute to conserving the planet.

Join an expedition in and around New York City to sample wildlife and habitat quality and learn about research methods. You may trap or camera-trap mammals, identify birds, or survey plant species. More than 250 species of birds have been observed in the five boroughs, along with raccoons, rabbits, deer, foxes, bats, mice, frogs, turtles, and other wildlife.

Research will be conducted at 10 protected areas: Central Park, New York Botanical Garden, Pelham Bay Park, Jamaica Bay Wildlife Refuge, Marshlands Conservancy, Great Swamp National Wildlife Refuge, Bear Mountain/ Harriman State Park, Ward Pound Ridge Reservation, Black Rock Forest Preserve, and Catskill Mountains.

Accommodations are at the Old Headquarters of Black Rock Forest, outside Cornwall, New York, surrounded by 4,000 acres of forest, hiking trails, lakes, and streams on the west shore of the Hudson River, only 50 miles north of New York City. The facility sleeps 16 people in several rooms, with shared bathroom facilities. There is a full kitchen, an air-conditioned common room, and a screened porch. Bedding and towels are provided, but if you opt to sleep outside, you must bring your own tent, sleeping bag, and sleeping pad. The expedition is for individuals 18 and older, but it may be possible for 16- and 17-year-olds to participate if accompanied by a parent or guardian.

Begin Volunteering Today

1-800-Volunteer.org says volunteering is easy and invites you to get involved. The Web site (www.1-800-volunteer.org) is a national database of volunteer opportunities that enables you to search for a place to volunteer, browse organizations, or find a volunteer center. The search feature allows you to type in a keyword (such as education, habitat, health, environment, etc.) a city and state, and the distance from that location you are willing to consider. Opportunities include the program or project name and the sponsoring organization, with dates that range from one-day events to longer-term commitments.

Monitor and Study Alaskan Fur Seals, St. George Island, AK: Earthwatch Institute (3 Clock Tower Place, Suite 100, P.O. Box 75, Maynard, MA 01754; 1-800-776-0188; 978-461-0081; fax 978-461-2332; www.earthwatch .org; info@earthwatch.org; 10 days, contribution of $3,246). St. George Island in the Bering Sea is one of the world's major breeding areas for northern fur seals, and it offers researchers an opportunity to monitor and study the fur seal population and a diverse marine ecosystem.

Volunteers spend four hours a day observing seals that breed on the island each summer, recording numbers, sexes, and ages. To reach the fur seal rookery, you must be able to hike a half-mile over rocky terrain, carrying a

On beautiful and remote St. George Island, volunteers help clear the runway of caribou, fox, and birds so the planes can land safely.

Alaskan fur seals on the rocks on St. George Island, Alaska.

backpack with your equipment. There are also opportunities to work with a local group monitoring sea lions or caribou, and to observe seabirds, including puffins, auklets, murres, and rare red-legged kittiwakes.

Accommodations are provided in a historic house with modern conveniences in the village of St. George. Your team of three to six volunteers (age 18 and older) will make breakfasts and lunches, and a cook will prepare your dinners and include local favorites—halibut pie and reindeer stir-fry.

St. George Island is part of a five-island volcanic archipelago known as the Pribilof Islands, located about 800 miles south-southwest of Anchorage, Alaska; it is often called the "Galapagos of the North." There is an Aleut saying that once you have visited the Island of Seals, you will always yearn to return.

Claudia's Story: Alaskan Fur Seals Study, St. George Island, AK

My greatest joy is getting out and doing things I never dreamed possible. I thought this was a very good year to stay in the United States, and the research project intrigued me. Hunting Alaskan fur seals had almost decimated the population and was outlawed about 25 years ago. Theoretically, without hunting, the population numbers should have increased; instead they continue to decline.

This is going to be a long-term study to figure out what is causing the problem. Researchers are considering many issues, including the food supply, predators, and commercial fishing. When one thing changes in the ecosystem, it affects everything else.

CLAUDIA SELDONS

Volunteers assist scientific researchers collecting data on the Alaskan fur seal population, St. George Island, Alaska.

It was a 10-day trip. One volunteer group had just left and another group was coming in behind ours. It turned out to be quite an experience getting there. I met two other people in my group at the Anchorage airport, but the airline was not able to fly that day. The following day, Peninsula Airways got us to St. Paul Island, but the weather was very bad in St. George, so we were stuck. There aren't any restaurants in St. Paul and it cost $75 for a cab ride to go to a general store to buy ramen noodles.

Members of the local school board put us up for the night. We met great people and experienced a different slice of life than we would have if everything had gone smoothly. It took us three days to get there. We missed counting the fur seal cubs and moms on the first day, but we knew everyone who worked at the airport by name, and people invited us over for dinner. I've actually enjoyed some of the problems associated with traveling. Airplane rescheduling can happen anytime. It's fun to experience the real life of where you go.

Monitor Diamondback Terrapins, Barnegat Bay, NJ: Earthwatch Institute (3 Clock Tower Place, Suite 100, P.O. Box 75,Maynard, MA 01754; 1-800-776-0188; 978-461-0081; fax 978-461-2332; www.earthwatch.org; info@earthwatch .org; 9 days, contribution of $1,950). Earthwatch expeditions teach you about critical ecological and cultural challenges and how you can take action. Choose the Barnegat Bay, New Jersey, expedition to study diamondback terrapins in their estuary environment. Your team will capture, tag, and track the terrapins, monitor turtle nests, measure sound disturbance, collect samples and temperature data, and mark and tag hatchlings.

BILL CROWELL

Endangered diamondback terrapins are monitored and studied through Earthwatch's program at Barnegat Bay, New Jersey.

Terrapin populations have been affected by land development and other human impacts along the Atlantic coast. Earthwatch scientists are studying the endangered ecosystem and the nesting ecology and habitat requirements of these colorful turtles. You can help with research while enjoying the scenic beauty of Barnegat Bay. In your free time you can canoe in the Pine Barrens; visit Old Barney, one of the most photographed lighthouses in North America, located on Long Beach Island; snorkel to view invertebrates; or swim at Island Beach State Park.

Your team will stay at the Lighthouse Center for Natural Resource Education, on 180 acres of undeveloped coastal

Diamondback hatchlings are minuscule when born and head right for the ocean.

habitat. The center has double rooms, air-conditioning, laundry facilities, a computer lab, lounge, and shared bathrooms with hot showers. Meals will be catered by a local chef and served in the dining room. The Barnegat Bay area is about an hour's drive from Philadelphia (the rendezvous site) and two hours from New York City.

Immersion Tip: Kayaks in New Jersey

New Jersey Kayak (409 East Bay Ave., Barnegat, NJ 08005; 609-698-4440; njkayak.com; sea touring kayak day rental, 6 hours, $75 single kayak, $140 double kayak; 1½ hour rental, $30 single kayak, $50 double kayak; 2½ hour rental, $45 single kayak, $70 double kayak; launch your own kayak, $10; lesson fees vary depending on group (4–12 people), semiprivate (2–3 people), or private, shorter expe-

riences for families with children ages 7–14, Beyond the
Basics for experienced kayakers, Rescue Classes, or 5-hour
Boot Camp). Kayak Boot Camp is a fast-track, five-hour
course for experienced kayakers with instructions, demonstrations, and exercises in the open water of Barnegat Bay
taught by ACA (American Canoe Association) certified
instructors. The program includes basic paddling,
advanced paddling, rescue techniques, and safety.

New Jersey Kayak is located within the Pinelands
Preserve and the New Jersey Heritage Coastal Trail, along
the coastline of Barnegat Bay. It offers rentals, instruction,
and guided kayak tours of the Edwin B. Forsythe National
Wildlife Refuge (www.fws.gov/northeast/forsythe).

**Wildlife Trails of the American West, Pierce Creek,
ID, and Red Butte Canyon, UT: Earthwatch Institute**
(3 Clock Tower Place, Suite 100, P.O. Box 75, Maynard, MA
01754; 1-800-776-0188; 978-461-0081; fax 978-461-2332;
www.earthwatch.org; info@earthwatch.org; 8 days, contribution of $1,946). Volunteer to help with a research project
that examines wildlife trails, and study animal movement
to understand how it uses available resources.

Wildlife has been isolated in areas that are not large or
diverse enough to sustain many of the species found in the
wilderness areas of the American West. This project will
ultimately design wildlife corridors that will ensure the
survival of these animals. Volunteers identify and count
tracks, map game trails and kill sites, survey vegetation,
and hike routes that are used by deer, moose, coyotes,
mountain lions, bobcats, black bears, and wolves.

Participants need to be physically fit, ready for unpredictable weather, and able to hike five or six hours a day
on sometimes slippery and steep slopes. Some of the trails
you will use are the same ones traveled by Lewis and Clark
two hundred years ago. The activity level of this trip is
rated strenuous.

Red Butte Canyon is in the Research Natural Area in the Wasatch Range, which is closed to the public. The Canyon's elevation is from 5,020 to 8,235 feet, with views of the Great Salt Lake Valley. The Pierce Creek project is in the remote and beautiful Beaverhead Mountains, in the Salmon-Challis National Forest, along the eastern border of central Idaho. The research area, along the western edge of the U.S. Continental Divide, is 32 miles north of Salmon, Idaho.

The project locations are Pierce Creek, Idaho, and Red Butte Canyon, Utah. Meeting sites are Idaho Falls, Idaho, or Salt Lake City, Utah. In Idaho Falls the accommodations are in a rustic mountain lodge, with heated cabins, hot showers, and shared cooking and cleanup chores. In Salt Lake City you will share rooms with bathrooms at the University (of Utah) Guesthouse, have breakfast at the guesthouse, lunch at the project site, and dinners at the student dining area.

Harriett's Story, Wildlife Trails, Salt Lake City, UT

It's very interesting to be part of a group of people from all over the world who choose to spend their vacations on an Earthwatch expedition collecting scientific data. It kind of self-selects the kind of people who will go and yet there's such diversity. On one project there was a 20-year-old college student and a retired 75-year-old, with the average age of the group about 45. We haven't been on any trip we haven't liked and always select something we haven't done before.

The volunteer coordinators do their best to make sure that when you are signing up for a trip it's a good fit. Some trips involve hiking, carrying loads, swimming, or changing altitudes. It's important to understand what's involved so you're surprised as little as possible.

I'm definitely a more well-rounded person for having participated in these expeditions. When you try out new things, it expands your life's experiences.

Salmon-Challis National Forest

Salmon-Challis National Forest (1206 S. Challis St., Salmon, ID 83467; 208-756-5100; www.fs.fed.us/r4/sc; mailroom/r4_s-c@fs.fed.us). The Salmon-Challis National Forest covers over 4.3 million acres in east-central Idaho. This includes 1.3 million acres of the Frank Church–River of No Return Wilderness Area. The Wild and Scenic Salmon River and the Middle Fork of the Salmon River are popular areas for wildlife viewing, fishing, white-water rafting, and other recreational activities.

The Frank Church–River of No Return Wilderness Area includes the Salmon River Mountains, the Clearwater Mountains, and the Bighorn Crags. It is the second-largest wilderness area in the lower 48 states—only California's Death Valley Wilderness is larger. It also has the deepest gorge in North America, the Salmon River Canyon.

Immersion Excursion: Scenic Byways and Ice Caves

Explore the **Sawtooth Scenic Byway** (www.byways.org/explore/byways/2400; www.idahobyways.gov), which runs along the Sawtooth Mountains to the towns of Hailey, Ketchum, and Sun Valley, Idaho, and then through the Sawtooth National Recreation Area. The route is 115.7 miles, and the trip takes about three hours, but it's recommended to plan the day exploring and stopping along the way. Visit the Shoshone Indian Ice Caves, a lava tube 1,000 feet long and between 8 and 30 feet high. The "ice" is caused by air currents that freeze subterranean waters. Take advantage of the many hiking and biking trails in the Sawtooth National Forest, and stop in Stanley, headquarters for white-water rafting in central Idaho and where the Sawtooth meets the Ponderosa Pine and Salmon River Scenic Byways. The National Scenic Byways Program

(www.byways.org) was established to recognize and preserve selected roads for their archaeological, cultural, historic, natural, recreational, and scenic qualities. There are
126 federally designated National Scenic Byways and All-
American Roads.

 **Rescued Wild Animals, Valentine, AZ: Keepers
of the Wild Nature Park** (13441 E. Hwy. 66,
Valentine, AZ 86437; 928-769-1800; www.keepersofthewild
.org; keepersoffice@hughes.net). Located at mile marker
87 on historic Route 66, Keepers of the Wild is a nonprofit
animal sanctuary and educational center founded in 1996.
It is permanent home to rescued and rehabilitated exotic
animals, including lions, tigers, jaguars, cougars, leopards,
and wolves. Some of the animals were abused by their
trainers; some were neglected by owners who kept them as
pets. At Keepers of the Wild, the animals are nursed back
to health and live the rest of their lives in a clean, safe,
and appropriate environment.

Volunteers at the park help care for the 100+ exotic animals that reside in the compound. People are needed to
lead tours, make presentations, and help with food preparation and rescuing animals. You can also consider working
in the gift shop or help with carpentry and other repair and
maintenance needs.

Volunteers are responsible for your own food, transportation, and lodging. Combine a wonderful volunteer
vacation with many opportunities to enjoy hiking, sightseeing, river rafting, horseback riding, and more.

Immersion Excursion: Grand Canyon Caverns

Ⓢ–ⓈⓈ **Grand Canyon Caverns and Inn** (Mile Marker
115, Route 66, Peach Springs, AZ 86434; 1-877-422-4459;
928-422-3223, www.grandcanyoncaverns.com; info@gc
caverns.com; reservations@gccaverns.com; private rooms,
RV sites, and tent sites; Cavern tours daily, every half-hour

from 10 AM to 4 PM, except Christmas Day, $14.95 adults, $9.95 children). Grand Canyon Caverns and Inn, on 800 acres at an elevation of 5,500 feet, is located on a plateau with the largest dry caverns in the United States. The caverns are huge—three football fields could fit inside—and air is drawn in from the Grand Canyon through miles of limestone caves. Visitors descend over 200 feet (21 stories) underground via an exploration elevator. Well-lighted trails are about .75 mile long, and half the tour is wheelchair accessible. Off-trail tours are also available. The 48-room inn, with an outdoor pool, restaurant and curio shop, has TV, Wi-Fi Internet access in the lobby, and a video library. There are also a night-sky observation deck and full RV hookups available in a private campground. Located a mile off Route 66 National Scenic Highway, six hours from southern California, two and a half hours from Phoenix or

Grand Canyon Skywalk

Grand Canyon Skywalk, Grand Canyon West, AZ (Grand Canyon Skywalk, Las Vegas, NV; 1-877-9378; www.grandcanyonskywalk.com; reservations@destinationgrandcanyon.com; $20 per vehicle permit and parking fee; $29.95 per person for Skywalk; package options available; no personal items, including cameras, allowed on Skywalk, lockers provided). The Grand Canyon Skywalk is a glass bridge 4,000 feet above the canyon floor, fully accessible to people with disabilities with an ADA-approved access ramp. You can take photos from the side of the bridge and a photo taken of you on the bridge can be purchased. Grand Canyon West, including the Grand Canyon Skywalk, is owned by the Hualapai Nation, a native people of the Southwest. Other Canyon West attractions include Guano Point, for spectacular canyon views, the Hualapai Market, and the historic Highpoint Hike. Native American dance performances, an Indian village with re-creations of tribe dwellings, and The Hualapai Ranch, a western town with cowboy performances, horseback riding, wagon rides, and a cowboy cookout, are at Eagle Point, near the Skywalk.

Las Vegas, the Grand Canyon Caverns and Inn are neighbors to the Hualapai Nation, with its Grand Canyon Skywalk.

 Turtle Rescue and Rehabilitation, Topsail Beach, NC: The Karen Beasley Sea Turtle Rescue and Rehabilitation Center (Sea Turtle Hospital, P.O. Box 3012, 822 Carolina Ave., Topsail Beach, NC 28445; www.seaturtlehospital.org; Loggrhead@aol.com). The Karen Beasley Sea Turtle Rescue and Rehabilitation Center is a private, nonprofit organization, founded in 1997, whose mission is the conservation and preservation of all species of marine turtles. The center protects nests, nesting females, and hatchlings, and is involved with the rescue, rehabilitation, and release of sick and injured turtles and with educating the public about sea turtles. Jean Beasley, the hospital's founder and director, was voted Animal Planet's 2007 "Hero of the Year."

The center is staffed by volunteers and there are plenty of opportunities for hands-on learning as you help endangered and threatened sea turtles. Responsibilities include the daily care of turtles, preparation of food and feeding, and cleaning tanks. You will also be involved in the medical attention the turtles receive, including the administering of some medicines.

The center is open to the public two hours in the afternoon, and volunteers talk with visitors about the turtles, their ailments, and the work done at the center. Your responsibilities will also include beach survey work, recording turtle tracks, relocating nests if necessary, and post-hatch data collection.

Internships with housing provided are available year-round for a minimum 12-week period. Interns work five and a half days a week, with Wednesday afternoon and Sunday off. Submit a letter with your contact and school information, length of internship desired, and a brief essay stating why you want an internship at the center and what your expectations are. Include two letters of recommendation, one from a teacher and one from a community leader.

Immersion Excursion: Surf and Turtles

Surf Camp, Inc. (530 Causeway Dr., Suite B-1, Wrightsville Beach, NC 28480; 1-866-844-7873; www.wbsurfcamp.com; info@wbsurfcamp.com; group lessons, $75 per person for a 2-hour clinic; private lessons, $65 an hour, 2-hour minimum; weekend group surf clinic, $150 per person for 4 hours of instruction; day surf camp, $350 per person for 4 days). Add surf lessons at Topsail Beach (or Carolina

TOPSAIL BEACH SURF CAMP

Add surf lessons at Topsail Beach's Surf Camp to your volunteer vacation on Topsail Island, North Carolina, home to the Karen Beasley Sea Turtle Rescue and Rehabilitation Center.

Beach) to your volunteer vacation at the Karen Beasley Center. You can take a two-hour clinic, a private lesson, or sign up for Surf Camp to combine with your volunteering experience. You can also register for certification in CPR/First Aid, for Lifeguard, Ocean Safety, or Surf Instructor. Topsail Beach is located on 26-mile-long Topsail Island, off the coast of southeastern North Carolina, about halfway between Wilmington and Jacksonville. Topsail Island is also known for its fishing, and the Jolly Roger Ocean Pier, on the south end of Topsail Island, has a motel, convenience store, bait shop, and the 850-foot fishing pier, which is open from March through November.

Topsail Beach, home to the Karen Beasley Sea Turtle and Rescue Center, is an important nesting ground for the endangered loggerhead sea turtle. Participants in overnight Surf Camp will have a private tour of the facility and meet Jean Beasley, Executive Director, and her staff. Surf Camp, Inc. donates a portion of your tuition to the Karen Beasley Sea Turtle Rescue and Rehabilitation Center.

Accommodations and Dining

⑤⑤–⑤⑤⑤ **Jolly Roger Inn and Pier** (803 Ocean Blvd., Topsail Beach, NC 28445; 1-800-633-3196; 910-328-4616; fax 910-328-0730). $85–125). Right on the beach, the inn has 65 rooms, including bedrooms, efficiencies, and suites, some equipped with kitchens, nonsmoking rooms available.

Popular with the locals for breakfast and lunch, **The Beach Shop and Grill** ($–$$; 701 S. Anderson, Topsail Beach; 910-328-6501) is known for fresh-squeezed orangeade, burgers, and hot dogs; you can dine in or travel to the beach. **Crab Pot**'s ($–$$; 508 Roland Ave., Surf City; 910-328-5001) Southern and Caribbean specialties include seafood gumbo, jerk chicken, and Key lime pie. There's beach music and shag lessons on summer nights.

(S) **The Wild Dolphin Foundation** (87-1286 Farrington Hwy., Waianae, HI 96792; 808-306-3968; www.wild dolphin.org/volunteer.html; info@wilddolphin.org). The Wild Dolphin Foundation (WDF) monitors progress and change, identifies gaps in knowledge of marine animals, and supports the preservation of their habitats. WDF volunteers play an essential role in the collection of data through observation, and help provide information on distribution, seasonal abundance, and trends through noninvasive and nondisruptive research. WDF also conducts reef surveys and checks to monitor the health of the coral reefs and fish sharing the dolphins' habitat, and it hosts the Great Annual Fish Count each summer.

There are both boat- and land-based volunteer opportunities available for those in good physical health. A strong

DANI GOBBO

WDF volunteers can earn college credit helping preserve habitat for wild dolphins.

DANI GOBBO

The Wild Dolphin Foundation monitors the health of the coral reefs and fish sharing the dolphins' habitat.

interest in wildlife and conservation is required, and a background in marine biology and environmental science is helpful. Enthusiasm, motivation, and good verbal and writing skills along with computer literacy are desirable, and the ability to work independently and as part of a team are both important. Volunteers interested in field research must be able to donate their time at least two days a week over an eight-week period. College credit internships are available; there is neither a charge nor compensation for the program.

Participants may assist with photography and recording data and sighting information, group activity patterns, upkeep of materials and vessels, naturalist programs, and reef monitoring at snorkeling sites. WDF is also looking for volunteers to perform shore-based observations and to design and present programs at hotels, local schools, and day camps.

If you are interested in working with WDF and protecting and restoring the natural habitats of dolphins, as well as gaining education and hands-on experience, apply by e-mail with a letter of interest detailing your personal goals, skills, experiences, and how your interests are compatible with the WDF mission. Include your availability: days, hours, and length of commitment. You will need to provide your own transportation and lodging on Oahu. For information, check Hawaii's official tourism site at www.gohawaii.com/oahu and the Oahu Visitor's Bureau Web site, www.visit-oahu.com.

Hawaiian spinner dolphins (so-called because of their high spinning leaps) are seen in the near-coastal waters of Oahu on a daily basis. The WDF has traced the Hawaiian dolphin population back at least eight hundred years. The spinners (called Nai'a in Hawaiian) can make seven complete turns before diving, through rapid underwater acceleration and the torque of their tails as they break the surface. Spins, and particularly their aftermath, are thought to be a form of communication since even distant dolphins would be able to pick up the sounds of their splashes through echolocation.

Because the Hawaiian spinner dolphins spend so much time in near-shore waters, WDF is able to observe their resting, socializing, mating, birthing, and other behavioral habits. Studies include determining the number of dolphins on Oahu's leeward coast, how many are transient or resident, and examining their habitat use. Be part of the effort to protect the dolphins and their habitats, and contribute to an important cause in a spectacular location.

For information on the Great Annual Fish Count, an event held every July to introduce divers and snorkelers to fish-watching and educate people about marine resources, contact www.fishcount.org. Events include dives, seminars, and social activities.

Jenny's Story, Wild Dolphin Foundation, Oahu, HI

I was a sophomore in college looking for a summer job. I was really into nonprofit conservation organizations and wanted to work outside, preferably on the water, and became a volunteer researcher and crew member, taking notes for the research staff on the dolphins we observed. Had they changed? How many were in the water? I noted the weather and cloud formations, speed of the boat, and identified the dolphins I saw by their dorsal fins. That was really great. It was also fun interacting with the people and being in the water with the dolphins.

I educated guests. The goal is to have a great time in the water and not impact the dolphins. It starts by sliding into the water to minimize the splash and looking to see where the dolphins are headed and merging in with them, like on a highway, not swimming directly into them or on top of them. Strong swimmers can often keep up with the pod.

Splashing will cause dolphins to become confused or suddenly swim off. Sometimes the dolphins will just hang out with us in the water. Spinner dolphins communicate by spinning around. I'm still really attached to dolphins and very interested in marine biology.

Accommodations

Oahu, and Hawaii in general, can be an expensive undertaking for a volunteer vacation that doesn't provide housing; however, there are alternatives to hotels, motels and condominium rentals to investigate. At Malaekahana Campground (www.coconutroads.com/CampMalaekahana.html) on Oahu's Windward side, pitch your own tent ($6 per person) or rent a yurt or a beach house (prices vary). For an added bonus, it's a great surfing spot.

About 10 minutes from Malaekahana, there's the Backpackers Vacation Inn and Plantation Village (59-788 Kamehameha Hwy., Haleiwa, HI 96712, 808-638-7838; fax 808-638-7515; www.backpackers-hawaii.com; info@back packers-hawaii.com) on Oahu's North Shore at Three Tables Beach, next to Waimea Bay. Prices range from $22 to $26 for a bed; cabins and vegetarian meals are also available. There's a complimentary shuttle service to and from Waikiki.

Preserving the Earth's Natural History, Thermopolis, WY: Big Horn Basin Foundation
(110 Carter Ranch Rd., Thermopolis, WY 82443; 307-864-2997, ext. 223; fax 307-864-5762; www.bhbfonline.org; foundation@wyodino.org). The Big Horn Basin Foundation (BHBF), in cooperation with The Wyoming Dinosaur Center

Volunteers are trained in dinosaur quarry mapping at the Big Horn Basin Foundation in Thermopolis, Wyoming.

BIG HORN BASIN FOUNDATION

Volunteer Bob removes rock surrounding an Apatosaurus femur.

(www.wyodino.org), offers a free training program at four levels asking a commitment of one week per level from its volunteers. The BHBF, a nonprofit educational organization tax-exempt since 1996, is dedicated to preserving and protecting the earth's natural history. The Wyoming Dinosaur Center (WDC), at the Warm Springs Ranch, has a museum and over 60 dinosaur dig sites on 500 acres.

Volunteers are required to complete certification programs before assisting staff. If you pass the basic level, which includes an introduction to the elementary requirements of fossil preparation, you may assist with hour-long programs and digs. Learn about proper documentation, identifying bones and abnormalities, applying glue, and prep processes. At the intermediate level you will prepare specimens and learn about the functions and rules of the prep lab. After passing the three-day intermediate prep course, you may assist with day programs and be eligible for the intermediate field certification course.

Basic field certification is an introduction to what to look for, how to recognize fossils, and how to dig with basic tools. Although the basic field course does not require completing the basic prep course, it is recommended by the BHBF/WDC volunteer program, which requires certification through at least the intermediate level in order to work at dig sites without staff supervision. Hill supervisors will assist volunteers in developing site plans. As you gain more experience you will be given more options to participate in projects. Contact the Big Horn Basin Foundation to schedule certification. Donations are not mandatory for instruction but are gratefully accepted.

If you are traveling as a family, consider the Kids' Dig for ages 8–12, or the Dinosaur Academy for high school students (www.Dinosauracademy.com). There are Elderhostel digs available as well. Visit the BHBF Web site for a list of accommodations (including tent and RV camping options) and attractions in the area, or contact the Chamber of Commerce (307-864-3192).

Warren and Betty's Prehistoric Story

My husband, Warren, has always had a real interest in dinosaurs. When we go on vacation we try to find places about dinosaurs. We visited the Wyoming Dinosaur Center's museum and dig sites, and were about ready to leave when we saw a sign in the gift shop that said "Ask us about our volunteer program." We did and returned the following summer as volunteers.

The training and experience are basically free. They trained us quite well on how to prep the dinosaur bones and how to use all of the tools: air scribes, sandblaster,

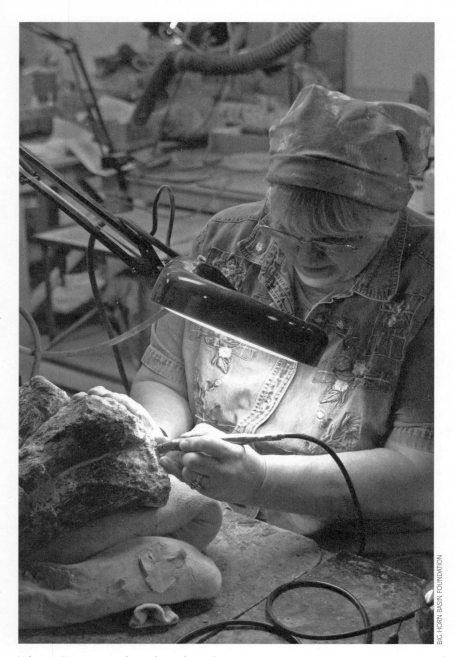

BIG HORN BASIN FOUNDATION

Volunteer Betty prepares the toe bones from a large Camarasaurus.

toothbrushes, dental picks, and matrix scrapes. Our job was to separate the rock from the bones so molds could be made. It's quite an experience to see how they are made and how long they take to construct.

The truth is, we get so involved with our bones we can hardly stay away. Warren just finished working on a bone that took 67 hours to prep—amazing. If anyone had ever told me that I was going to love using my summers sitting and working over dinosaur bones eight hours a day, week after week, I'd have said, yeah, right.

Paleontology, Hell Creek Formation, ND: Marmarth Research Foundation (P.O. Box 5, Marmarth, ND 58643; 610-937-7916; June–Aug, 701-279-6601; www.mrfdigs.com; tyler.lyson@mrfdigs.com; adults: 1 week, $1,000; 2 weeks, $1,900; additional weeks, $850/week; high school or college students and teachers: 1 week, $900; 2 weeks, $1,700; additional weeks, $775/week). Volunteer with the Marmarth Research Foundation (MRF), a nonprofit corporation tax-exempt since 2006, in the Hell Creek Formation of North Dakota, and assist professional paleontologists with the excavation of dinosaur bones.

Project activities may include removing overburden (the top, sterile layer of rock and soil), going through the bone layer, or prospecting. Fossils with no scientific merit may be kept as souvenirs. A lunch break is followed by work in the field until 3–4 PM. There may be lectures after a buffet dinner, but most evenings are free. The prep lab is open between 7 and 9 PM, and many volunteers choose to help with cleaning and repairing bones and preparing them for study or display.

Last year more than 86 volunteers participated in this summer program. Students between the ages of 14 and 17 must be accompanied by an adult, which makes this a great family project as well as an opportunity for anyone who is fascinated by the prospect of discovering fossils and prepping bones at the foundation's lab.

The fees include three meals a day, lodging, an MRF T-shirt, transportation to and from dig sites, and equipment. Accommodations are in a bunkhouse maintained by the Marmarth Historical Society. There is a communal bathroom with showers, and towels and bed linens are provided. Coin-operated laundry facilities are available. There is Wi-Fi, but bring a calling card for long-distance calls, as most cell phones are unable to receive a signal.

View the current schedule on the MRF Web site, along with a list of what to bring and information on past and ongoing excavations. There is a registration form you can download and print. The closest airport is in Rapid City, South Dakota, and transportation for the 180-mile trip to the foundation costs $60 per person, roundtrip.

Jack's Story, Dinosaur Dig, Marmarth, ND

Participating in this program for the past five years has greatly enriched my life. I travel there from my home on the East Coast, and people converge from all over, of all ages, working together. I'm a septuagenarian embracing the experience of finding a dinosaur and digging it out of the ground. Depending upon what day it is and what you are doing, walking and digging in the hot sun is hard work. The main attraction is that new discoveries are continually being made, and you can only keep doing that by digging up old bones.

I experience firsthand all phases of paleontology. I go out and search, dig it up, and ready it to ship back to the lab. Then I prepare it for display. All of the parts of it add up to the total experience. We dig on private property around Marmarth, a very isolated spot with

about 138 residents. I enjoy every part of it, from learning from the experts to sleeping in a bunkhouse and
eating hot breakfasts and dinner with everyone talking
about the dig.

Defenders of Wildlife

Defenders of Wildlife (1130 17th St., NW, Washington, DC 20036;
1-800-385-9712; www.defenders.org; defenders@mail.defenders.org). Defenders of
Wildlife is a national nonprofit membership organization, founded in 1947, dedicated
to the protection of all native animals and plants in their natural habitats and committed to saving endangered wildlife through advocacy and political campaigns.
Defender's Wildlife Volunteer Corps connects people with volunteer opportunities to
help protect, monitor, and recover wildlife, habitats, and ecosystems. Corps volunteers work with others who share their interests and contribute to the conservation
of wildlife. Register on the Web site and Defenders of Wildlife will contact you when
there is an opportunity in your area.

**Study Moose and Wolves, Isle Royale, MI: School of
Forest Resources & Environmental Science** (Michigan
Technological University, Houghton, MI 49931; www.isle
royalewolf.org; lmvuceti@mtu.edu). Apply for a four-week
internship, early May to mid-June, to help researchers from
Michigan Technological University with an ongoing project
that studies the predator-prey system. Find the full listing
in Chapter 5, "National Treasures."

**Fisheries Science Center's Survey Cruises,
Woods Hole, MA: The National Oceanic and
Atmospheric Administration (NOAA) Ocean Life
Sampler** (166 Water St., Woods Hole, MA 02543; 508-495-
2342; www.volunteer.noaa.gov; www.volunteer.noaa.gov/
fisheries_oceanlife.html; katherine.sowers@noaa.gov).

Volunteers are welcome on most of the Northeast Fisheries Science Center's survey cruises on a space-available basis. Get hands-on experience aboard a research vessel and participate in an exciting volunteer vacation at sea. Cruises are usually two to three weeks in duration and monitor fish abundance and survival, the geographic distribution of species, ecosystem changes, biologic rates of the stocks, and environmental data.

Volunteer work varies depending on the type of survey and will be described to you at a pre-cruise meeting. There are spring and fall bottom-trawl surveys, sea-scallop dredge surveys, summer and fall trawl surveys, marine mammal sighting surveys, and surveys of fish eggs and larvae. There will be hands-on demonstrations aboard ship.

There are two 12-hour watches around the clock, seven days a week. Off-watch time is your own to sleep, read, write, exercise, sunbathe, and do laundry. All boats have exercise facilities and televisions, with movies shown daily. Meals are served cafeteria-style, and several choices are available, including vegetarian by previous request.

It is also possible to arrange to arrive the day before your cruise sails and spend the night aboard the ship. Cruises are out of Woods Hole, a seaside village on Cape Cod between Buzzards Bay and Vineyard Sound. Check the NOAA Web site for a schedule of current surveys with dates and vessels; read about each type of survey and find full descriptions (with photos) of the vessels, including living arrangements.

Volunteers will be contacted by the Chief Scientist or his or her representative a week before the cruise to verify departure time and answer any questions.

Travel Plans

T. F. Green, serving Warwick/Providence, and Logan in Boston are the nearest airports. There is a bus depot in

Woods Hole, a short walk from the ships and laboratory. Call the bus station (508-548-7588) for a schedule. If you rent a car, the nearest drop-off point is in Falmouth, 4 miles from Woods Hole, with trolley service from the end of May through Labor Day.

Animal Care, Kanab, UT: Best Friends Animal Society (5001 Angel Canyon Rd., Kanab, UT 84741; 435-644-2001; network.bestfriends.org; volunteers@bestfriends.org). Best Friends Sanctuary volunteers visit for a few hours, a day, a week, or longer, and it is a great trip to take as a family. Children between the ages of 6 and 17 may work with animals at the discretion of staff and must be accompanied by an adult. Spend your time with dogs and cats, birds, rabbits, horses, potbellied pigs, and other wildlife, helping with cleaning, grooming, feeding, walking, and socializing the animals. There are two volunteer sessions a day, morning and afternoon.

About 2,000 animals live at the sanctuary, a nonprofit corporation, tax-exempt since 1971; they are sent from shelters and rescue groups all over the country. Some of the animals are up for adoption, while others spend their lifetimes on site. Each year, 20,000 people visit as a sole destination or while exploring southern Utah. Best Friends is in the center of the Golden Circle of national parks in beautiful red-rock country. You can plan a visit to the Grand Canyon, Zion National Park, Bryce Canyon, Grand Staircase–Escalante National Monument, and Lake Powell, as well as explore Angel Canyon, which has ties to the ancestral Puebloans.

Travel and Accommodations

The closest major airport is Las Vegas, and driving from Las Vegas to Kanab takes four hours. There are also commuter flights to St. George, Utah, from Salt Lake City and Los Angeles. The drive from St. George is about an hour and a half.

There are eight one-bedroom guest cottages in the red cliffs of Angel Canyon, which overlook the horse pastures. They are $125 per night double occupancy (high season, March 1 to November 30) with $10 a night for each additional person. Best Friends members receive a discount.

Cabins are available on sanctuary property. They are studios with one queen-sized bed and a kitchenette, available for $82 a night and suitable for one or two people. There are two new, fully equipped RV sites, with beautiful views, for $45 a night or $270 per week. Stays are limited to 14 consecutive nights.

Immersion Excursion: The People Who Came Before

Angel Canyon is the ancestral home of the Anasazi, the "people who came before," or "the ancient ones," who planted corn, peppers, beans, squash, and other plants native to the area. The earliest Anasazi in the Southwest were known as Basket Makers. They wove baskets that were then covered with mud and baked, and they used plant and animal materials to make their clothing, sandals, and cooking utensils. Ruins and rock art from the Basket Maker period can still be found in Angel Canyon. The rock art tells us that the Anasazi used celestial movements to schedule their planting, harvesting, and other ceremonies—the same ceremonies celebrated by the Hopi and other Pueblo tribes today. There are no depictions of any violence in the rock art, unlike almost all other ancient civilizations. The Anasazi's legacy of peace and harmony is still present among the modern Hopi people, and alive in Angel Canyon.

Visit Petroglyph Rock, carved about one thousand years ago; Kanab Creek and Crossing; Angel's Landing; Angel's Rest pet cemetery; the Underground Lake, which is rumored to be the place where the Aztec King Montezuma hid his treasure; Red Canyon; and the rock formation known as Shaman's Needle.

⑤ Wildlife and Environmental Support, Orr, MN: American Bear Association

(P.O. Box 77, Orr, MN 55771; 218-757-0172; www.americanbear.org; bears@americanbear.org). The American Bear Association, a nonprofit corporation since 1995, offers an opportunity to volunteer at the Vince Shute Wildlife Sanctuary (VSWS). Located on 520 acres in the North Woods of Minnesota, two hours northwest of Duluth, VSWS is a seasonal home to many black bears. There are aspen forests, open meadows, cedar swamps, marshes, beaver ponds, and a primary stream, and these habitats are shared with white-tailed deer, bald eagles,

JOHN DERYCH JR.

Alphie is most often found hanging out in his favorite tree.

JOHN DERYCH JR.

Two black bear cubs.

mink, pine martens, fishers, timber wolves, red squirrels, bobcats, owls, ducks, songbirds, ravens, and other wildlife. An elevated platform allows visitors to view and photograph the wild bears that come to the sanctuary each summer.

Volunteering outdoors in an extraordinary setting, meeting people from across the county and visitors from abroad, and learning about the bears and other wildlife and their habitats are rewarding and exciting experiences. The work varies, and your interests and skills are matched to appropriate jobs when possible. Most activities involve manual labor, so good health and stamina are necessary, along with enthusiasm.

Jobs range from daily cleanups to cooking meals for staff and volunteers, picking up and unloading supplies, maintaining the property, planting, mulching, weeding, road maintenance, and preparing bear food. You may also

JOHN DERYCH JR.

Peanut is a very happy bear at the Vince Shute   A mother bear nursing her cubs looks content.
Wildlife Sanctuary (VSWS) in Orr, Minnesota.

greet visitors, park cars, educate the public and answer their questions, or work in the gift shop.

Volunteer days begin early and may end late, with time off in the afternoon, from May 1 through September 30. You may volunteer for a weekend or the entire summer, or any period of time in between.

While it is not possible to provide housing for everyone, efforts are made to accommodate long-term volunteers. Some people stay at nearby Cabin O' Pines Resort (218-757-3122, www.cabinopines.com), which offers a discount to sanctuary volunteers. The town of Orr offers a variety of accommodations, including motels, resorts, and camp-grounds. Contact the Orr Tourist Information Center at 1-800-357-9255.

Volunteers enjoy social events together, relaxing around campfires, enjoying barbeques and picnics, and swimming in nearby Pelican Lake. There's also fishing, boating, and canoeing in area lakes, and hiking at the International Wolf Center, Superior National Forest, and at Voyageurs National Park.

John's Story, Vince Shute Wildlife Sanctuary, Orr, MN

My passion is photographing and learning more about bears. I first visited Minnesota in 1991, when I joined a biologist to check on hibernating bears in the middle of the winter. I have continued to return at least twice a year to the Vince Shute Wildlife Sanctuary. My photography skills have greatly improved, as has my knowledge of bears.

Five years ago I took over the volunteer job of editor for our quarterly and weekly newsletters, *Bear in Mind* and *Volunteer Voice*. My full-time job is working for the U.S. Postal Service in Long Island, NY, but 99 percent of my spare time is spent getting updates from the sanctuary for future publications, checking out about 40 other bear Web sites for pertinent information, and responding to e-mail questions about bears.

The American Bear Association asks visitors and volunteers to stop by and get to know the bears.

I do all of these volunteer jobs because of my love for bears and my desire to share the information I have gained with others. When I volunteer, I give talks to visitors on the viewing deck, answer their many questions, and correct misconceptions. Bears are one of the true great survivors in nature.

Sea Turtle Preservation, Savannah, GA: Caretta Research Project (P.O. Box 9841, Savannah, GA 31412; 912-447-8655; fax 912-447-8656; www.carettaresearch project.org; WassawCRP@aol.com; registration fee, $650). The primary goal of the Caretta Research Project (CRP) is to monitor loggerhead sea turtle activity and protect nests on Wassaw National Wildlife Refuge in Chatham County, Georgia. CRP, a nonprofit environment organization founded in 1972, educates the public about conservation and management of marine turtles. Volunteer for a week and help protect the turtles and improve their chances of survival as you collect data, watch the turtles lay their eggs, and follow the hatchlings on their trip to the sea.

Volunteer work varies, and includes working at night during egg-laying season. All nests are covered with screens to protect them from small animals. Turtles are measured and tagged, and nests may need to be relocated. You need to be in good health and able to do a lot of walking, dig out nests, and carry buckets of eggs.

Volunteers stay in a small, rustic cabin with an indoor bathroom and outdoor shower. There is no air-conditioning. A second cabin has a kitchen, dining area, and staff bunkroom. Electricity is available in the kitchen cabin only. Meals are included. Team members help with housekeeping, dinner prep, cooking, and cleanup. Each team has six volunteer spaces and participants must be 16 years or older if traveling alone or with friends the same age.

Call to check week availability, and submit reservations on or after January 2 for egg-laying season, mid-May through early August, or hatchling season, late July through September. Download an application on the Web site. No special gear is necessary, and a suggested packing list is provided. Leisure time is built in to explore Wassaw Island, swim, hike, relax on the beach, photograph the wildlife, and make new friends

National Wildlife Federation

National Wildlife Federation (11100 Wildlife Center Dr., Reston, VA 20190; 1-800-822-9919; www.nwf.org; volunteer team, 1-800-247-7387, ext. 6177 or volunteer-match@nwf.org). The National Wildlife Federation (NWF), a nonprofit organization founded in 1936, inspires people to protect wildlife for future generations. Register to become a NWF volunteer on the Web site or by contacting NWF. Opportunities include becoming a Habitat Ambassador, a Global Warming Ambassador, or a Wildlife Literacy Ambassador. You can also join a group to help restore wildlife habitat in Louisiana, or be a behind-the-scenes volunteer at NWF offices or from your home. An even more unusual volunteer opportunity is a frog- and toad-monitoring program, which collects information to help protect these amphibians. Find more information about Frogwatch USA, including how to observe and report on frogs, on the NWF Web site.

Work with Primates, Saugus, CA: Gibbon Conservation Center (P.O Box 800249, Santa Clara, CA 91380; 661-296-2737; fax 661-296-1237; www.gibbon center.org; gibboncenter@earthlink.net; ages 20+). Volunteer at the Gibbon Conservation Center (GCC) and assist with feeding, data collection, and maintenance. GCC, a nonprofit corporation since 1995, is dedicated to the study and preservation of gibbons and the education of the public about these endangered primates. All staff members at the center are volunteers.

Resident volunteers need to commit to a minimum of one month of service. You will be responsible for your

Female and infant male gibbons at the Gibbon Conservation Center, Santa Clara, California.

Female and male white-cheeked gibbons.

C. CUNNINGHAM

Gibbon Conservation Center director Alan Mootnick gives a tour to college students as a volunteer feeds gibbons.

travel costs and food, vaccinations, and medical tests. To secure your place, send a $200 deposit at least three months in advance; it is refunded after you complete your service commitment.

Housing is provided at no charge, in a trailer, possibly shared with another volunteer. Bedding, towels, dishes, and access to kitchen, laundry, and bathroom facilities are included, or you may stay in a nearby hotel at your own expense. There are openings year-round, and GCC usually has more need of volunteers from September through April. There is an application on the GCC Web site, which must be accompanied by a résumé and two letters of recommendation.

GCC needs volunteer Primate Keepers to prepare gibbon food, feed gibbons, change water, and clean the kitchen, bathroom, and enclosures. This position requires a full day of work, from about 7 AM to 5 PM, seven days a week. Other responsibilities may include behavioral observations, medicating gibbons, and doing library research, depending on your skills, experience, and the center's needs.

Center Assistants may do grounds and enclosures maintenance work, behavioral observations, cleaning of food-preparation areas, library research, fundraising, and word processing. Clerical Assistants do word processing, research, and fundraising. Both Center and Clerical Assistants are required to keep a minimum distance of 6 feet from gibbon enclosures. All resident volunteers should be self-motivated, love animals, and able to work alone. You also need to be comfortable in a rather isolated location. GCC is located in Saugus, California, about an hour north of Los Angeles. It's a perfect getaway for volunteers who enjoy biking, hiking, reading, bird-watching, and other solitary pursuits.

The GCC Web site has specific guidelines for being in close proximity to the gibbons, along with required medical tests and vaccinations. There is also a suggested reading list, to prepare you for your volunteer experience.

Fiona's Story, Gibbon Conservation Center, Santa Clara, CA

> For anyone with a love of animals wanting to get "up close and personal" with primates, GCC is a wonderful opportunity. I volunteered at the center for four weeks and thoroughly enjoyed becoming part of the gibbons' day-to-day life. You quickly learn their different personalities and how to interact with them during the

nine feeding sessions a day, and it is fascinating to observe behaviors and hierarchies in the social pairs and groups.

The volunteer accommodations are very comfortable, and it was great to work so closely with experts and volunteers alike. GCC continued my learning of patience, tolerance, and understanding that I have developed from volunteering all over the world, as well as the fun of being out of my comfort zone. I learned new skills, made good friends, and took away experiences that very few people can match.

Volunteer Fiona has an armful of gibbon babies.

Care for Wildlife; Sanibel Island, FL: Clinic for the Rehabilitation of Wildlife (P.O. Box 150, Sanibel Island, FL 33957; 239-472-3644; volunteer coordinator, ext. 1; fax 239-472-8544; crowclinic.org; crowclinic@aol.com). The Clinic for the Rehabilitation of Wildlife (CROW), a non-profit corporation since 1973, is dedicated to the rescue, care, rehabilitation, and release of sick, injured, and orphaned native wildlife. Volunteer to help with daily wildlife care; organize food and diets; rescue and/or transport injured birds, mammals, and reptiles; repair cages; and help with grounds maintenance, fundraising, and education programs.

You can impact the health and welfare of wildlife and contribute to the education of the public to ensure people respect and protect wildlife and their habitats. Work involves cleaning cages and other daily chores. Volunteers may also be taught to feed baby birds, prepare diets for CROW patients, transport wildlife to veterinary hospitals, and, with specific training, help capture injured wildlife.

Grounds maintenance includes tree-trimming, mowing, general landscaping, and gardening. Volunteers are needed to help with fundraising events from event planning and invitations to selling tickets, working booths, parking, and other tasks. Training is provided for outreach presentations to service clubs, schools, and other organizations. CROW's staff, with the help of volunteers, provides care for more than 4,000 patients a year and over 160 different wildlife species.

Marine Mammals/Education and Research, Grassy Key, FL: Dolphin Research Center (DRC, 58901 Overseas Hwy., Grassy Key, FL 33050; 305-289-1121; fax 305-743-7627; www.dolphins.org; drc-vr @dolphins.org). DRC is a nonprofit education and research facility founded in 1984, and home to a family of Atlantic bottlenose dolphins and California sea lions. DRC assists marine mammals in distress and has rehabilitated whales

Keenly Observed

Vacationing in Florida? This is a great family activity and for people of all ages. Consider assisting in a very worthwhile cause while enjoying the beach. **Marine Resources Council of East Florida** (MRC Headquarters, 3275 Dixie Hwy. NE, Palm Bay, FL 32905; 321-725-7775; fax 321-725-3554; www.mrcirl.org; council@mrcirl.org) requests that everyone on or near the beaches between November and April 1 call the whale-sighting hotline at 1-888-97-WHALE whenever they see a North Atlantic right whale. These are highly endangered whales in need of protection. When a call comes into the hotline, a response team goes out to document the sighting and ensure the whale is not injured or entangled.

and dolphins; it includes endangered manatees in its efforts. Volunteer at DRC and assist staff working in the fish house; answering visitors' questions; monitoring interactive programs and tours; and helping with maintenance chores and administrative tasks.

Volunteers are needed throughout the year, and work 40 hours a week with a minimum four-week commitment. There are also 12- to 18-week internships, which would be a great gap year option. Internships are offered year-round and concentrate on specific areas: animal care and training, special-needs education, research, and visual communications.

Housing and transportation are not provided for volunteers; however, you will be given a list of local housing and transportation services so that you can make your own arrangements. Besides the obvious benefits of your experience and the satisfaction of helping in the care of the dolphins, you will also be enjoying a wonderful location on the Gulf of Mexico, in the Florida Keys, and making new friends who share your interests.

Immersion Excursion: A Dolphin Day

One-Day Specials with the Dolphin Research Center (DRC, Grassy Key, FL; www.dolphins.org; drc-vr@dolphins.org; 305-289-0002; $650). Only have a day to spare? Use it well. Get to know a dolphin by signing up for one of DRC's great dolphin programs: meet a dolphin, swim with a dolphin, play with a dolphin, or paint with a dolphin. Yes, you will create a one-of-a-kind T-shirt work of art with a dolphin. If dolphins are your passion, consider planning ahead to be a dolphin researcher or trainer for a day. The Trainer-for-a-Day program pairs you with a professional for an entire workday and teaches you about animal training techniques. The day will include learning how to prepare the dolphins' meals and interacting with the dolphins in behavioral sessions, and playing and communicating with them using hand cues. At day's end you'll have a better idea of what the life of a dolphin trainer is like, along with new skills, photographs, and a trainer whistle. Family groups of up to six people can be accommodated by special arrangement. Adults must accompany children under 12. Special-needs programming is also available. This activity is handicap accessible.

Ⓢ **Humpback Whale Research, Lahaina, HI: The Hawaii Whale Research Foundation** (P.O. Box 1296, Lahaina, HI 96767; www.hwrf.org; Research Director, Dr. Dan Selden, dsalden@siue.edu). The Hawaii Whale Research Foundation (HWRF), a nonprofit corporation since 1994, is staffed by skilled, committed volunteers who conduct field research on humpback whale social affiliation, behavior, and communication. Volunteer opportunities exist for independent researchers who want to work with Hawaiian humpback whales. Off-island volunteers are expected to make a minimum commitment of four weeks.

Applicants should be researchers and doctoral students interested in marine mammals, and whales in particular.

Data collection involves note taking, photographing identifying features, and videotaping whale behavior. HWRF accepts a small number of research associates to assist with data collection from January through May.

Staff members, including visiting researchers, are not paid, and travel and living expenses are your responsibility. HWRF may be able to assist you in finding reasonable housing.

Immersion Excursion: Lahaina

Lahaina is in West Maui, in Maui County, Hawaii, where you can enjoy beautiful sunsets and numerous water activities. Whales are visible from Mala Wharf, the harbor just north of town. There are great restaurants, shopping, diving, and whale watching boats available. Kaʻanapali Beach is Maui's equivalent of Waikiki, just not as big or busy. The island of Maui offers many recreational and sightseeing options: helicopter rides, volcano sightseeing flights, ATV tours, sailing cruises, hiking, kayaking and snorkeling adventures, deep-sea fishing trips, surfing and sailboarding lessons, paragliding, and horseback riding tours. For more information on Lahaina, travel, lodging, dining, services, and things to do, visit www.lahainahi.com.

Volunteer Host, Multiple Locations, OR: Oregon Department of Fish and Wildlife (ODFW Volunteer Host Program, 7118 NE Vandenberg, Corvallis, OR 97330; 541-757-4186, ext. 230; www.dfw.state.or.us; vol.program @state.or.us). The Oregon Department of Fish and Wildlife (ODFW) offers opportunities for volunteers to participate in resource-management activities. Help support their programs and work to protect fish and wildlife by donating your time in a variety of positions, including maintenance of equipment and facilities, improving interpretive trails, removing invasive plants from wildlife areas, conducting surveys, collecting biological samples, monitoring fish

OREGON DEPARTMENT OF FISH AND WILDLIFE

A litter patrol volunteer with the Oregon Department Fish and Wildlife (ODFW) in Corvallis.

Collecting fish for research analysis is enjoyable and rewarding volunteer work.

populations and their habitats, and building fish-viewing platforms.

The ODFW Volunteer Host Program provides hookups for your own RV if you live and work for a month or longer at one of the ODFW fish hatcheries, offices, or wildlife areas. Volunteers donate 20 hours a week per person at 46 locations with host sites throughout the state. Respon-

OREGON DEPARTMENT OF FISH AND WILDLIFE

If you have your own RV, a popular summer activity is to be a campground host in a national or state park.

sibilities vary with location and needs, and may include greeting the public, giving tours, assisting with farming to benefit wildlife, feeding fish, gardening and grounds maintenance, carpentry, data entry, clerical and computer work, and working at special events.

This is a great program that allows plenty of time to enjoy Oregon's natural areas, meet other RV owners from across the nation, use your skills or gain new ones, interact with the public, give something back to the wildlife and the habitats you care about, and enhance the experience for others. Most RV hookups are located close to recreation opportunities. Go to the ODFW Web site to download a Volunteer Host Booklet and Host Application, and to check current host site availability.

Elaine and Bruce's Story, Oregon State Department of Wildlife and Fisheries, Corvallis, OR

We have a 40-foot motor home, which lets us get away and see different places. For years we volunteered as campground hosts in state parks until we found an advertisement, in the *Good Sam Camping* magazine, for the Oregon State Department of Wildlife and Fisheries, to work (or volunteer, or work as volunteer hosts) at a fish hatchery. They raise hatchery steelhead trout, hatch the eggs, and stock local lakes and rivers.

The first year we worked with the hatchery we signed up for two months and then asked for an extension. We trade 20 hours of work a week each for a hookup for our motor home. We do general maintenance and yard work and on the weekends clean the offices. The people are very easy to work for. If something comes up that we don't want to do, we don't do it. On our time off we volunteer at the local food bank and visit a lot of the old towns around here.

Research Vessel Whale Watch Trips, Gloucester, MA: The Whale Center of New England (P.O. Box 159,Gloucester, MA 01931; 978-281-6351; fax 978-281-5666; www.whalecenter.org; info@whalecenter.org; $110 per person for members; $125 per person for nonmembers; $50 of fare is tax deductible). The Whale Center of New England (WCNE) accepts up to six people per cruise, two days a week during the summer, on the research vessel *Mysticete*. Full-day cruises are conducted by the Whale Center staff and U.S. Coast Guard licensed captains.

Research may include photo-identification censuses, behavioral observations, and surveys of whale prey. Volunteers on WCNE cruises have access to areas that public whale watch boats are not permitted to enter, and while there are no guided tours, there's the opportunity to interact with and engage Whale Center scientists in informal discussions. This is a great day trip or activity to plan a weekend excursion around, or add to an already planned trip to Gloucester. Reservations are required.

WCNE, a nonprofit organization, was founded in 1980 to study whales in the waters off the Massachusetts coast. Its mission is to contribute to the understanding and protection of marine mammals and their habitats though research, conservation, and education. Summer volunteer positions are open to college undergraduates after their junior year or to recent graduates; WCNE is looking for volunteers with enthusiasm, science backgrounds, and strong communications skills. Room and board are not provided, but there is no fee for the program. Volunteers are put in touch with each other to find shared accommodations, and are guaranteed two days off a week.

Fall and spring internships are also available, and college credit may be arranged. Interns pay $1,000 for their experience, which includes shared housing, utilities, education, staff support, and a weekly food stipend. Applications are accepted on a rolling basis, and positions are very competitive. Visit the WCNE Web site for internship details, requirements, and how to apply.

Immersion Tip: A Multitude of Tours

Gloucester, Massachusetts (www.gloucesterma.com) is the country's oldest seaport. It is part of Cape Ann, about 30 miles northeast of Boston. Most of Gloucester is an island, connected by bridges to the cape, which also includes the towns of Rockport, Manchester, and Essex. American painters Fitz Hugh Lane, Winslow Homer, Milton Avery, and John Sloan painted in Gloucester, and it is said that the light in Gloucester is unique. The Rocky Neck Art Colony in East Gloucester is the oldest continuously operating art colony in the country. Poetry, theater, dance, sculpture, music, and many other cultural offerings are available to residents and visitors year-round. You can tour Gloucester by sea or by land, with choices that include a harbor loop, river cruise, sail charters, sea kayaking, bus tours, walking tours, bike tours, and seasonal whale watching. Local train service out of Boston has a special car for bikes and bike riders on weekends. Don't forget to check out the beautiful beaches, whale-watching cruises, the historic lighthouses, and downtown Gloucester, where many of the art galleries are located.

Ⓢ Caring for Pigs, Marana, AZ: Ironwood Pig Sanctuary (P.O. Box 35490, Tucson, AZ 85740; 520-631-6015 or 520-575-8469; ironwoodpigsanctuary.org; ironwoodpigs@yahoo.com). The Ironwood Pig Sanctuary, a nonprofit organization founded in 2000, wants to eliminate the suffering of potbellied pigs by promoting spaying and neutering and providing a permanent home for those that are abandoned, abused, or neglected. The sanctuary, home to approximately 540 potbellied pigs, also assists pig owners and other refuges. Accommodations are available for volunteers who can donate a week, or more.

There is work at all times of year, cleaning up, feeding the pigs, watering, making repairs, adding shelters, or socializing the pigs. If you have skills that you think the pig sanctuary can use, tell them what you can do and when you are available to volunteer. If you prefer to help out at the sanctuary during your stay in Tucson, you can work in the office with data entry, organization, filing, typing, mailing, and other clerical duties.

The Ironwood Pig Sanctuary takes in more pigs as they find homes for others, trying to keep their numbers stable. Some pigs live out their lives in this safe and caring environment located in Marana, Arizona, a one-hour drive from Tucson, on 80 acres of Sonora Desert habitat. This is a premier bird-watching area, and there are mountains nearby for hiking.

Whale Conservation

The American Cetacean Society (P.O. Box 1391, San Pedro, CA 90733; 310-548-6279; fax 310-548-6950; whale watch information, 310-548-7821; trip information, 310-548-7821; www.acsonline.org; memberships $25 and up). The American Cetacean Society (ACS), a nonprofit organization founded in 1967, is the oldest whale conservation group in the world. ACS protects whales, dolphins, porpoises, and their habitats, and members can become involved by volunteering for the society's yearly gray whale census, counting dolphins, reporting strandings, training as naturalists, or participating in special projects or events. Members can also join ACS Whale Watch trips accompanied by certified naturalists for a great learning vacation. ACS chapter meetings are free and open to the public.

 Exotic Animal Refuge, Tampa, FL: Big Cat Rescue (12802 Easy St., Tampa, FL 33625; 813-920-4130; fax 813-920-5924; www.bigcatrescue.org; Kathryn Quaas, Big Cat Rescue Intern Manager, 813-426-5948; Intern1@bigcatrescue.org; Info@BigCatRescue.org). Big Cat Rescue (BCR), in Tampa, Florida, a nonprofit educational sanctuary founded in 1992, offers three-month internships with three-month extensions available to qualified candidates, depending on available housing. The Intern Program has 6–12 positions, overlapping throughout the year. Training classes include Animal Observation, Animal Emergency, Small Cat Cleaning, Guest Relations, Human First Aid, Events, Big Cat Cleaning, Animal Feeding, Enrichment, Operant Training, and Tour Guides.

Level 1 internships, open to ages 18 and older, are full-time positions that provide an introduction for those with little or no exotic animal training. The work is primarily physical and outdoors in all weather. You are responsible for your own food, transportation, and long-distance calls. Housing is provided free of charge in group houses that can accommodate two to four interns. The commitment is to a five- or six-day week of 50+ hours, with a 10:00 PM curfew for the duration of the internship.

Level 1 responsibilities include enclosure cleaning, diet preparation, feeding, operant conditioning, and behavioral enrichment for Siberian and Canada lynx, servals, caracals, bobcats, ocelots, jungle cats, Geoffrey's cats, leopard cats, fishing cats, and other exotic cats. Tigers, lions, leopards, snow leopards, and cougars are not cared for by interns. Ground maintenance includes cage renovations, landscaping, and building maintenance. An additional part of the programming is the opportunity to interact with guests and assist with educational tours and programs.

⑤ Rescued Exotic Animals, Zolfo Springs, FL: Peace River Refuge and Ranch (P.O. Box 1127, 2545 Stoner Lane., Zolfo Springs, FL 33890; 863-735-0804; fax 863-735-0805; peaceriverrefuge.org; volunteer@peace riverrefuge.org). Peace River Refuge and Ranch is a nonprofit exotic animal sanctuary, tax-exempt since 1999, dedicated to the care of abused, neglected, confiscated, or unwanted exotic animals. The animals, rescued from potentially harmful situations and given permanent homes, include tigers, cougars, leopards, wolves, bears, primates, small wild cats, and bats. Natural habitats are provided on the 90-acre compound, and the animals' medical, nutritional, and emotional needs are met by the skilled staff.

Volunteers at Peace River Refuge and Ranch engage in hard work and strenuous exercise. There are many different activities available, and your help will make a difference in the lives of these animals. The animals are not accustomed to human interaction and require special handling by experienced staff. The program focuses on proper management of captive wild animals, and does not promote private ownership of exotic animals.

On-site accommodations are not provided for volunteers. However, there are exotic-animal-care internships offered that do provide room and board for students enrolled in an animal-related college curriculum, or who have graduated with a degree in animal-related studies such as zoology, biology, or animal psychology. Information about accommodations, application guidelines, an internship job description, and a downloadable application form is on the Web site.

Accommodations

⑤⑤ **The Double M Ranch** (4202 Sweetwater Rd., Zolfo Springs, FL 33890; 941-735-0266, call after 6 pm; www.seekon.com/L/US/FL/Zolfo_Springs; $65 per night for double occupancy, single occupancy $55 per night; breakfast includes fresh-squeezed orange juice from the ranch groves; no children under 13). The Double M Ranch Bed and Breakfast is a working citrus and cattle ranch in Hardee Country, central Florida, two hours from beaches, Walt Disney World, Busch Gardens, Sea World, Cypress Gardens, Gatorland, and other attractions.

Immersion Excursion: The Cracker Trail

On November 20, 2000, the Florida Cracker Trail was selected as a Community Millennium Trail; a partnership among the White House Millennium Council, the Department of Transportation, Rails-to-Trails Conservancy, the National Endowment for the Arts, and other public agencies and private organizations. The goal of Millennium Trails is the creation of a nationwide network of trails that protect the natural environment, interpret history and culture, and enhance alternative transportation, recreation, and tourism.

The historic Florida Cracker Trail is a route originally used both by cattle and horses that runs approximately 120 miles from east of Bradenton to Fort Pierce. Today the

Cracker Trail shares sections with interstate highways. There is an annual Cracker Trail ride in February to bring attention to Florida's horse and cattle heritage. The five-day Pioneer Days Festival and the Grand Prix car race in nearby Sebring are held in March. There's also excellent bird-watching and extensive hiking, biking, and horseback-riding trails.

 Endangered Elephants, Hohenwald, TN: The Elephant Sanctuary (P.O. Box 393, Hohenwald, TN 38462; 931-796-6500; fax 931-796-1360; www.elephants .com; elephant@elephants.com; ages 15+, volunteers under 18 must be accompanied by an adult). The Elephant Sanctuary, a nonprofit organization since 1995, is the

THE ELEPHANT SANCTUARY

Four of the Elephant Sanctuary's favorite girls: Delhi, Sissy, Tina, and Winkie.

THE ELEPHANT SANCTUARY

These Elephant Sanctuary divas are happily living out their days in Hohenwald, Tennessee.

country's largest natural-habitat refuge specifically designed to meet the needs of old, sick, or needy elephants retired from circuses and zoos. On more than 2,700 acres, it has separate environments for endangered Asian and African elephants, with pastures, forests, spring-fed ponds, and heated barns. The sanctuary's mission also includes providing education to the public about these endangered creatures.

Volunteers can spend a day working on a sanctuary-directed project, or sign up to help at a fundraiser or awareness booth at a special event. Volunteer Days are both inside and outside, without any direct contact with elephants, but your contribution will benefit the elephants in many ways. Projects may include painting fencing, renovating existing structures, or helping clean up new areas of habitat. The sanctuary needs 12 crew members per Volunteer Day and accepts both individuals and groups.

You need to be in good physical condition, and a tetanus shot is recommended. Volunteer Day hours are 8:45 AM to 3 PM, with check-in by 8:30 AM. Reservations are required, and a map is provided when your registration is accepted. Bring a sack lunch and enough water for the day. A small camera is suggested to record your visit. Be prepared for inclement weather, as rain will not cancel volunteer activities, and wear proper insect repellents, work boots, long pants, sunscreen, and sunglasses. Latex gloves are recommended for painting projects; you will have the opportunity to clean up before returning to your vehicles.

Accommodations

ⓈⓈ–ⓈⓈⓈ **Aveleen Springs Bed and Breakfast** (7619 Hwy., 412 East Linden, TN 37096; 931-589-2857; www.bbonline.com/tn/avaleen; avaleenspringsretreat@msn .com; rooms, suites, and cabin from $85 to $179; breakfast included; midweek discount and special packages available). This B&B, in a rustic setting on more than 160 acres, offers hiking, walking trails, and a fishing lake. There is a small basketball court, horseshoes, croquet, and other activities on site, with many other attractions nearby, including the Antebellum Trail and Shiloh Civil War Battlefield, Amish and Mennonite communities, state parks, golf, and canoeing.

Ⓢ–ⓈⓈ **Many Cedars Campground and Trail Ride** (233 Pollock Cemetery Rd., Hohenwald, TN 38462; 931-796-4384; www.manycedarscamp.com; info@manycedars camp.com; open daily, Feb. 1–Oct. 31; camping and riding per person, $16 per day for adults; $5 per day for children 7–12; children under 6 free; $5 reservation deposit a week prior to stay; no charge to picket horses; includes potable water at site and electric hookups, bathhouse with hot showers and restrooms; 5 fully furnished cabins from $60 to $85, reservation deposit $25). There are 70 spacious, shaded campsites, with some sites on the banks of the Buffalo River. Riding trails range from easy to difficult, with rivers, streams, and springs on approximately 3,200 acres. Reservations for campsites and cabins are strongly suggested.

Juanita's Story, The Elephant Sanctuary, Hohenwald, TN

You can always give money, but the reward is truly for giving of yourself to something you are truly passionate about. Elephants are my favorite animals. I was watching *The Urban Elephant* on PBS. They had a program with one of the sanctuary elephants, Shirley, being transferred from a New Orleans zoo. I went directly to www.elephants.com and read the entire Web site to figure out what I could do to help these animals.

I've always loved elephants and wanted to do something, but how do you get involved with an elephant? Sure enough, the sanctuary has monthly volunteer days. I made vacation plans to go down there; it's a 12-hour drive from my home in Livonia, Michigan, to Hohenwald, Tennessee. I've gone down myself, with friends, and with my husband and daughter. It's hard work: taking fences down, weed whacking, digging trenches. There's no interaction with the elephants, but I get to see them with my own eyes, be on their sanctuary grounds, and I feel connected with them. I plan a vacation a year around volunteering with this awesome organization.

When you volunteer, you learn more about the plight to free elephants, and I have become that much more passionate about them. They do not belong in zoos.

Thoroughbred Adoption, Chapters in NJ, NY, KY: ReRun, Inc. (P.O. Box 113, Helmetta, NJ 08828; 732-521-1370; www.rerun.org; Qzee30@hotmail.com). ReRun, Inc. is a nonprofit thoroughbred adoption program that helps former racehorses find a second career. Horses are evaluated and rehabilitated, then placed with qualified adopters. ReRun, with chapters in New Jersey, New York, and Kentucky, is supported by grants, fundraising, donations, and volunteers.

ReRun needs volunteers to help with fundraising, event planning, marketing, and photography of horses and events. There is an annual horse show in September at the New Jersey Horse Park in Allentown, so if you are scheduling a trip to the area, be sure to contact volunteer coordina-

Thoroughbred Lifetime Care

Thoroughbred Retirement Foundation (P.O. Box 3387, Saratoga Springs, NY 12866; 518-226-0028; fax 518-226-0699; www.trfinc.org; diana@trfinc.org). The Thoroughbred Retirement Foundation (TRF) is a nonprofit organization founded in 1982 to save thoroughbred horses no longer able to compete on the racetrack from possible abuse, neglect, or slaughter. TRF says it is the world's largest organization dedicated to equine rescue.

It is also unique in its agreement with the State of New York Department of Correctional Services, which provides land use and labor in return for a vocational program—designed, staffed, and maintained by TRF—in equine care and management for inmates. The prison program has spread to include TRF farms at correctional facilities in Kentucky and in Maryland. You can help save thoroughbreds by adopting a horse, retiring a horse, sponsoring a horse, or making a donation.

tor Suzanne DeForne at the above e-mail address. Put "volunteer help" in the subject line, give your contact details, and list the skills you can contribute.

Riders can participate in the Annual ReRun Benefit Trail Ride. Pay at the gate; the donation is $15 per rider. Check the Web site for the date and place, and join ReRun for a great time for a great cause. For more information contact Debbie at 845-781-3420 or DebbieSchiraldi@hvc.rrr.com.

You may even want to adopt a retired thoroughbred, retrained from the racetrack to a new career in a show ring. Since ReRun was founded in 1996, 500 horses have been placed in new homes. If you are interested in adopting a horse, you need to fill out an application on the Web site and provide photographs of your stable.

Wolf Rescue, Candy Kitchen, NM: Wild Spirit Wolf Sanctuary (378 Candy Kitchen Rd., HC 61, Box 28, Ramah, NM 87321; 505-775-3304; fax 505-775-3824; www.wildspirit wolfsanctuary.org; info@ wildspiritwolfsanctuary .org; ages 21+). Wild Spirit Wolf Sanctuary, a non-profit organization incorporated since 1994 and tax-exempt since 1995, rescues abused and abandoned wolves and wolf-dogs and provides education to the public. More than 50 animals live at the sanctuary, a safe, permanent home.

MARY HILL

Wolves and volunteers develop very close relationships.

Fi meets Dakota the timber wolf for the first time while Allison, his caretaker, looks on.

Volunteers must commit to two months or longer; they receive housing, food allotments, and perhaps a stipend after 30 days, depending on funding. These long-term volunteers care for the animals and take part in animal-enrichment programs. The sanctuary asks that volunteers be respectful and compassionate toward all living creatures, self-motivated, responsible, and self-sufficient.

Weather can be harsh in the high desert, and primitive housing ranges from hogans, cabins, and trailers to dormitories. Wild Spirit Wolf Sanctuary invites you to challenge yourself, learn more about wolves and how a nonprofit organization works, and to make a difference working and caring for the animals. Applications are available on the Web site.

Fiona's Story, Wild Spirit Wolf Sanctuary, Ramah, NM

The Wild Spirit Wolf Sanctuary in Candy Lake, New Mexico, is huge and much more of everything than I expected. It was a big adjustment living in a trailer in the New Mexico desert, with 15 people sharing a shower. Adjusting to the heat, dryness, and altitude was tough, with hard physical work all day, raking scat, preparing feed, sweeping out, scrubbing, and socializing the animals.

None of these wolves was taken from the wild; they were bred in captivity in zoos or cross-bred with dogs because breeders mistakenly thought offspring would make good pets. A 12-week-old wolf cub looks like a puppy but grows to be enormous at one year, and at two starts testing for dominance for his place in the pack.

They are predators, big dangerous animals, not at all like dogs. Part of the training process is going into the enclosure with the wolves. Each volunteer is assigned a few animals to be responsible for, and you need to spend a lot of time with them so the wolves become comfortable sharing their space. You're a new thing, and they are frightened of anything new. The rewards are so amazing when you get to the stage where you are interacting with your wolves and taking a wolf for a walk.

Protecting Wolf Populations, Ely, MN: International Wolf Center (3410 Winnetka Ave. North, Suite 101, Minneapolis, MN 55427; 218-365-4695; fax 763-560-7368; www.wolf.org; bettym@ties2.net). Volunteers help the International Wolf Center advance their mission: the survival of wolf populations by educating people about wolves, their relationship to wild lands, and the human role in their future. The Ely, Minnesota, facility is situated in the heart of the largest wolf population in the lower 48 states. The center, a non-profit corporation since 1987, is actively involved in wolf research and public education, and has a wolf-viewing theater, classrooms, laboratory space, and a permanent exhibit, "Wolves and Humans."

The Ely facility has plenty of opportunities to volunteer and get involved. You can serve as a host or docent, conduct education programs, help maintain exhibits and facilitate children's activities, respond to information requests, do grounds maintenance, help with data entry, catalog library material, and perform other office tasks. If you are going to be in Minneapolis, you can contribute office support, staff Twin Cities–area events, assist with mailings and marketing, and help plan educational events and activities.

If you have professional skills to offer and want to work on grant writing, printing, graphic design, advertising, Web programming, or writing for *International Wolf* magazine, contact the Development Director at development@ wolf.org.

Ask about the Volunteer Rendezvous Schedule. There are sessions at the Wildlife Science Center, volunteer get-togethers, a volunteer appreciation night, and other events.

There are a variety of educational programs offered for adults and families including howling trips, radio tracking, snowshoe treks, family activities, dogsledding, videos, presentations, flights over wolf territory, demonstrations, and hikes.

Ely, Minnesota, is the perfect place for a weekend immersion excursion, with the wild beauty of the Boundary Waters Canoe Area Wilderness and first-class shopping, arts, and modern resorts. Read the full listing: **Trail work on portage trails, Boundary Waters Canoe Area**

Wilderness, Superior National Forest, MN: Wilderness Volunteers, Chapter 5, "National Treasures" for an additional activity in this area. Contact the Ely Chamber of Commerce, www.ely.org, for additional information on lodging, dining, and events.

Immersion Excursion: A Year-round Park

Voyageurs National Park (3131 Hwy. 53 South, International Falls, MN 56649; 218-283-9821; fax 218-285-7407; www.nps/voya/) is located on the northern edge of Minnesota where the United States borders Ontario, Canada. The park contains 218,054 acres, which include 83,789 acres of water. The park was named for the French-Canadian voyageurs, who traded goods and furs between the Canadian Northwest and Montreal. Visit in summer to fish and explore the waterways by motorboat, canoe, kayak, or by houseboat. The fall is a great time for hiking, and in winter you can enjoy snowshoeing, ice-fishing, cross-country skiing, and snowmobiling. Consider renting a winter villa complete with a cozy fireplace right on the park. Be sure to bring along your binoculars to view black bear, wolves, white-tailed deer, moose, red squirrels, and bird species including common loons, great blue herons, and white pelicans.

Accommodations

ⓈⓈ **Kettle Falls Hotel** (10502 Gamma Rd., Voyageurs National Park, MN 56669; 218-240-1724 or 218-240-1726; www.kettlefallshotel.com; kettlefalls@frontier.net: open May–mid-Oct.; rooms $50 per night adult, $20 per additional adult, $15 per child; air-conditioned villas and villa suites also available, daily or weekly rates). Kettle Falls Hotel is the only lodging within Voyageurs National Park and is accessible only by water. A free shuttle service is available from the docks to your room. With construction supposedly financed by Nellie Bly (American journalist, author, industrialist, charity worker, and adventurer), the hotel has hosted travelers since 1913. It was placed on the National Register of Historic Places in 1976 and renovated by the National Park Service in 1987.

Reintroduce the Wolf into Its Natural Habitat, Grand Canyon Region, AZ: Grand Canyon Wolf Recovery Project (P.O. Box 1594, Flagstaff, AZ 86002; 928-202-1325; www.gcwolfrecovery.org; info@gcwolfrecovery.org; Paula Lewis, Project Director, paula@gcwolfrecovery.org). Grand Canyon Wolf Recovery Project (GCWRP), founded in 2004, is a grassroots, nonprofit group, tax-exempt since 1998, whose mission is to bring back wolves and restore ecological health to the Grand Canyon Region. Volunteer to help

GRAND CANYON WOLF RECOVERY PROJ

The Native American group Futures for Children visited the Grand Canyon and volunteered with the Grand Canyon Wolf Recovery Project.

with outreach programs at the South or North Rim of the Grand Canyon, and commit to a few hours over one or more days to manage educational or interactive table displays. If you volunteer four or more days in a row, you will be eligible for a stipend. This is a great volunteer opportunity to expand an already planned trip to the Grand Canyon. Become educated about the history of the wolf in its natural habitat and then share your knowledge with others. Volunteers provide information, answer questions, hand out flyers, and encourage visitors to consider lending support by signing petitions, helping with mailings, and fundraising. Training will be provided at the City of Flagstaff Public Library; you can find training session and program dates, along with a Volunteer Request Form, on the GCWRP Web site.

Damien's Story, Northern Arizona University, Flagstaff, AZ

My experience is immersion travel in action. I'm from New York but was living in the Southwest completing my master's in Environmental Sociology. I have a strong interest in how culture is reflected in individual perceptions of wildlife, and I used the wolf as a metaphor for environmental consciousness.

My intention was to query visitors about their observations and how their perceptions of the wolf changed or stayed the same. As much as we want to be objective, by going through the human experience we become subjective.

I contacted the Grand Canyon Wolf Recovery project for a chance to do an internship and had a transformative experience. My project ended up with my being more than an intern. I developed a strong relationship with people in the organization and with wolves.

I observed people at the Grand Canyon and gathered information on their perceptions of wolves and their place in the natural environment. It all lumped together beautifully—the experience of living in the Southwest, my research in southwestern communities, and the Wolf Recovery Project.

I learned that travelers no longer simply want to travel and consume. Tourists today are interested in immersion travel—becoming part of the community they visit, giving a little of themselves, and taking something back home with them.

Habitat Restoration, Pelican Island National Wildlife Refuge, FL: Sierra Club (85 Second St., 2nd Floor, San Francisco, CA 94105; 415-977-5500; fax 415-977-5799; www.sierraclub.org; information@sierraclub.org; 1 week, $295). The membership-supported, nonprofit Sierra Club, founded in 1892, is the country's oldest, largest, and most influential grassroots environmental organization. This service trip to Pelican Island National Wildlife Refuge, America's first national wildlife refuge, is an ongoing project to restore wetland and hardwood-hammock habitats for the benefit of wildlife. The project involves removing invasive plants and contributing to the refuge's public facilities plan, which includes a quarter-mile boardwalk, an 18-foot observation tower, and a half-mile wildlife drive through restored wetland habitat.

Help preserve mangrove nesting grounds and roosting habitat, and enhance hiking and bird-watching opportunities in the refuge, located within the Indian River Lagoon on Florida's central eastern coast, the most diverse estuary in the country. The lagoon, which covers 156 miles and has six inlets that connect to the Atlantic Ocean, provides habitat for more than 2,200 animal species, 2,100 plant species, 700 species of fish, 310 species of birds, and 36 endangered species. Located on the Atlantic flyway, a bird-migration route that follows the Atlantic coast, the refuge has the most diverse bird population in North America. The Pelican Wildlife Refuge also provides habitat for one-third of the nation's manatee population.

You will have a day off to enjoy recreational activities, which might include kayaking/canoeing to view the Pelican Island rookery, fishing in the Indian River Lagoon or Sebastian Inlet State Park, boat tours, bird-watching, hiking, surfing, or just relaxing. Your trip leader will schedule evening ranger programs about the impact of humans on the Indian River Lagoon, the cost of controlling invasive plants and animals, the preservation of turtle nesting beaches, the reduction of pollution, and the conservation of energy and water.

Accommodations are at a campsite in Sebastian Inlet State Park, located 3 miles north of the Pelican Island Wildlife Refuge. Meals are planned by staff, and all trip participants assist with cooking. A current tetanus shot is required, and you must submit a medical-information form signed by a healthcare professional. A complete packing list will be sent upon registration.

Immersion Excursion: Spanish Gold

Be sure to visit the **McLarty Treasure Museum at Sebastian Inlet State Park**. It is located at the site where survivors of nine Spanish ships, lost in a 1715 hurricane, set up camp and spent the next few years trying to salvage sunken treasure. The Spanish filled treasure-hunting ships with silver and gold from the mountains of Mexico and South America and then made the long trip back to Spain along Florida's east coast. The McLarty Treasure Museum tells the story of the 1,500 survivors of the 1715 storm and their salvage efforts and displays found artifacts.

Service and Whales, Maui, HI: Sierra Club (Outings Department, 85 Second St., 2nd Floor, San Francisco, CA 94105; 415-977-5522; www.sierraclub.org; national.outings @sierraclub.org; 10 days, $1,979). The Sierra Club offers this volunteer vacation combining different activities in a fabulous setting: Sun, Service and Whales, together on Maui, Hawaii. The adventure begins in Hana, where volunteers stay for three nights before traveling to Honokowai Valley, a farming community between A.D. 1400 and 1900, now a large archeological site protected by Maui Cultural Lands, Inc., which preserves historic sites on the island. Work in Honokawai Valley includes weed-cutting and digging. Participants need to be able to hike a moderate-to-steep incline.

Immerse yourself in local culture, learn about native and nonnative Hawaiian plant life, and observe humpback whales on days off from the work site. The whales come to Hawaii between November and April to breed, give birth, and rest before returning to Alaskan waters during the summer. There is time for a snorkel excursion and relaxation built into the seven-night stay in the Honokawai area.

Transportation is provided to and from the Kahului airport on the first and last days of the trip. Accommodations in Hana are in a large, family-style hostel with shared bedrooms. In the Honokawai area you will stay in condominiums, with two participants sharing a bedroom and several group members assigned to each unit. All meals except for one dinner are included.

Immersion Excursion: A Hawaiian Treasure Trove

Hasegawa General Store (Highway 360, Hana, HI 96713; 808-248-8231) is a must-stop in Hana. Three generations of the Hasegawa family have owned, managed, and run the gas station and store, carrying Hawaiian delights from fresh leis and grass skirts to Spam musubi, a popular

Hawaiian snack with a slice of Spam on top of a block of salted rice wrapped in nori (dried seaweed).

Conservation, Education, and Rescue, Mebane, NC: Conservators' Center (P.O. Box 882, Mebane, NC 27302; 336-421-0883; www.conservators center.org; volunteer@conservatorscenter.org; for internships, keeper@conservatorscenter.org). The Conservators' Center, a nonprofit organization founded in 1999, provides educational programs, rescues and places animals in need, and has a captive-breeding program for threatened and endangered small carnivores, including New Guinea singing dogs and binturongs. There are scheduled tours, by appointment, of the facilities, and the center provides outreach programs to schools and community groups.

Learn about the animals at the center, including lions, tigers, leopards, servals, caracals, bobcats, wolves, red foxes, ring-tailed lemurs, kinkajous, and genets. Work includes cage construction, maintenance, landscaping, clerical work, food transportation, and fundraising. Only those with experience will be considered for help with animal care. All volunteers must participate in training.

There are regularly scheduled workdays once or twice monthly when you can join a crew to work on different projects; no experience is necessary. If you want to be added to a workday notification list, e-mail the volunteer coordinator with "workday notification" on the subject line.

Internships are available to students from local colleges and universities and adults from across the country and abroad looking for wildlife-keeper experience. Applicants must be committed to an intense program and able to perform physically demanding work in all weather conditions. Responsibilities include learning to feed the animals, cleaning cages, helping with cage construction, maintenance, fundraising, and other tasks necessary to run a nonprofit wildlife facility. Participants need to purchase a $15 orientation and safety booklet for personal use. Call or e-mail to request an application.

Accommodations and Dining

Ⓢ **Econo Lodge** (2133 W. Hanford Rd., Burlington, NC 27215; 336-227-1270; fax 336-227-1702; www.econolodge.com). This local lodging has 122 rooms, complimentary continental breakfast, high-speed wireless Internet access, and a seasonal outdoor pool conveniently located near Alamance Battleground, city parks, lakes, Burlington Historic District, and restaurants.

ⓈⓈ **Holiday Inn Express Hotel & Suites** (149 Spring Forest Dr., Mebane, NC 27302; 1-877-865-6578; www.ichotels group.com). The hotel has 61 rooms, serves a complimentary continental breakfast, and is located on two major Interstates (I-84 and I-40) near Duke University. Amenities include fitness center, outdoor pool, and high-speed Internet access.

Ⓢ **Smithfield's Chicken 'n Bar-B-Q** (1710 South NC-119, Mebane, NC 27302; 919-563-2440). One of several locations for eastern-style North Carolina barbecue and fried chicken, in a family-friendly restaurant serving lunch and dinner.

Ⓢ–ⓈⓈ **La Cocina** (1239 S. Fifth St., Mebane, NC 27302; 919-983-7002; fax 919-938-7004; www.lacocinanc.com; lacocina3@msn.com). Offering traditional Mexican food, La Cocina serves lunch and dinner with popular dishes like quesadilla Cocina and Texas fajitas.

Songbirds of the Tetons, Grand Teton National Park, Northwestern WY: Earthwatch Institute: Live in Grand Teton National Park for nine days and help monitor resi-

Volunteer Trips for All Ages

National Wildlife Federation's Expeditions Travel Program (NWF, 11100 Wildlife Center Dr., Reston, VA 20190; 1-800-606-9563; www.nwf.org; www.nwf.org/expeditions; expeditions@nwf.org). The National Wildlife Federation (NWF), founded in 1936, inspires Americans to protect wildlife for future generations. NWF offers a variety of trips that vary from year to year and include many opportunities to volunteer with wildlife and the environment. Check out their Family Trails program for a meaningful experience.

dent and migratory songbirds. Read the complete listing in Chapter 5, "National Treasures."

Protect Birds of Prey, Kempton, PA: Hawk Mountain Sanctuary (1700 Hawk Mountain Rd., Kempton, PA 19529; 610-756-6961; fax 610-756-4468; internships at the Acopian Center for Conservation, 570-943-3411; www.hawkmountain.org; info@hawkmountain .org). Hawk Mountain Sanctuary, a nonprofit organization, tax-exempt since 1946, is located along the Appalachian Flyway in eastern Pennsylvania. A wonderful one-day immersion excursion and a sight rarely equaled elsewhere, about 18,000 hawks, vultures, falcons, and eagles fly directly by Hawk Mountain between August and December.

Hawk Mountain is part of the Kittatinny Ridge (Blue Mountain), which has been named a critical corridor by the Pennsylvania Game Commission–State Wildlife Management Agency. The ridge extends 200 miles, crosses 12 counties, and has been designated an Important Bird Area by Audubon Pennsylvania. It is also one of the largest forests in southeastern Pennsylvania and essential for wildlife dependent on forest habitats.

You will find a volunteer-interest form on the sanctuary Web site. Select the activities that work best for you:

Archives/Library, Biological Survey, Bookstore, Computer Data Entry, Community Outreach, Education, Gardening, General Maintenance/Groundskeeping, Group Greeter, Information, Invasive Plant Removal, Mailings, Parking, Photography, Special Events, Raptor Care, Trail Maintenance, and more.

Longer-term opportunities as an intern in Conservation Science are available to qualified candidates committed to a career in conservation. There are 12–14 two- to four-month internships; you would work with at least one senior staff member and complete an independent project in one of three areas: research, monitoring, or environmental education. A modest stipend and some travel assistance are usually provided.

Protect Seabirds, Mid-Coast, ME: National Audubon Society (Seabird Restoration Program, 159 Sapsucker Woods Rd., Ithaca, NY 14850: 607-257-7308; www.project puffin.org; puffin@audubon.org; ages 18+; contribution requested). Join the National Audubon Society (NAS) and about 30 other avid birders, naturalists, aviculturists, students, and biologists who work with Audubon research staff at seven sanctuaries in the Gulf of Maine managed by NAS. A nonprofit organization founded in 1886, Audubon has been working to protect birds and other wildlife, and their habitats, for over a hundred years.

NAS began "Project Puffin" in 1973 to learn how to restore puffins to nesting islands in the Gulf of Maine. Since that time, work has expanded to restoration and management of other seabird species, including terns, murres, and petrels. The project is based in Ithaca, New York, at the Cornell Lab of Ornithology, and at Maine Audubon's Todd Wildlife Sanctuary, Mid-Coast, Maine.

Restoring seabird colonies takes years of work. Depending on the time of year, you will participate in banding, band reading, burrow monitoring, feeding, and productiv-

ROBERT F. BUKATY

Charlie with a tern on his back.

ity studies. Volunteers must make a minimum two-week commitment between June 1 and July 30, depending on schedule openings. Previous field research experience is desirable. Those contributing $1,500 or more will receive preference.

Volunteers stay in rustic or primitive camps at each field station and need to be flexible and able to live and work in close proximity to others. Exercise areas are limited, since the majority of the space on the islands belongs to the nesting seabirds. Three-hour observation shifts require sitting in a small wooden observation blind with enough room for a spotting scope and backpack. The

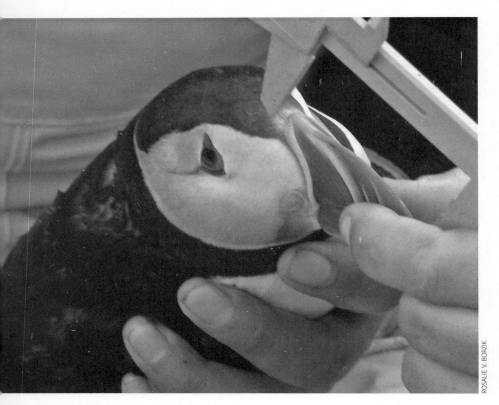

ROSALIE V. BORZIK

Researchers measure the head and beak of an Atlantic Puffin on Eastern Egg Rock, Maine.

terrain is rugged, and potable water must be carried to the islands. Participation requires your being able to hike over boulders, and boat landings necessitate stepping on slippery rocks, seaweed, and into the water. Communication with the mainland is limited.

Bring binoculars, sleeping bag, pad, and a waterproof tent that can withstand high winds. A tarp to fit over your tent is recommended. Predator (gull) control may be necessary, and while you are not required to participate, you may not interfere with it. This is a spectacular opportunity to contribute to research and have an experience that will stay with you for a lifetime.

Anthony's Story, Puffin Project, Eastern Egg Rock, ME

I'm a nature lover. It's one thing to send money to the Audubon Society. It's quite another to spend time and effort doing something very concrete that can improve the outlook for particular kinds of wildlife. Birds have historically been part of Maine's feather trade and subsistence way of life.

In the 1700s and 1800s, puffins were decimated for food, feathers, and flesh for baiting traps. Steve Kress started Project Puffin in 1973, based on the knowledge that puffins and other seabirds return to where they were born to nest and raise their young. Seal Island National Wildlife Refuge was a natural habitat for the puffin; human activity had wiped them out. Steve Kress brought in puffin chicks that have slowly established a community. Last summer two hundred puffin pairs nested on Seal Island.

Volunteers do not need to be expert birders, but they do need to make a two-week time commitment. Conditions are spartan. Volunteers live in tents, use outhouses, and carry potable water onto the island. Everyone pitches in on the chores; we work in shifts, and the food is provided. There's no cell phone service or Internet. It's an isolated experience that is hard work, but I find it a very refreshing break from my high-stress job as a medical microbiologist in a hospital.

Immersion Tip: Adopt a Puffin

Help **Project Puffin** by adopting an Atlantic puffin. You will receive a certificate of adoption, individual information, statistics about your puffin from ongoing research, and an update on your puffin's behavior and activities. Adoptions can be renewed annually. Project Puffin's operating budget comes mostly from private contributions; tax-deductible gifts to Project Puffin are dedicated entirely to protecting and restoring Maine seabirds, and the Adopt-a-Puffin program is one of the chief fundraisers. The adoption fee for one nesting season is $100. Call them or visit the Web site to adopt online.

4

Environment: Conserve and Protect Natural Resources

Restoration and Improvements, Trail Building and Maintenance, Ecology, and Sustainable Living

I went to the woods because I wished to live deliberately, to front only the essential facts of life, and see if I could not learn what it had to teach, and not, when I came to die, discover that I had not lived.

—HENRY THOREAU, *WALDEN*

Volunteer immersion excursions devoted to protecting, preserving, and intelligently using natural resources are timely and of rapidly growing interest. These opportunities include enjoying the great outdoors, participating in multiple levels of physical activity, and becoming educated about green and sustainable living. You can help out in parks, preserves, forests, camps, farms, deserts, mountains, coastal regions, islands, and on the waterways and oceans across the country.

Volunteering for some environmental projects involves hard work and physical challenges. Not only might you be required to hike several miles over rugged terrain, you might also be carrying heavy equipment, items you've collected, or camping supplies. As one participant points out, it is very difficult to swing a pickax when the temperature is 105 degrees. Despite the physical demands, many of the volunteers say the rewards and benefits to both people and the environment are immensely satisfying.

If you know you have certain limitations, you need to take them into account when asking questions and planning your trip. Collecting field data for environmental studies may be less physically challenging than cutting and maintaining trails, but it can be just as difficult, depending on the weather, terrain, and altitude, among other variables. Most organizations tell you what to expect; if they don't, ask what a day is like from morning until night. Usually, work goes on rain or shine. There are many less rugged options to choose among, including working on a kitchen crew instead of on a trail, or as a teaching assistant in a nature center, or at an environmental day camp for children.

The physical demands of individual trips are often rated as easy, moderate, difficult, or strenuous. Ask for written definitions of their rating system to make sure that your definition of "moderate" matches the organization's interpretation. Planning ahead might make it possible to train and prepare for an active trip you'd really like to take and a goal you hope to achieve. But there are a variety of tasks that can be done with less physical challenge and many different ways to contribute. Such options include living in a state park and working as a campground host, interacting with park visitors, or volunteering as an administrative assistant helping staff with filing, data entry, telephone inquiries, scheduling, and correspondence.

Consider how you can prepare yourself physically, emotionally, and intellectually for your volunteer experience. Several organizations offer training sessions. Another option is to choose a shorter, less intensive experience

D ACRES

Volunteer housing can be so diverse—sometimes it's in a tree house.

your first time out and work your way up to more demanding trips, perhaps even becoming a trip leader at a later
date. A volunteer in a wilderness location in the western
United States recommends physically scouting a location
and becoming familiar with it before committing to longer-
term volunteer work. Research the areas you'll be visiting;
there may be suggested reading lists about your destination and related environmental studies available on an
organization's Web site.

Some volunteer vacations mean living and working
closely with other people from diverse backgrounds, and
others call for being on your own and working independently, isolated in a remote location. Challenge yourself, but
consider the limitations of your comfort zone. Meeting and
volunteering with people from across the United States and
visitors from other countries can be a large part of the

D ACRES

Volunteer Clay mulches potatoes at D Acres.

pleasure of your immersion experience, along with getting to know the local people and places.

Most organizations specify minimum ages for volunteers; again, if they don't, inquire. If the trip is not age-specific, ask about the median age or range of ages of the participants. Some projects can accommodate younger participants if accompanied by a parent or other responsible adult, even if younger children are not permitted on the actual work site. Some environmental volunteer vacations are specifically designed for families, and there are many volunteer opportunities that focus on teen crews, internships, and gap year programs; however, if you find something of particular interest and think it might not include your age-group, it's worth a call to find out for sure. Often decisions are made on individual applications and specific circumstances.

Find out exactly what is included in the program fee. Ask how the fees are allocated to the project and what percentages are used for services. This information is often available on the organization's Web site. Inquire about what portion of your trip fee is tax deductible. Some trips are entirely tax deductible. Most membership organizations offer a discount to members; ask about membership fees and benefits.

Also note that a number of the offerings in this category are fee free or close to being free with nominal fees. There are many exciting opportunities to choose from offering outdoor, scenic, and memorable locations, along with the benefit of seeing the contribution of your work almost immediately, and enjoying a very reasonably priced volunteer vacation.

Accommodations are sometimes described only in general terms on an organization's Web site or in other materials provided. Ask specific questions about campsites, bunkhouses, dormitories, and "rustic" housing. Discuss dietary restrictions and preferences beforehand; some organizations offer vegetarian alternatives even on camping trips. It may be possible for you to borrow or rent camping equipment if you do not own your own, usually by prior arrangement.

Not all accommodations involve camping out or basic facilities. There are condos or private homes you may rent on your own, or your trip may include hotel stays. There are also ways to build volunteer activities around an already-planned trip. Some organizations offer a trade of services, with or without an additional fee, for room and board. Be sure to find out how many hours you are expected to work, and if you volunteer as a couple whether work hours are per-person.

Another consideration is the amount of free or leisure time built into your volunteer vacation. This can vary greatly from trip to trip. Some organizations provide planned excursions and facilitate leisure activities, while others simply give you time off. Relaxing at a campsite, under the stars, may be just what you need after a day on the trail, but you might also want the opportunity to bike, kayak or canoe, observe and photograph wildlife, or visit nearby attractions. Remember, you always have the option of extending your trip on your own and adding a nearby destination to your itinerary before or after your volunteer commitment.

Be sure you know what you'll need to bring; there may be a packing or equipment list for volunteers on an organization's Web site, or you may be sent one after your application has been accepted. If a project sparks your interest, contact the organization for details and current trip dates and have your list of questions prepared before you call. Get in touch with the local Chamber of Commerce or Visitors Bureau to learn more about an area and what it offers, and find links online for lodging, dining, travel, cultural attractions, recreational opportunities, and practical information about the climate, geography, and population.

Remember to ask how to contact people who have experienced the trip you are considering. Once you make the decision to join in, ask about e-mail contact with the others in the group. More and more volunteer vacationers are reporting that it is very common to develop e-mail relationships before the trip.

If a particular activity strikes your fancy but you are not attracted to the location, research similar activities in other parts of the country using the resources provided. Many of the clearinghouses included in this book offer a state-by-state choice of activities, if you type in a keyword like "environment." You can make a difference in so many ways and in so many places across the USA, and have a fantastic time while you're at it.

Island Conservation and Preservation, Avalon, CA: Catalina Island Conservancy (P.O. Box 2739, Avalon, CA 90704; Volunteer and Visitor Services Department, Scott Dennis, Director, 310-510-2595 ext. 102; fax 310-510-2594; www.catalinaconservancy.org; Catalina Adventurer, ages 18+, 4 days of service and a naturalist activity, $180 per person, contact Lesly Lieberman at llieberman@catalina conservancy.org or call 310-510-2595 ext. 112; Catalina Explorer, ages 12+ accompanied by a parent, Sun. through Sat., $575 per couple or $287.50 for individuals, accommodations booked separately, contact janet@catalinavacations .com or call 1-800-631-5280). The Catalina Island

ROB RHEIN

Volunteers are housed in the lower campground facilities at Catalina Island Conservancy.

A Catalina Island Conservancy custom is that local California volunteers make dinners and desserts for the visiting volunteers.

Conservancy is a nonprofit organization, formed in 1972, dedicated to the conservation and preservation of the island; by agreement with Los Angeles County, it guarantees public recreational and educational use consistent with the goals of the conservancy. Santa Catalina Island, 22 miles off the coast of southern California, is the perfect location for a volunteer vacation. Help restore the ecosystem and pre-serve native plants and animals with a choice of two levels of involvement.

Option A is the Catalina Adventurer for people who enjoy a physical challenge. Stay at a private camp with stunning coastline views, sleep in padded bunks in canvas tents on raised decks with access to shared bath houses on site. An outdoor kitchen is provided, and themed dinners are prepared by restaurants and local volunteers. Activities may include hiking up to a mile on rough terrain, monitor-ing seedlings, and removing invasive plants, and they might require handling heavy tools. Projects are rated moderate to strenuous.

Option B is the Catalina Explorer, for adults and children who seek more of a balance between a traditional vacation and a volunteer experience. Accommodations are in private cottages or condos booked through Catalina Island Vacation

Rentals (CatalinaVacations.com; reservations@catalina vacations.com), and prices vary depending on the home you choose. Special weekly volunteer vacation rates are available. Enjoy island tours and a free day for your own planned activities, as well as assisting with a half-day beach clean-up, working at a native plant nursery, and maintaining trails. The project rating is light to moderate.

The Catalina Explorer package includes membership in the conservancy, a conservancy T-shirt and water bottle, two tickets to the Wrigley Memorial Botanical Garden, two tickets to the Catalina Botanical Museum, lunches served in the field on full-service days, a historical walking tour of Avalon, and a Jeep eco-tour. Six participants are required for each Explorer package, so bring your family and your friends, become involved, and create a memorable volunteer vacation.

Half- and full-day volunteer activities are also available at the Catalina Island Conservancy. For example, Mornings at the Nursery (Thursdays 8 AM–noon) needs helpers to perform a variety of essential horticultural tasks while learning about Catalina's unique environment and the native plant species found there. The Windward Beach Clean-Up (second Saturday of each month) is a beachcomber's delight, raking the sand for debris. Locations rotate throughout the year to keep all four windward beaches beautiful. Transportation and beverages are provided.

Mike's Story, Catalina Island Conservancy, Avalon, CA

I always wanted to get into the interior of Catalina Island and selected a six-day trip of physical labor, staying at a base camp overlooking the ocean. The conservancy had planned different work activities for us every day: trail building, working at the nursery, painting, and tree trimming. We worked three hours in the morning, had lunch, and then worked until about three o'clock, had dinner and relaxed. I paid $180 to go somewhere I really wanted to be for a week in June, stay in a beautiful campsite, sweat, and work really hard.

I loved it. Catalina has over 25 miles of trails, and our job was cutting a new trail into the hillside with pickaxes and shovels. What really concerned me is that some of the people on the trip weren't physically able to do such difficult work in 105-degree weather.

Two people suffered from heatstroke within the first few hours on our first day. It's very important to understand what will be asked of you physically. Swinging a pickax in 105-degree weather is extremely difficult work. The interior of Catalina is a rather hostile desert environment, with cactus, rattlesnakes, and lots of bugs.

Fortunately, our group leader was very flexible and well organized. People who could not handle the hard physical labor shifted to seed gathering and plant work. I took time off from my job to go work on the nature trails because I knew it would be enriching and fulfilling. I plan to go again next year with my wife and a few of our friends.

Nancy's Story, Beach Cleanup, Catalina Island, California

I've been volunteering for the past seven years on Catalina Island. I love the island, the enthusiastic people who work for the Conservancy, and the other volunteers. My favorite task is beach cleanup, because it's like a treasure hunt and always ends with a swim. I have learned so much and appreciate all aspects of nature more than ever before—and how what I contribute fits into a much larger picture.

Service in Loess Hills National Natural Landmark, IO: Sierra Club (85 Second St., 2nd Floor, San Francisco, CA 94105; 415-977-5500; fax 415-977-5799; www.sierraclub .org; information@sierraclub.org; 9 days, $645). Join the Sierra Club, a membership-supported, nonprofit environmental organization founded in 1892, in its effort to preserve the unusual land formations of Iowa's Loess Hills. Formations like these are found in only one other place in the world—along the Yellow River in China—and were created from the silt left exposed to the wind and other elements after glaciers retreated from the Midwest, between 14,000 and 24,000 years ago.

The Loess Hills cover more than 650,000 acres, with about 18,000 acres managed by a federation of state, county, and private partners. Because over 95 percent of the Loess Hills are on private land, they are not protected as a national park but have been designated by Congress as a National Natural Landmark. The Sierra Club works with private owners in protecting the land and helping restore the prairie, oak savannahs, and other original ecosystems.

Help harvest and process seeds of native grasses, expand conservation efforts, preserve native oak savannahs, remove invasive species, seed new areas of prairie, and prepare seed plugs for planting. Some activities are rated moderately strenuous, and you need to be in good physical condition and able to climb steep hills. The trip is nonsmoking.

Accommodations are in a cottage and rustic bunkhouse, with an option of camping on the grounds of the homestead with your own gear. All foods are provided, and meal preparation will be a shared responsibility. A detailed equipment list will be sent to registered participants.

National Outings Program, Service Trips, Multiple Locations: Sierra Club (85 Second St., 2nd Floor, San Francisco, CA 94105; 415-977-5500; fax 415-977-5799;

www.sierraclub.org; information@sierraclub.org). The Sierra Club's National Outings program offers about 90 service trips each year with a wide variety of options in locations and projects and donates about 25,000 work-hours annually to state and federal land agencies.

Volunteer to clear and maintain trails in Chaco Canyon, New Mexico, or in the Chiricahua Wilderness area in southern Arizona. Participate in a research study of forest health on Monhegan Island, 10 miles off the coast of Maine. Assist the National Forest Service in designating campsites along the Prince William Sound in south-central Alaska. Help protect the ecosystem of Santa Cruz Island in Channel Island National Park, California.

All service trips include a balance of group activities and free time, and you will be able to explore your surroundings and engage in a variety of activities depending upon your location. You will meet and work with the people who know the area best and form friendships with other participants who share similar interests.

The cost and length of trips vary, with meals provided and accommodations ranging from tents at campsites to bunkhouses and cabins. Tools and equipment for service projects will be provided; you are responsible for your personal gear, airfare, and transportation. Trips are rated for difficulty, and complete itineraries of current trips are available on the Web site, along with clothing and equipment lists, information about trip leaders, and a description of both service and leisure activities.

Sierra Club Outings was recognized as one of the 2008 Best Travel Companies on Earth by the editors of *National Geographic Adventure Magazine* (http://atr.nationalgeo graphic.com/outfitters/outfitterDetail.action?id=51). The Sierra Club also offers group service outings through its chapters nationwide.

Edna's Story: Sierra Club Family Trip, Stehekin, WA

My family and I have a very busy and demanding lifestyle. My husband is an anesthesiologist, and I'm a pediatrician. Our two children, 9 and 11, were over-programmed with activities and schedules. We started taking Sierra Club family trips to give them time with us in natural, beautiful settings without a tight structure. We've visited spots all over the United States, often rustic settings without television, radio, or shopping malls.

We leave the laptops and cell phones at home and set aside time to read, think, and explore. Now that they are 13 and 15, the children take turns selecting our trips and setting our goals. Together we've become outdoors enthusiasts and most of our conversations are about where we will go, who we will meet, what we need to accomplish before we go, and what we will be doing when we get there. I was really thrilled when each of my kids wanted to invite friends on all our family trips, including volunteer vacations.

Habitat Restoration, Pelican Island National Wildlife Refuge, Indian River County, FL: Sierra Club: The complete listing for this ongoing project to restore wetland and hardwood hammock habitats for the benefit of wildlife can be found in Chapter 3, "Wildlife."

Park Resident Volunteer, Los Ojos, NM: Heron Lake State Park (New Mexico State Parks, 1220 South St. Francis Dr., Santa Fe, NM 87505; 1-888-NMPARKS; 505-476-3355; fax 505-476-3361; www.emnrd.state.nm.us; nmparks@state.nm.us). Receive a free campsite and

These seasoned volunteers recommend writing directly to the park that interests you. They most enjoy volunteering at the annual Osprey Festival, Heron Lake State Park, Los Ojos, New Mexico.

hands-on training in exchange for a commitment of 24 hours a week for eight weeks. Heron Lake State Park, in Los Ojos, New Mexico, is designated a "quiet lake," known for its sailing, fishing, cross-country skiing, and hiking.

Become a New Mexico Volunteer in Parks (NMVP) and choose to serve as an administrative assistant helping staff in the operation and management of the park office. Duties include filing, data entry, telephone inquiries, scheduling, correspondence, and light office maintenance. Computer skills are a plus.

Volunteer as a campground host and work with visitors directly, providing information, collecting fees, doing facility maintenance, and assisting staff with various projects. A current driver's license and proof of insurance are required to drive a state vehicle. Operating lawn mowers, chainsaws, and other tools might also be involved.

Apply for a position as an interpretive assistant, to coordinate or arrange interpretive programs, assist speakers with planning and materials, and possibly develop and conduct your own interpretive programs. Applicable skills include experience or education in cultural or natural resources, communication and interpersonal skills, and the ability to research materials and information.

The New Mexico State Parks also need Night Sky Interpreters, Site Stewards, Boating Volunteers, and Visitor Center Associates. There are 84 state parks in New Mexico. To apply, fill out an application online, clearly stating your preference for a region or park or job.

Immersion Excursion: Osprey Festival

Heron Lake State Park (505-588-7470, www.nmparks.com) in Los Ojos, New Mexico, hosts an annual Osprey Festival in July. Ospreys are one of the largest birds of prey in North America, with wingspans as wide as 54 inches. They feed on the fish in Heron Lake and since 1990 have been breeding there as well. There are viewing stands for the public, and a docent with a spotting scope helps visitors view the nests during the summer. The festival includes music and food, live raptor exhibits, pontoon boat tours, and osprey-related artwork and souvenirs. There is no fee to attend the festival, but normal day and camping rates apply to park visitors. Money raised during the festival is used to support two co-hosts of the festival, the Friends of Heron and El Vado Lake State Parks.

Trail Work Weekend, Blairstown, NJ: Appalachian Mountain Club (AMC Main Office, 5 Joy St., Boston MA 02108; 610-868-6906; www.outdoors.org; mohican_trail_crew@verizon.net; $6 contribution; register for bunk space at no extra charge by calling the MOC Reservations and Trails Lodge at 908-362-5670). This is a fun, family-oriented trail crew in the mid-Atlantic region, with housing at the

Environmental Awareness

Friends of the Crooked River (2390 Kensington Rd., Akron, OH 44333; 330-657-2055; ohgreenway@aol.com; www.cuyahogariver.net; www.epa.gov/adopt). Friends of the Crooked River is a Watershed Alliance founded in 1990 to raise awareness of the recreational, cultural, historic, and environmental resources of the Cuyahoga River, promote responsible use, and alert the public to the causes of deterioration of water quality and wildlife habitat. It is an all-volunteer effort that can use your help.

A watershed is an area of land where all the water that is under it, or that drains off it, flows into a common waterway such as a stream, lake, estuary, aquifer, wetland, or the ocean. The U.S. Environmental Protection Agency (EPA) Web site allows you to "Surf Your Watershed," a feature that helps you locate your local watershed by city, state, or zip code.

You will find a database of citizen-based watershed groups, learn about the environmental health of your watershed, and find out what you can do to protect it. There are links to resources for organizing a volunteer monitoring program, and to sites for kids, including suggested games, activities, and educational materials to teach children about pollution and the environment, estuaries, wetlands, marine

Mohican Outdoor Center (MOC) in the Delaware Water Gap National Recreation Area in Blairstown, New Jersey. Bring your children six years and older; Trail Work Weekends are every second Saturday and Sunday from April to November, except in June. The Appalachian Mountain Club, founded in 1876, is the country's oldest nonprofit conservation and recreation organization.

Arrive at the Mohican Outdoor Center Friday afternoon and begin work Saturday morning following a description of the weekend's projects and a tool-safety talk. Hike to the work site from the trailhead. There are water and lunch breaks, and the crew returns to the MOC in the afternoon and can attend an optional spaghetti dinner for a fee of $6. On Sunday, the workday ends at 3 PM.

Accommodations are in a bunk-style cabin with a kitchen. There will be time to relax, listen to stories, play games, and enjoy getting to know fellow crew members. On days off enjoy the camp and surrounding area or hike to the Appalachian Trail. On most Saturday nights there is music in the main lodge.

Trail Maintenance, Locations Throughout Washington State: Washington Trails Association (2019 Third Ave., Suite 100, Seattle, WA 98121; 206-625-1367; www.wta.org/volunteer/vacations; alyssa@wta.org; $150 per person, $125 WTA members, $75 for subsequent trips; ages 18+). Washington Trails Association (WTA) asks you to give them a week, and in return they will make it great. Join the WTA, a nonprofit organization tax-exempt since 1980, for a week of volunteer trail maintenance in premier backcountry locations throughout Washington State.

Volunteers of all ages contribute to repairs and renovations on WTA trails.

You might choose to spend your volunteer vacation in the Alpine Lakes Wilderness, working on trails from the junction of Colchuck to Stuart Lake, one of the gateways to the Enchantments. Or, if you sign up for the Holden Village trip, your week will begin with a boat ride up Lake Chelan, then a bus ride to the historic mining village. Or volunteer with your family (with children ages 10–14) on the Hyas

Lake Family Trip, staying at a lakeside camp with other families and swimming, fishing, and exploring on your day off.

Trail work includes rebuilding treads, installing drainage, and clearing brush. Morning and evening you will help with in-camp jobs, with plenty of time to relax and socialize. Wednesday is your day off, and there will be great options for exploring your surroundings and the spectacular scenery. Food is provided and can accommodate a hearty appetite and most dietary needs. Find a sample menu on the WTA Web site, an online application, a list of what to bring, and a schedule of available trips and dates.

Environmental Children's Camp, Anchorage, AK: Volunteers for Alaska (1413 N St., Anchorage, AK 99501; volunteersforalaska.org; info@volunteersforalaska.org). Volunteers for Alaska (VFA) is a nonprofit organization, founded in 2004, that places volunteers from all over the world in conservation positions in Alaska. VFA encourages environmental awareness, supports community development, and ensures that the beauty of Alaska is preserved for future generations.

Anchorage is Alaska's largest city, located on the shores of Cook Inlet. Volunteer at a camp for children, ages 10–14, from all economic, social, and cultural backgrounds. The camp is located on 740 acres of wilderness, and camp programs focus on the environment and educational experiences for the campers. Volunteers teach natural history, nature crafts, and outdoor stewardship skills.

Service projects—planting trees, maintaining trails, and working on streambed erosion projects—are an important part of the camp experience. The youngest campers help by watering and picking up litter. Volunteers also lead groups on backpacking, kayaking, mountain biking, and floating trips for older campers. It's a 40-hour week with weekends free.

Accommodations

Spenard Hostel International (2845 W. 42nd Ave., Anchorage, AK 99517, 907-248-5036; www.alaskahostel.org; Stay@AlaskaHostel.org; $21 per night cash; $22 credit card) is centrally located between the bike-trail system and the Coastal Trail. Hostelers and budget travelers are welcome. Additional hostel locations throughout the state are listed, with contact information, at www.alaskahostel.org/html/alaska_hostels.html.

Alaska Vacation Rentals, Homes, Villas and Condos (www.vacationrentals.com/vacation-rentals/Alaska.html) continually updates its rental property listings. Longer-term volunteers often find it economical to rent a home or apartment together.

Alaska State Parks (DNR Public Information Center, 550 W. 7th Ave., Suite 1260, Anchorage, AK 99501; www.dnr.state.ak.us/parks/cabins/index.htm; for reservation-request contact information, go to www.dnr.state.ak.us/parks/cabins/cabininfo.pdf; prices range from $20 to $65 per night, depending upon location and season). Alaska State Parks offers 56 cabins for rent in 18 state parks in a variety of locations, including Fairbanks and Ketchikan. Depending on their size, the cabins accommodate between 2 and 12 people and come equipped with wooden sleeping platforms, a wood-burning stove, a table, and benches or chairs. Many are in remote locations, and some are road-accessible.

Immersion Excursion: An Amazing State Park

Anchorage, Alaska (Anchorage Convention and Visitors Bureau, 524 W. Fourth St., Anchorage, AK 99501; 907-276-4118; fax 907-278-5559; www.anchorage.net; info@anchorage.net) has 120 miles of paved and 300 miles of unpaved trails and is a great place for hiking and biking. The Coastal Trail is designated as a National Recreation Trail for its amazing views. Neighboring Chugach State Park, the third-largest state park in the USA, has snowcapped mountains, alpine wildflowers, and wildlife, including Dall sheep, mountain goats, moose, black and brown bears, eagles, and wolves. There's hiking, biking, horseback riding, rafting, climbing, camping, boating, fishing, and glacier travel.

Baxter State Park Crew, Baxter State Park, ME: Appalachian Mountain Club (AMC Main Office, 5 Joy St., Boston, MA 02108; 617-523-0636; fax 617-523-0722; www.outdoors.org; information@outdoors.org; two-week program, ages 18–80+; contribution, $175 member, $195 nonmember). Baxter State Park, Millinocket, Maine, maintains its trails almost solely through volunteer efforts. Appalachian Mountain Club (AMC) and Baxter State Park staff members provide the needed training. There will also be time to swim, photograph wildlife, relax by the fire after dinner, and enjoy canoeing on one of the park's many ponds. The Appalachian Mountain Club, founded in 1876, is the country's oldest nonprofit conservation and recreation organization.

Projects may include clearing drainage ditches, cutting out trail corridors, painting blazes, clearing larger brush and trees, constructing bog bridges, or building rock stairs. Volunteers should be physically fit and able to carry heavy loads; this is one of AMC's more strenuous adult programs. Pry bars, grip hoist rigging systems, and other tools may be needed to move rocks. Workdays are Monday through Thursday, with Friday through Sunday unscheduled so you can enjoy the park at no additional charge. The base camp is near vehicle-accessible campgrounds; tents, cooking and safety equipment, tools, and all other group gear will be provided by AMC.

Young Members Alpine Crew, White Mountains, NH: Appalachian Mountain Club (AMC Main Office, 5 Joy St., Boston, MA 02108; 617-523-0636; fax 617-523-0722; www.outdoors.org; one-week program, ages 20s–30s; contribution, $175 member, $195 nonmember). This volunteer vacation is a great opportunity for people in their 20s and 30s to meet, work, and spend leisure time together. Work is strenuous, and performed rain or shine. But there will be plenty of time to relax, appreciate the views, enjoy wonderful food, and get to know your fellow volunteers.

The trip begins on Sunday evening with dinner and orientation, and Monday's project will be near the base camp. On Tuesday your crew will pack into another camp at the base of an alpine peak, with your crew leaders, for the next three nights. Packs usually weigh from 40 to 60 pounds, and the hike is demanding. Projects may include building cairns and scree walls, or installing drainage, rock steps, and bog bridges.

Crew members return to the base camp for the Friday-night barbecue and may stay Friday night, which is included in the program cost, as is breakfast Saturday morning. Base camp is at AMC Camp Dodge Volunteer Center, where there are bunkhouses, bathroom facilities, hot showers, and a full kitchen. Dates, schedule, and application are available upon request.

Trail Crews: Appalachian Trail Conservancy (799 Washington St., P.O. Box 807, Harpers Ferry, WV 25425; 304-535-6331; fax 304-535-2667; crew information 540-953-3571; www.appalachiantrail.org; info@appalachian trail.org or crews@appalachiantrail.org). Spend a week or more volunteering to help build and protect the Appalachian National Scenic Trail, a marked hiking trail from Maine to Georgia, stretching 2,175 miles through

14 eastern states. Projects vary and may include trail relo-
cation and rehabilitation, rock work, maintenance, and
bridge and shelter construction. Volunteers must be
18 years or older—no experience is necessary. The
Appalachian Trail Conservancy is a private nonprofit
organization, tax-exempt since 1950.

Program options include the Konnarock Crew, which
covers the Appalachian Trail (A.T.) from Rockfish Gap,
Virginia, to Springer Mountain, Georgia; the Maine Trail
Crew, with projects along 280 miles of scenic woods; the
Vermont Long Trail Patrol, which does heavy construction
projects on the co-aligned Appalachian and Long Trails; the
Mid-Atlantic Crew, which works on the A.T. from Virginia to
the New York/Connecticut line; and the Rocky Top Crew,
which works on the portion of the A.T. that passes through
the Great Smoky Mountains National Park.

**Estuarine Research, Wells National Estuarine
Research Reserve, ME: Volunteers For Peace** (1034
Tiffany Rd., Belmont, VT 05730; 802-259-2759; fax 802-
259-2922; www.vfp.org; vfp@vfp.org; 3-week program, ages
18+, $300). The Wells National Estuarine Research Reserve
is the host for this project, sponsored by Volunteers For
Peace (VFP), a nonprofit organization, founded in 1982, that
promotes international voluntary service as a means of
intercultural education and community service.

This project is located on the coast of southern Maine
and involves improvements on wildlife habitat and trail
work at the reserve, and maintenance on historic buildings.
Help is also needed with projects for partner conservation
organizations. The main activity will be preparing for and
staffing a large Nature Crafts Festival fund-raising event
with setup and takedown, also assisting with food, parking,
recycling, and other jobs.

Housing is in a new dorm with a modern kitchen and a
common room. Bicycles are available for your use, and the

reserve has a private beach and nature trails. Wells is located a half-hour south of Portland, Maine, and a half-hour north of Portsmouth, New Hampshire. The reserve, covering 1,600 acres, includes scenic uplands, coastal marsh, and historic farm buildings, and is a sanctuary for endangered plants and wildlife.

Restoration and Maintenance, Gulf Coast, FL: Wilderness Volunteers (P.O. Box 22292, Flagstaff, AZ 86002; 928-556-0038; fax 928-222-1912; www.wilderness volunteers.org; info@wildernessvolunteers.org; 1-week trip, ages 18+, $259). Caladesi Island State Park is a Gulf Coast barrier island, home to 43 species of birds, including the brown pelican, American oystercatcher, bald eagle, osprey, and piping plover. Wilderness Volunteers, a nonprofit organization founded in 1997, organizes and promotes volunteer service to America's wildlands, working with the National Park Service, the Forest Service, the Bureau of Land Management, and the U.S. Fish and Wildlife Service

Volunteers spend a week on the island doing trail maintenance and exotic-plant removal, painting buildings, and completing various other tasks. Free days are enjoyed at the beach, swimming, hiking, fishing, kayaking, and birding. Accommodations are at tent camps in the park. The trip is rated physically active with several miles of walking each day, carrying lumber, sawing, hammering, lifting, and hauling. The average age of participants is about 40, with a range from 18–75+. Transportation and your camping equipment are your responsibilities. Food and cooking equipment are provided.

No experience is required, but you must be physically fit. Trip leaders are chosen from among previous trip participants, based on recommendations by staff. People with extensive outdoor experience may be invited to become assistants on a trip with a senior trip leader, with performance evaluated by staff before being invited to begin leading trips. Wilderness Volunteers offers a training course and a mentoring program for prospective leaders.

The Wild Horses of Assateague Island, Maryland and Virginia

There are several wonderful stories about the origins of the ponies that inhabit Assateague. The most popular is that the ponies swam ashore from a Spanish ship that had run aground. Another story claims that pirates brought them to Assateague. Legends aside, they were most likely brought to barrier islands like Assateague by their owners to avoid fencing laws and taxation. The National Park Service manages the Maryland herd, and the Chincoteague Volunteer Fire Department oversees the Virginia herd, which grazes on Chincoteague National Wildlife Preserve by a special permit issued by the U.S. Fish & Wildlife Service. The cooperating agencies balance the needs of the horses with the need to protect their habitat. Help support this effort through a Foster Parent project by visiting the Assateague National Seashore Park Foster Horse program at www.assateaguewildhorses.org/index.cfm?fuse action=foster and choosing a horse from the online photo album. For your donation you will receive a photo of your horse, a certificate that recognizes your contribution, a biography of your horse with a map of the island showing you where your horse can be found, and *Horsin' Around,* a newsletter.

Habitat Restoration, Assateague Island, VA: Elderhostel (11 Ave. de Lafayette, Boston, MA 02111; 1-877-426-8056; fax 1-877-426-2166; www.elderhostel.org; registration@elderhostel.org; 5 nights, $536 per person). Volunteer at the Chincoteague National Wildlife Refuge on the Virginia end of Assateague Island and have the opportunity to experience parts of the refuge closed to the public. Projects vary and may include building boxes for birds or the endangered Delmarva Peninsula fox squirrel, improving access for disabled visitors, and working on the fencing to protect the dunes and control the herds of wild horses.

Volunteers work five to six hours a day, leaving time for sightseeing and other leisure activities. Accommodations are at the Quality Inn on Chincoteague Island (757-336-6565), within walking distance of the historic downtown area. All meals will be provided at a variety of local restaurants for a "Taste of the Island." The program is rated activity level three, which means you need to be able to handle your own luggage, climb a few flights of stairs, and walk on uneven surfaces for up to 2 miles. Most work is outdoors, and you will use simple tools: hammers, pliers, and post diggers. No previous experience is necessary.

Elderhostel is a nonprofit organization providing educational travel for adults 55 and older since 1975. By participating in Elderhostel's service learning programs, you will experience new areas, meet new people, and learn through hands-on activities and from your fellow Elderhostelers, project staff, and members of the community.

Trail Work, Multiple Locations in CO: Volunteers for Outdoor Colorado (600 S. Marion Pkwy., Denver, CO 80209; 1-800-925-2220; 303-715-1010; www.voc.org; volunteer@voc.org). Spend your vacation in Colorado, volunteering to help maintain trails, stop the spread of invasive weeds, and protect natural wildlife habitats. Volunteers for Outdoors Colorado (VOC), a nonprofit corporation tax-exempt since 1993, offers many opportunities to make a difference.

Each spring the selection committee evaluates and selects projects for the coming year from among those proposed by various land management agencies. Some are trail or boardwalk construction projects; others include planting trees, shrubs, and native grasses. Each project addresses the protection, restoration, and enhancement of natural resources.

Connect with Other Outdoor People

Volunteers for Outdoor Colorado has a feature called **V Outdoors** (www.voutdoors.org) which connects people with volunteer opportunities all over Colorado. You may do a search by location and activity in a database called V Match, which includes more than 150 land managers and nonprofits working to preserve and protect parks, wildlife, trails, rivers, and open spaces. V Match makes it easy to find ways to get involved, volunteer, and give back.

No experience is necessary—the crew will be working under the supervision of an experienced leader who will show you what you need to know. Some projects that are appropriate for children will be noted in the project description. Children under 16 must be accompanied by an adult. There is a difficulty rating attached to each project so you can match your abilities with requirements.

Once the project list is released, check the VOC Web site for locations, dates, and scheduled activities, and then register online. Detailed project information, sent to you 10 days prior to the project, will give you the background of the project as well as information about how to get there, what to bring, what meals will be provided, where to camp, and where to stay if you don't want to camp.

Conservation, Edmund Niles Huyck Preserve, Rensselaerville, NY: BTCV Holidays (BTCV Holidays, Sedum House, Mallard Way, Potteric Carr, Doncaster, England DN4 8DB; 011-44-1302-388-883; fax 011-44-1302-311-531; www2.btcv.org.uk; international@btcv.org.uk; 14 nights' accommodations and meals, £450, approximately $765 depending on current exchange rate; ages 18+). BTCV is the United Kingdom's largest conservation charity, established in 1959. Join British tourists for a unique volunteer experience. BTCV Conservation Holidays combine physical

The Edmund Niles Huyck Preserve in Rensselaerville, New York, has trees that are over 200 years old.

work with all the perks of a great vacation: new people, beautiful scenery, and time to relax, explore your surroundings, and socialize.

The Edmund Niles Huyck Preserve is about 30 miles southwest of Albany, New York. The preserve includes a variety of habitats, birds, and animals, 200-year-old hardwood stands, Lake Myosotis, Lincoln Pond, and Rensselaerville Falls. It is one of the oldest biological research stations in the country studying a range of concerns in botany, ecology, and zoology.

One volunteer says, "I never imagined how inspiring it could be to clear trails."

Help prevent and repair the results of heavy use of the trails and the effects of weather erosion. Projects include rebuilding historic rock walls and nature trails; volunteers need to be reasonably physically fit for digging, carrying, and walking.

Accommodations are in Lincoln Pond Cottage, which dates from 1790, a modernized wooden cabin overlooking the lake. The cottage includes a full kitchen, dining room, living room, bathroom, and shared bedrooms. Recreational options include hiking, fishing, swimming, and kayaking. Evenings and weekends are free, and there will be informal presentations on animals, geology, and history of the preserve.

Native Ecosystem Resources, Kaua'i, HI: The Koke'e Resource Conservation Program (P.O. Box 1108, Waimea, Kaua'i, HI 96796; 808-335-0045; www.krcp .org; rcp@aloha.net). Volunteer in the tropical paradise of Kaua'i, the northernmost of the main Hawaiian Islands, 20 minutes by air from Honolulu. The Koke'e Resource Conservation Program (KRCP), a community-based non-profit created in 1998, provides natural-resource management and invasive-weed control, concentrating on the preservation of the island's native forest. KRCP volunteers remove invasive species and promote public awareness of the need to protect the ecosystems of Koke'e State Park and Alaka'i Wilderness Preserve. This project involves strenuous hiking and the use of herbicides.

Rustic housing at the Koke'e Civilian Conservation Corps Camp (CCC Camp) is available for volunteers. The CCC Camp serves as a field station and volunteer center for research and conservation work. There is a large bunkhouse with bunk beds, hot showers, and a communal kitchen.

KRCP provides transportation to and from the airport, grocery, post office, etc., but the camp is isolated and volunteers need to find transportation for leisure activities and to get to the beaches—the camp is 15 miles from the coast. There are hiking trails in the park and a public bus route on the island. Volunteers work four days a week and have three days off.

This volunteer experience is for people who are self-sufficient and enjoy solitude. There are no formal evening programs. For more information about the island, visit the "All About Kaua'i" Web site at www.kauai.gov, where you will find airport and travel information, car-company contact numbers, bus schedules, and activities.

Immersion Excursion: Find Puff

Puff the magic dragon certainly thrives in Hanalei. Kaua'i is one of the most beautiful places in the United States, and the kayaking is superb. Rent everything you need for a morning glide up the Hanalei River, being careful not to disturb the nesting egrets along the banks. Pack a lunch to eat on a secluded beach on Hanalei Bay after snorkeling by the reefs. In a land known for its sunsets, none is more beautiful than those in Hanalei.

Protect the Environment, Maui, HI: Pacific Whale Foundation (300 Maalaea Rd., Suite 211, Wailuku, HI 96793; 1-800-WHALE-11; 808-249-8811; fax 808-243-9021; www.pacificwhale.org). The Pacific Whale Foundation, a nonprofit organization founded in 1980 with support from the Hawaii Tourism Authority and County of Maui Office of Economic Development, offers a "Volunteering on Vacation" program. This is a way to give back to the places you visit, meet people who share your interests, and learn about the local environment and culture. Combine a trip to Hawaii with volunteer work to help restore native plants, remove invasive species, protect cultural sites, and clean up the beaches.

Participants receive a free Volunteering-on-Vacation T-shirt, learn about the history of natural areas, meet local

experts, and share experiences with other like-minded volunteers. There is no charge for this program, and you will
gain the satisfaction of having made a difference on behalf
of Maui's environment. If you volunteer in Hosmer Grove in
Haleakala National Park or another venue that charges
admission for visitors, your free admission is included in
the program.

Each Saturday there is a project in Honokawai Valley, an
area closed to the public. Learn about this archaeological
site and Hawaiian culture and history, remove invasive
weeds, and plant native species. On the third Sunday of the
month there is a program in Haleakala National Park, led by
a Pacific Whale Foundation group leader who teaches you
about the wilderness area. This program includes three
hours of work and a short hike and picnic.

Volunteer on Friday mornings with the Island Fish Pond
Restoration project. Your group leader will talk about the
coastal area and its history, birds, and some of the last
sand dunes on Maui. On Monday mornings, help maintain a
new oceanside trail at Hoaloha'aina, another great area for
bird-watching. Join the Kanaha Beach project on Tuesday
mornings, removing invasive species, clearing marine
debris, and planting native species at Kanaha Park, with an
opportunity for a swim.

If the current group projects do not fit your schedule,
you can pick up a kit and plan your own project. The beach
cleanup kit includes directions to a local beach, rubber
gloves, trash bags, and instructions on how to dispose of
litter. This is a great activity for families with children, who
can learn to give back to the places they visit.

Immersion Excursion: Haleakala

Waking up at 3 AM to drive up Haleakala Mountain for the
sunrise might not sound too exciting, but it is definitely a
must-see when visiting Maui. The sunrise up and over the

crater on top of the mountain is eerily magnificent—and quite cold. Have extra layers handy. Throughout the year, summit temperatures range from below freezing to highs of 50°–65°F, on average a 20-degree drop between daytime and nighttime temperatures. Be sure to stop at the Proteas Farm on the way back down. The native flowers are spectacular and dry beautifully too. For the superadventurous, consider a Haleakala Biking Tour (www.bikemaui.com), with a ride up in a van and an amazingly fast bike ride down the volcano after sunrise.

Protect Hiking Trails, Multiple Locations: American Hiking Society (1422 Fenwick Lane, Silver Spring, MD 20910; 301-565-6704; americanhiking.org; volunteer@ americanhiking.org; member, $245 for a first trip, $220 if registering before the end of February; nonmember, $275 for a first trip, $250 if registering before the end of February, including a one-year membership. Additional trips in the same calendar year, $175). Join the American Hiking Society, a nonprofit organization tax-exempt since 1977, for a weeklong immersion excursion building and maintaining trails across the country.

Select the state or region you are interested in visiting on an online chart that includes hosting organizations, dates, difficulty levels, and accommodations from tents to bunkhouses and cabins. View a current schedule of 75 stewardship projects in 25 states, with new locations and shorter projects highlighted. Tools and supervision are provided by the hosting organization.

No experience is necessary, but participants must be in good physical condition. Trips are scheduled from February through November, with alternative spring break trips for college groups throughout the month of March. The American Hiking Society partners with the Leave No Trace Center for Outdoor Ethics, an organization that promotes responsible outdoor practices.

Coral Reef Conservation, Key West, FL: Reef Relief
(631 Greene St., Key West, FL 33040; 305-294-3100; fax
305-293-9515; www.reefrelief.org; reef@reefrelief.org).
Reef Relief is a nonprofit, membership organization,
founded in 1987, dedicated to preserving and protecting
living coral reef ecosystems. With a new headquarters and
environmental center in Key West, Reef Relief is looking
for volunteers to provide tours of the educational facility
and introduce visitors to the coral reef ecosystem of the
Florida Keys.

REEF RELIEF

The Florida Keys are home to this barracuda.

REEF RELIEF

College student Rob Schaudt organized a reef cleanup during his spring internship with Reef Relief.

Reef Relief needs help distributing educational materials and arranging special events and children's educational activities, including Coral Camp, the Discover Coral Reefs School Program, and Reef Ranger Program. College students may apply for internships. Training is provided, and program areas include environmental center operations, educational programs, and special events. If you are a diver or boater on vacation in Key West visiting coral reefs, you can monitor the condition of the reefs and share your observations, documenting findings with photographic images.

Missy's Story, Reef Relief, Key West, FL

During the summer, we run a Kids Reef Relief Camp, educating children about how what we do impacts the environment and how they can help to keep it clean. I really love working with kids ages 6–13 through camp and school programs to help them make a difference in their own lives and ours.

I'm always surprised by how much the students learn. Jordan was a very shy and quiet 13-year-old. He kept to himself and didn't talk much until the last day of camp, when we have a pizza party, parents tour the center, and the kids teach the parents what we've taught them.

REEF RELIEF

Sea turtles thrive in the reefs off Key West, Florida.

Jordan had made a series of drawings showing how one cigarette butt contaminates 60–80 gallons of water, and since we live on an island 4 feet above sea level, when it rains the drains overflow and the dirt on our streets contaminates the ocean. He told the group how the course had impacted him and changed his life, and that being conscious of the reefs was the best thing that ever happened to him. He not only had a great time, he also knew he wanted to study and work in the field, possibly in environmental biology, and to make a difference. It was totally awesome.

Protect and Rehabilitate Reefs, Multiple Coastline Locations, CA: Reef Check Foundation (P.O. Box 1057, Pacific Palisades, CA 90272-1057; 310-230-2371; fax 310-230-2376; www.reefcheck.org; rcinfo@reefcheck.org; $200 for 2-day boat dive class). Reef Check Foundation, an international nonprofit organization founded in 1996, with volunteer reef-monitoring teams around the world, is based in the United States with offices in Hawaii and California. Volunteer divers can participate in a training course over two weekends and become certified to do Reef Check California (RCCA) surveys, monitoring rocky reefs following a specific research protocol.

Reefs are in a state of crisis, threatened by overfishing, destructive fishing, pollution, and global warming. By helping to monitor the marine environment, you help support marine conservation and management. Once you are certified, you may survey any rocky reef in California and add this volunteer opportunity to your travel plans. Check the RCCA Web site for locations and dates of training weekends, as there are many possibilities for great vacations in Santa Rosa, Monterey, San Luis Obispo, Santa Barbara, Los Angeles, and Orange County.

Immersion Excursion: Aquarium on the Bay

The Monterey Bay Aquarium (886 Cannery Row, Monterey, CA 93940; 831- 648-4800; www.montereybay aquarium.org; 3-hour day sails, $69 adults, $59 youth ages 10–17, $10 discount for members; 90-minute sunset sails, nonmembers $55 per person, members $45 per person). Join aquarium staff aboard a 65-foot sailboat, departing from Fisherman's Wharf, and gather plankton, test water samples, and learn about the Monterey Marine Sanctuary. Take a turn at the helm, learn about navigation and sailing, and see harbor seals, California sea lions, sea otter, harbor porpoises, whales, and the coastal bottle-nose dolphin—all common visitors to the Bay. Monterey has fine restaurants, boutiques, galleries, inns, and well-known sights such as Cannery Row. Carmel-by-the-Sea is known for its charming downtown shopping streets and beautiful beaches

Conservation Adventures, Locations in AZ, CO, UT: Plateau Restoration (P.O. Box 1363, Moab UT 84532; 435-259-7733; www.plateaurestoration.org; info@plateau restoration.org; one-day volunteer events and opportuni-ties range from $20 to $75 per person). Plateau Restor-ation, a nonprofit organization since 1995, is a licensed guide and outfitter that offers land-based excursions, river journeys, and custom trips throughout southern Utah, western Colorado, and northern Arizona. They provide meaningful, fun-filled opportunities for people to partici-pate in the preservation and rehabilitation of public lands through service learning, volunteer vacations, and adven-ture education programs. Service learning is defined as educational enrichment programming integrated with active, hands-on community service.

Plateau Restoration's focus is on building a connection with nature and encouraging an active role in long-term

PLATEAU RESTORATION

These students from Northwestern University built a fence with Plateau Restoration during their spring break.

conservation. Activities include trail building, fencing, revegetation, seed collection, controlling exotic species, research, and monitoring recreation impacts.

Programs emphasize the interconnections between soil, vegetation, wildlife, humans, and the landscape. Interactive, multienvironment experiences encourage you to become better informed about desert ecosystems and the forces that give rise to the dramatic landscapes.

Plateau Restoration programs feature instructor/guides with over 20 years of field experience leading and teaching courses in the canyon country. University credit is available for many programs.

PLATEAU RESTORATION

College students who selected a Plateau Restoration spring break enjoyed hiking and river rafting.

Brad's Story, Plateau Restoration, Moab, Utah

I had so much fun. I flew out to Moab, Utah, from Johnson City, Tennessee, to volunteer with five groups of college kids on service-learning vacations. It was absolutely wonderful. That's one of my favorite things to do, and I'm very proud to be part of it.

We did projects in a number of locations around Moab. We worked and stayed at Ken's Lake, named for a former mayor. We did trail maintenance and rerouting trails, where we actually had to go in and create new trails, building water breaks and cribbing high-erosion areas. The biggest project was at Arches National Park by Delicate Arch. We were removing some vegetation, digging out roots—holey moley, some were 3 to 4 feet long. Hard work when it's so hot; those kids just ate it up.

I go on a service-learning vacation every year. It's awesome, and the kids really benefited from it and enjoyed themselves, and so did I. It was my vacation, time away from my job, and as always, it was time very well spent. I returned home revved, revived, rejuvenated, and looking forward to next year.

Jason's Story, Yale University Junior, New Haven, CT

After one spring vacation in Daytona Beach, Florida, I decided I was much more suited to exploring alternative spring vacations. I like volunteering during spring break and returning with memories to last a lifetime rather than returning from spring break without any memories at all.

Education, Service, Adventure, and Conservation, Locations in AZ, CO, NM, UT: Four Corners School of Outdoor Education (P.O. Box 1029, Monticello, UT 84535; 1-800-525-4456; www.fourcornersschool.org; fcs@four cornersschool.org, $925–1,200). Four Corners School (FCS) is a nonprofit organization, founded in 1984, dedicated to building a community of people committed to conserving the natural and cultural resources of the Colorado Plateau located in Arizona, Colorado, New Mexico, and Utah.

Southwest Ed-Ventures are adventures with an educational mission. There are several trips offered each year; costs vary with length and destination. Past trips have included Archaeological Excavation in Southeast Utah (7 days, $925 per person), where participants learned excavation, mapping and photo methods, artifact classification, identification, and storage techniques. Butler Wash Archeology, Rock Art, Monument Valley (7 days, $1,200 per person) equipped volunteers to assist with locating and surveying cliff dwellings, rock art, and surface ruins, and help with site documentation.

Since 1984, FCS has served 25,000 participants ranging in age from 6 to 90, has repaired or rehabilitated hundreds of miles of trails and roads, and has worked to conserve over 20 archaeological sites.

Park Volunteer, Multiple Locations in FL: Florida State Parks (3900 Commonwealth Blvd., Tallahassee, FL 32399; 850-245-2157; www.floridastateparks.org). Combine a vacation to Florida with a volunteer opportunity in one of Florida's 161 state parks. Greet visitors, conduct tours, remove invasive plants, maintain trails, beaches, and waterways, or be a campground host and receive a free campground site in return for your services. The Florida State Parks Web site has all of Florida's state parks listed with contact information and a link to each park's home page.

Decide which park or region of Florida you would like to visit. Fill out and submit the application located on the main volunteer page of the Web site and your application will be forwarded to the park or area of your interest. If you are interested in camping accommodations, inquire as early as possible, as most parks book winter volunteers a year in advance. Smaller parks and those in northern Florida are more likely to have openings in the winter months on shorter notice.

Dominick's Story, Paynes Prairie State Park, FL

I've been a photographer for 50 years. I was going to different parks, and then I started visiting Paynes Prairie State Park pretty regularly. It was reasonably close by, with plenty of beautiful places to shoot. One day I dropped a picture off at the ranger's station and they asked, "Why don't you become a volunteer?" So I asked what that would mean and the answer was, "Just keep taking pictures." I've gotten quite involved there. I do shows for the Prairie Friends, and they call me the Paynes Prairie Photo Ambassador.

Ginny's Story, Florida State Parks, Destin, FL

You don't have to be retired to enjoy RV life. My children are young, and I work more than full time. But getting away with your own housing all-in-one is a great break from everyday life. Living in Louisiana, the Florida State Park system is quite an accessible gem. You just pull up with your RV and there are so many jobs where they need help that you can basically stay there as long as you want, contributing skills they need. We stayed in Destin, which is next door to San Destin at Topsail Hill

Preserve State Park, with beautiful, pristine white sand beaches. It's a great way to travel.

Ⓢ **Environmental Education, Durango, Southwest Colorado, and the Four Corners: Durango Nature Studies** (1309 East 3rd Ave., Suite 34, Durango, CO 81301; 970-382-9244; fax 970-382-9273; www.durangonature studies.org; sally@durangonaturestudies.org). Durango Nature Studies (DNS), founded in 1994, is a nonprofit organization dedicated to providing nature, science, and environmental education to the Four Corners, an area that covers 12,000 square miles. DNS has a small core staff and relies on volunteers, interns, and contractors to serve about 6,000 people a year, mostly children.

Volunteer opportunities include being a Volunteer Naturalist, a Summer Teaching Assistant, working at special events, office support, and nature center maintenance. If you love working with children and being outdoors, DNS offers weeklong day camps for children ages 8–12. Camps focus on hands-on learning at the nature center or at Spud and Haviland Lakes. No special training is required to help staff with games, hikes, and art projects.

Accommodations

Ⓢ **Durango Hometown Hostel** (736 Goeglein Gulch Road, Durango, CO 81301, 970-385-4115, www.info@durango hometownhostel.com; info@durangohometownhostel.com; room rates $22–30; check-in 3:30–8 PM daily or by arrangement). Minutes away from the historic downtown district, the Durango Hometown Hostel offers affordable lodging in male, female, or coed dormitory style bunk bedrooms. There's a communal kitchen, shared bathroom facilities, and common living areas with computers and Internet access. Durango Hometown Hostel has some of the area's most popular hiking and mountain-biking trails out its front door.

Ⓢ–ⓈⓈ **Randy's** (152 E. College Dr., Durango, CO 81301; 970-247-9083; www.randysrestaurant.com) is known for their lunch salads, daily specials, steaks, and seafood with an Italian flair.

Ⓢ **Durango Doughworks** (2411 Main Ave., Durango, CO 81301; 970-267-1610; www.durangodoughworks.com) is where you'll find the locals over coffee, bagels, doughnuts, and a daily list of luncheon specials, open 6 AM–2 PM daily.

  Organic Farming and Sustainable Living, Rumney, NH: D Acres of New Hampshire
(P.O. Box 98, Rumney, NH 03266; 603-786-2366; www.dacres .org; info@dacres.org; interns, $20 per week; apprentices, $125 per week). D Acres, founded in 1997, is a nonprofit educational center that teaches and applies skills of sustainable living and organic farming. Participants share a communal living situation and work together to raise awareness about people's impact on the environment, to limit consumption of fossil fuels and other resources, and to encourage on-site pro-

The barn, silo, and grounds at D Acres in Rumney, New Hampshire.

Joe Vachon: Artist-in-residence, blacksmithing.

duction and consumption. D Acres provides training for the development of skills relating to organic farming, forestry, landscaping, eco-friendly construction, and cottage crafts.

Apply for either an apprenticeship or an internship and trade a minimum of 26 hours, and a weekly fee, for food and accommodations in a tree house, tent site, room in the Community House, or converted barn space. The policy is that no one will be denied access to D Acres workshops and events due to an inability to pay.

Work is primarily in the gardens, forest, and on building projects, and is related to the development, maintenance, and long-term economic viability of the community. All residents share cleaning and cooking tasks. Perks include access to a large commercial kitchen, living room, laundry, woodshop, research library, reading library, yoga space, wireless Internet, telephone, and the forested property. In your free time you can explore the White Mountains and the Lake District.

Ariel's Story, D Acres Organic Farm, Rumney, NH

I'm a 19-year-old sophomore at Brown University in Providence, Rhode Island. I do a lot of farming, I'm involved in the sustainable food campaign to use more sustainable foods at school, and have worked in a community garden. I found D Acres online, and it struck me as cool that it was much more than farming, including education, forestry, art, poetry, and animals. It definitely taught me a new way of life.

I didn't really know what to expect, immersing myself in an intentional community with other people, eating whole, seasonal foods, and sharing a common space with people of all ages. There is also a hostel on the farm with guests coming and going.

The lifestyle was just so different for me from school or home in Schenectady, New York. It's a strong community able to develop very meaningful bonds between people in short amounts of time. I went with a desire to experience something new, and open to change. I worked, did chores, and had time to just be there, focus on art projects, read at the library, and learn independently and from others. I had a really great time. I've already returned for a visit and plan to return again.

Immersion Excursion: The Mountains of New England

The White Mountains (www.fs.fed.us/r9/forests/white_ mountain/recreation; www.theoutdoorforum.com/New Hampshire/WhiteMountain.htm), formed by glaciers that retreated over 10,000 years ago, are considered the most rugged mountains in New England. The White Mountain National Forest covers almost 800,000 acres in north-central New Hampshire, extending into Maine, and includes 100 miles of the Appalachian Trail. The forest contains the largest alpine area east of the Rocky Mountains and south of northern Quebec, and is one of the most heavily used forests in the country. Alpine regions (about 5,500 feet and above) are high mountain ecosystems with low temperatures, strong winds, unstable soils, and short growing seasons. The Presidential Range includes Mt. Washington at an elevation of 6,288 feet. You can backpack, camp, picnic, bike, climb, fish, ski, and enjoy scenic drives, water activities, geocaching, horseback riding, wildlife viewing, photography, and dogsledding.

Restoration, Black Rock Desert Project, NV: BTCV Holidays (BTCV Holidays, Sedum House, Mallard Way, Potteric Carr, Doncaster, England DN4 8DB; 011-44-1302-

388-883; fax 011-44-1302-311-531; www2.btcv.org.uk; international@btcv.org.uk; www.nevadaoutdoorschool .org; fee £300, approximately $448, depending on current exchange rate, does not include transportation). BTCV Conservation Holidays, established in 1959 and today the United Kingdom's largest conservation charity, is partnering with the Nevada Outdoor School (NOS) to help with desert restoration and other volunteer projects. The Black Rock Desert Restoration Project requires volunteers to camp and work in the wilderness for a two-month commitment, with the legendary Burning Man Festival as the trip's grand finale.

The trip begins with orientation and training, teaching Leave No Trace ethics. Projects include trail building, invasive species removal, fence construction and restoration, road rehabilitation, helping with NOS activities, and assisting in setting up the Burning Man Festival.

The Black Rock Desert is the largest designated wilderness in Nevada.

Fieldwork is for eight days at a time, with tent camping throughout the trip. All equipment is provided. When at base camp in Winnemucca, you will stay in an RV park, with a large yurt as communal space and access to the park's facilities. Between trips there will be two days off at a time to tour, play, and relax.

This will be an immersion experience, getting to know the people in town by attending their barbecues and sporting events. The Black Rock Desert is the largest designated wilderness in Nevada. It is surrounded by the Pahute Peak Wilderness and the North and South Jackson Mountains Wilderness areas. Hike at Water Canyon, swim in the Rye Patch Reservoir, enjoy natural hot springs, and travel to Reno—two and a half hours away.

Louise's Story, Black Rock Desert Restoration Project, Nevada

After working as a land surveyor for seven years in the UK, I decided to return to college to pursue an outdoor, countryside-based program and wanted to do something over the summer that would help with that course. I looked up the BTCV (Conservation Holidays) to see what was available and came over on a tourist visa for a nine-week working holiday at the Nevada Outdoor School. Then I was offered a year's job, to be a volunteer with a living stipend. I needed to return to the UK to secure a one-year volunteer visa.

My title is NCA (National Conservation Area) Transportation Specialist and basically I GPS roads within the Black Rock Desert National Conservation Area. So I'm mapping and finding open roads, closed roads, legal roads, and campgrounds. I also served as the crew leader for the BTCV groups that came over this summer.

I think the key thing is that you need to come and visit before making any long-term commitment. I work and live in Winnemucca, Nevada, in the middle of nowhere with extreme temperatures and intense conditions, which might not be for everyone. It's worth researching the area that you're actually planning to go to. Here there are antelope, wild horses, rattlesnakes, scorpions, and a large species of lizard I've never encountered before.

This experience has totally changed my life. I am far happier than ever before, more comfortable with myself, more outgoing, and I absolutely love it here and can't get that point across enough. Being here has instilled in me the love of being outdoors and working outside, and made me realize this is exactly what I want to do.

Immersion Excursion: A Famous Event

The Burning Man Festival (www.burningman.com; questions@burningman.com), founded on a small beach in San Francisco in 1986, has grown into a city that comes together in the Black Rock Desert for one week out of the year. It is an event that allows participants to connect with fellow community members and to express themselves creatively around art themes, art installations, and theme camps. It is an experimental community of 48,000+ people who decide for themselves how they want to contribute to the experience. The city is built and then completely dismantled after the participants leave. Two thousand volunteers work before, during, and after the event to ensure its viability and success. Burning Man takes place the week prior to and including Labor Day Weekend.

Protect Coastal Regions, San Clemente, CA, and other Coastal Locations: Surfrider Foundation (P.O. Box 6010, San Clemente, CA 92674; 949-492-8170; fax 949-492-8142; www.surfrider.org; info@surfrider.org). Volunteers are always needed at the Surfrider Foundation, in San Clemente, California, and its 60+ chapters on the East, West, Gulf, and Hawaiian coasts. Surfrider, a nonprofit organization founded by Malibu surfers in 1984, believes all people should have access to beaches and supports initiatives to reduce pollution and ensure that coastal environmental resources are protected.

Volunteers participate in beach cleanups, collecting and testing water samples, giving presentations, and speaking to state and federal agencies. There are many levels of volunteering, which are listed in the Volunteer Menu Book on the Surfrider Web site. Entry-level volunteer activities include collecting debris on the beach, participating in petition drives, storm-drain stenciling (to inform the public that street gutters lead to the ocean), member outreach, and general assistance.

Intermediate-level volunteer activities include the Blue Water Task Force, a program to test water samples to determine pollution patterns, and Respect the Beach, a coastal and surf education project. Get involved in Beachscape and help gather additional information to promote sustainable coastal-resource management by documenting small portions of the coastline and noting pipes, structures, debris, beach access, rideable waves, and river mouths.

Stewardship, Southwest CO: San Juan Mountains Association (P.O. Box 2261, Durango, CO 81302; 970-385-1310; fax 970-375-2319; www.sjima.org; kathe@sjma .org). The San Juan Mountains Association (SJMA) promotes education, volunteer stewardship, and hands-on involvement on public lands in southwest Colorado. SJMA, a nonprofit organization since 1976, has access to opportunities from federal, state, local, and tribal programs.

Volunteer to monitor archaeological or cultural sites, build trails, and educate other people. Some programs require a longer-term commitment and training, while others fit short-term traveling plans. Contact the volunteer coordinator with suggestions for projects you'd like to do.

The San Juan Public Lands include 2.5 million acres crossing five Colorado counties and ranging from high-desert mesas to alpine peaks. Cultural resources include historic mining towns and ancestral Puebloan cliff dwellings. Because of the varied ecosystems, there is an abundance of native fish, wildlife, and plants; geological resources include rock formations, minerals, caves, and fossils.

Sustainable Living Skills, Mendocino County, CA: Mendocino Ecological Learning Center

(4651 Bear Canyon Rd., Willets, CA 95490; 707-456-0779; www.melc.us; inquiry@melc.us). The Mendocino Ecological Learning Center (MELC), founded in 2003, is a nonprofit educational organization and ecological reserve that practices sustainable stewardship of lands, plants, animals, and energy systems. The center seeks innovative solutions to the problems caused by destructive farming, housing, land management, and energy practices. MELC offers research and training to people interested in finding and implementing long-term solutions.

Support community-based agriculture, land management, natural building and housing alternatives, and renewable energy production. Apply to a work-exchange program to learn more about sustainable living skills and practices. Activities include site design, infrastructure improvements, and assistance with daily operations. There are two short-term residential positions offered in a work/trade program in which you receive lodging, use of

Benefits for Everyone

The Land Trust Alliance (1660 L St., NW, Suite 1100, Washington, DC 20036; 202-638-4725; fax 202-638-4730; www.landtrustalliance.org; info@lta.org). Created in 1982, the nonprofit Land Trust Alliance includes 1,700 organizations conserving over 37 million acres, saving forests, farms, waterways, and natural areas. Contribute your time and skills in communities where you live, work, or travel by connecting with a local land trust. Learn how to conserve land, promote conservation, and get involved. Volunteer at the annual rally, become a tour guide, work on a trail maintenance crew, clean up a stream, or help in an office with e-mail and flyers. Find a member land trust by searching by state and county on the Land Alliance Web site. There are nationwide, statewide, and local land trusts listed with links providing contact information, demographics, and acres conserved.

facilities, meals, and work experience. You will be a part of a growing nonprofit while living and working in a beautiful and educational setting.

MELC, located in northern California, is on 31 acres of second- and third-growth forestlands. With windy hilltops and fast-flowing creeks, the area provides possibilities for solar, hydro, and wind energy production. MELC is looking for people with positive and enthusiastic attitudes and the desire to learn and contribute.

To apply, send a cover letter and résumé describing your interests and experiences, and what your goals are for your participation in the work-exchange program. Include work and personal references with phone numbers.

Damaged Ecosystems, New Orleans, LA: Earthwatch Institute (3 Clock Tower Place, Suite 100, P.O. Box 75, Maynard, MA 01754; 1-800-776-0188; 978-461-0081; fax 978-461-2332; www.earthwatch.org; info@earthwatch.org; 11 days, contribution of $2,346). Earthwatch is an international nonprofit organization, founded in 1971, that supports scientific research by engaging volunteers in the effort to contribute to environmental sustainability. Volunteers join scientific research teams to collect field data in the areas of rainforest ecology, wildlife conservation, marine science, archaeology, and more.

Help researchers and work in ecosystems damaged by Hurricanes Katrina and Rita by collecting caterpillars and other insects to restore an important greenhouse collection. This project tracks the parasitoids (insects that lay eggs inside other species) to find out how caterpillars defend themselves and how they have been affected by weather conditions and events. You can also help update the forest caterpillar database, which tracks biodiversity in the region.

After spending three nights in the Park View Guest House in New Orleans (www.parkviewguesthouse.com) you will stay at a research station in the Pearl River Wildlife Management Area. The one-room, air-conditioned building has eight bunk beds, a full kitchen, dining area, bathroom, and shower. Your team will prepare meals with the help of the research staff.

The guesthouse is located across the street from Tulane University and Audubon Park, and near the French Quarter, Central Business District, Riverwalk shopping, D-Day Museum, and the Aquarium of the Americas.

Immersion Excursion: A New Orleans Delight

Enjoy walking along the Mississippi River, and be sure to stop at Café Du Monde, famous for chicory coffee, powdered sugar beignets, and local servers with entertaining stories about the people and the place.

Claudia's Story, Earthwatch Field Representative

There are about 60 field representatives across the country. I am in Detroit, and we have two official reps

in the area. It is a totally volunteer position I've done
for about five years. Usually we make our own schedules and that depends on the things going on in any
particular area.

We have partnered with the Detroit Zoo, the New
Detroit Science Center, Cranbrook Institute of Science,
and the Science Teachers Association, among others.
Members also give talks to local organizations when
they return from a trip.

I have been on 11 Earthwatch trips, five of them
with my husband and six on my own. I can't think of
one that I regret taking. I enjoyed my nursing career, but
if I had it to do all over again, I would want to work in
scientific research.

**Trail Maintenance/High School Students, Multiple
Locations in Washington State: Washington Trails
Association** (2019 Third Ave., Suite 100, Seattle, WA
98121; 206-625-1367; www.wta.org/volunteer/youth;
alyssa@wta.org; $150 per person, $125 members, $75 for
subsequent trips). Washington Trails Association (WTA), a
nonprofit organization, tax-exempt since 1980, offers
Youth Vacations for high school students, ages 14–18.
Participants learn about building and maintaining trails,
safety, and teamwork. There are opportunities near the
ocean, in the Cascade Mountains, and in northeast
Washington.

WTA provides experienced crew leaders, challenging
and exciting projects, camping gear, and food. Weeklong
trips run from Sunday afternoon to Friday afternoon and
require hiking to and from the project site and working at a
moderate pace through the day. Meet new people from different backgrounds, learn new skills, and have fun while
contributing a valuable service. At the end of your trip you

may contact the WTA office to request a letter of service for up to 40 hours of community service credit.

For those with previous trail work experience with either WTA or other organizations, there are Advanced Backcountry trips. These trips, for ages 15–18, run from Saturday morning to the following Saturday, and will enable you to further your trail skills and learn leadership techniques under the supervision of a WTA crew leader. Trips are rated easy, moderate, difficult, and strenuous.

Volunteers have a day off on Wednesday and time to relax, engage in recreational activities, explore the surroundings, and learn about the area. Front-country volunteers stay in tents at campsites within state parks and U.S. national forests, while advanced backcountry volunteers hike into camp and stay in tents. You will prepare your own food, sometimes over a campfire, and pack your own lunches. A parent consent form, trip schedule, and a short documentary about the youth program are available on the WTA Web site.

Two-Week Teen Spike Crew, White Mountains, NH: Appalachian Mountain Club (AMC Main Office, 5 Joy St., Boston, MA 02108; 617-523-0636; fax 617;523-0722; www.outdoors.org; information@outdoors.org; ages 16–18, contribution, $465 member, $500 nonmember). The Appalachian Mountain Club (AMC), founded in 1876, is the country's oldest nonprofit conservation and recreation organization. Make new friends when you volunteer with AMC in the White Mountains of New Hampshire. You will practice Leave No Trace ethics as you contribute to the conservation and preservation of our natural resources.

This program offers ten days of trail work and two days of recreation. After arrival Sunday afternoon and one night at base camp, the crew packs food, equipment, and personal belongings into the woods. Project work may include

Protecting Lands and Water

The Nature Conservancy (4245 North Fairfax Dr., Suite 100, Arlington, VA 22203; 1-800 628-6860; 703-841-5300; www.nature.org; info@nature.org). The Nature Conservancy, a nonprofit organization founded in 1951, works in all 50 states and around the world to protect lands and water for nature and people. The conservancy partners with indigenous communities, businesses, governments, multilateral institutions, and other nonprofits. You can help nature and the environment by volunteering and contributing your time and skills. To find available volunteer opportunities, select the state in which you live or the state you are planning to visit and choose from among work days, ongoing projects and activities, and special events. Download job descriptions and find contact information for questions you might need answered.

PLATEAU RESTORATION

Plateau Restoration provides service-learning, volunteer vacations, and adventure education programs.

clearing brush, installing drainage, and building rock steps and bog bridges. There will be time to enjoy the views, swim, socialize, and enjoy great food.

Crew members assist with food preparation and clean-up, and after dinner enjoy board games, tell stories, discuss conservational and environmental ethics, and relax. AMC supplies all tents and cooking equipment. Each morning your group is contacted to see if more supplies are needed, before hiking to the project site with water, lunch, rain gear, tools, and safety equipment.

After five days on the trails, the crew returns to base camp for the Friday-night barbeque, and Saturday rock climbing with guides from Eastern Mountain Sports Climbing School, Conway, New Hampshire. Sunday activities are decided by the group. On Monday the crew returns to the backcountry for five more days of trail work, returning to base camp again in time for the Friday-night barbecue.

Volunteering with AMC is a wonderful way to spend part of your vacation, and a great opportunity if you are interested in future work with the Park or Forest Service, a seasonal job with a paid work crew, or any other environmental work. It is also a great time on its own, with terrific people who enjoy the outdoors.

Trail Work Weekend, Little Lyford Pond Camps, ME: Appalachian Mountain Club (AMC Main Office, 5 Joy St., Boston MA 02108; 617-523-0636; registration 603-466-2727; fax 617-523-0722; www.outdoors.org; information@ outdoors.org; $20 per night). All abilities are welcome and no experience is necessary to join one of these three-day trail-crew weekends. Arrive at Little Lyford Pond Camps Friday afternoon, within Maine's 100-mile Wilderness, and get to work after breakfast on Saturday. Projects range from clearing brush to building shelters and bridges.

AMC provides all the tools, and Lyford Pond Camps has hot showers and provides great food. Breakfast and dinner

are family-style, and a trail lunch is provided. Bring a sleeping bag or bed linens for use in a comfortable bunkhouse.
The trail crew returns to the camps after 2:30 PM for rest
and recreation, showers, and dinner.

Try fly fishing in two ponds at the camps or the west
branch of the Pleasant River, or hike the many trails to
enjoy viewing wildlife and plants, or paddle on the ponds
with canoes and kayaks provided. The camp is a 2-mile
hike from Gulf Hagas and the Appalachian Trail.

Two-Week Teen Stewardship Crew, Berkshires, MA: Appalachian Mountain Club

(AMC Main Office,
5 Joy St., Boston, MA 02108; 617-523-0636; fax 617;523-
0722; www.outdoors.org; information@outdoors.org; ages
16–19, contribution, $285 member, $315 nonmember).
Volunteer for two weeks in the beautiful Berkshires in
Massachusetts, spending ten days on a trail crew in the
backcountry and two days in a Leave No Trace course.
The Appalachian Mountain Club, founded in 1876, is the
country's oldest nonprofit conservation and recreation
organization.

After arrival Sunday at the AMC office in Western
Massachusetts, followed by an orientation, crew members
begin trip preparations to pack in food, tools, camping
equipment, and personal belongings to the project site.
Trail work may include installing rock water bars, cleaning drainage, building rock steps, painting blazes, and
clearing downed trees. After five days in the backcountry,
the crew attends a two-day skills session, then returns
to the backcountry and a new project site for the last
five days.

The program cost includes food, supervision by two
experienced trail crew leaders, transportation from the
office to the work site, skills sessions, and camping for 12
nights. Current trip dates, additional trip options, and a
registration form are available on the Web site.

Teen Trails Leadership Crew, White Mountains, NH: Appalachian Mountain Club (AMC Main Office, 5 Joy St., Boston, MA 02108; 617-523-0636; fax 617-523-0722; www.outdoors.org; information@outdoors.org; three-week program, ages 17–19; contribution, $795 member, $860 nonmember). This volunteer vacation includes Leave No Trace certification and a SOLO (Stonehearth Open Learning Opportunities, Conway, NH) Wilderness First Aid (WFA) course and certification. Crew members will enjoy a day of rock climbing and receive AMC's *Complete Guide to Trail Building and Maintenance*. Volunteers arrive at base camp on Friday afternoon, spend the night there, and begin their Leave No Trace studies. During the three-week program, crew members participate in a variety of maintenance projects, which may include brushing, drainage cleaning, rock work, bog bridging, trail construction, and training in backcountry living. Crews pack out food, tools, camping equipment, and personal belongings while working on trails in remote sites.

Your second weekend includes the SOLO WFA course, and the third weekend offers rock climbing with the Eastern Mountain Sports Climbing School, Conway, New Hampshire. After each week of trail work the crew returns to base camp for the Friday night barbeque.

Service Projects for High School Students Multiple Locations Across the Country: Landmark Volunteers (P.O. Box 455, 800 North Main St., Sheffield, MA 01257; 413-229-0255; fax 413-229-2050; www.volunteers .com; landmark@volunteers.com; 2-week summer program, $1,400; 1-week spring program, $750). Landmark, a nonprofit organization founded in 1992, offers a variety of volunteer opportunities for motivated students entering 10th, 11th, or 12th grades. Make a difference and work for a cultural, environmental, historic, or social service organization during your school vacation.

Time is built in for fun and friendship. Leisure activities may include swimming, hiking, tennis, campfires, movies, and participating in community and special events and festivals. Jobs include clearing trails, building, painting, and grounds maintenance, or working with children at a summer camp, with projects determined by the needs of the hosting nonprofit organization.

Choose six programs in order of preference, taking into account your interests, the type of work you want to do, the geographic location of the program, the type of accommodations (ranging from dorm rooms to wilderness camping), and the dates available. The application requires an essay and parent endorsement.

Upon completion of service, students receive community service credit (up to 80 hours for a two-week session and 40 hours for a one-week session) and letters of recommendation.

 High School Conservation Crews, Nationwide: Student Conservation Association (P.O. Box 550, 689 River Rd., Charlestown, NH 03603; 603-543-1700; fax 603-543-1828; www.thesca.org; ask-us@thesca .org: ages 15–19; application fee only). High school students can volunteer for three to five weeks, joining a Student Conservation Association (SCA) national crew building hiking trails, protecting natural habitats, constructing footbridges over marshlands, and more, in national parks and forests, on beaches and riverbanks, at fisheries and on volcanoes. SCA is a nonprofit organization founded in 1957 to restore and protect the country's public lands.

Share this volunteer experience with other crew members from across the United States and two experienced adult leaders. A preference for a particular region of the country can be specified on the application, but you are not guaranteed a placement at a particular site. There are

There's a sense of great accomplishment in removing a tamarisk stump.

PLATEAU RESTORATION

opportunities in all 50 states, and there is a list of possible placements on the SCA Web site.

Crews of six to eight members, similar in age but with diverse backgrounds and experience, are split evenly between boys and girls, with both a male and a female crew leader. Friends are not placed together, as making new friends is an important part of your experience. There are trips at the end of each program, planned by the crew leaders, which range from backpacking in nearby mountains to day trips near the work site and canoe trips.

Volunteering with SCA is tuition-free, after a $25 application fee. SCA provides tents, community equipment, and food. Travel costs are your responsibility, along with your personal equipment. If you do not have and cannot borrow a backpack, sleeping bag, and pad, SCA has some equipment you may use if arranged beforehand.

You will be instructed which airport to fly into, and a crew leader will meet you and provide transportation to the campsite. A financial aid form is included with the acceptance package, and if qualified you may be reimbursed for some of your travel costs. The maximum award is $400.

SCA accepts applications year-round and begins reviewing them in January. Applications require references, crew signature form, medical health history, and physician recommendation forms. Acceptance letters begin going out in April and continue until all crews are complete.

Interdisciplinary Environmental Opportunities: Student Conservation Association (P.O. Box 550, 689 River Rd., Charlestown, NH 03603; 603-543-1700; fax 603-543-1828; www.thesca .org; internships, www.thesca.org/more-environmental-conservation-internships; admissions@thesca.org; 18+).
Student Conservation Association internships are perfect gap year programs, varying from 3- to 12-month commitments, in more than 50 disciplines, for young adults who want to make a difference and help preserve environmental and cultural resources. Internships include Interpretation and Visitor Services, Invasive Species Control, Resource Management, GIS/GPS, Environmental Education, and Wildlife Management. A comprehensive list of positions is available on the SCA Web site, with a great feature called Weekly Staff Picks that includes some of the most interesting and unusual SCA internships across the country.

Spend your gap year as a Wilderness Volunteer Coordinator in the Yuki Wilderness (California), or as an Interpreter in the Chattahoochee River National Recreation Area (Georgia). Learn about botany and fire effects at the

Bandelier National Monument (New Mexico), or Marketing and Communications for the Texas Parks and Wildlife Foundation (Texas). Be a Wilderness Ranger in Wasatch-Cache National Forest (Washington), or a GIS (Geographic Information Systems) Specialist at the Petersburg National Battlefield (Virginia).

To search for an internship (by location, discipline, or availability) you must have an application on file. Apply online or contact SCA for more information. SCA offers many benefits: personal, financial, and global. Since SCA internships are volunteer positions, you will receive a subsistence allowance for basic food expenses. Housing is provided at no cost, and grants may be awarded to help with expenses for roundtrip travel to work sites.

AmeriCorps Education Awards are available and may be used to pay college tuition or education loans. SCA interns are covered by accident insurance, and medical coverage/insurance is offered to all long-term interns at no cost. You will also benefit from the specialized training you receive, and in some cases academic credit or professional certifications are available.

5

National Treasures: Preserve Federally Protected Areas

Conservation, Maintenance, and Stewardship

Camp life suited me; it was just naturally no trouble for me to settle into it. Many people have asked me: "How did you manage the children way off there in the mountains?" Well, all I can say is that it was simpler there than in town.

—MARGARET MURIE, AUTHOR, *TWO IN THE FAR NORTH*

There's a great history and connection between concerned citizens, artists, writers, activists, and national parks. Preserving our national treasures involves everyone. Fully appreciating, enjoying, and celebrating our national parks, forests, lakes, trails, seashores and scenic highways through conservation, maintenance, stewardship, and education is both a responsibility and a gift.

National treasures are found throughout the United States with thousands upon thousands of miles of trails that need our help in order to protect and preserve them for future generations. The Pacific Crest National Scenic Trail and the Continental Divide Trail, among many others highlighted in this chapter, are significant resources for the enjoyment of hikers and equestrians and for the value of wild and scenic lands to everyone.

Volunteers help restore, maintain, and build new trails. On a volunteer trail crew, some people might be able to move rocks while others can do less rigorous work. Whatever your skills, interests, or passions, there's a place for you to share your energy and talents. You can monitor songbirds; collect data about stream habitat, water quality, and fish populations; work on archaeological sites and artifact processing; assist with botanical surveys; report on ski trail conditions; provide commentary aboard a moving train; or volunteer as a living-history volunteer on a canal boat.

It's important to understand your limitations and consider the requirements of the activity you will be doing. Begin by asking yourself what your true level of physical conditioning is. How much time can you comfortably work outdoors? Are you willing to work in all weather conditions? If you don't currently have the skills you need, can you acquire them in the time you have to prepare for your volunteer vacation?

Find out from the sponsoring organization about the trip's physical requirements, and if there is orientation or training required and provided. Accommodations can range from a light-keeper's house to an apartment, dormitory, campsite, pad for your RV, lodge, or rustic cabin. Ask what "modest living quarters" means, and if you are responsible for your own meals, so that you know exactly what to expect. As one seasoned volunteer puts it, the more questions asked up front, the fewer surprises later.

National parks are very special places that need and use a multitude of volunteers in many different ways: to restore natural habitats, monitor wildlife, maintain trails and buildings, care for the park's exhibits, patrol the park, educate visitors, and staff the park's visitor centers.

Volunteering enables you to experience a national park in a whole new way, with many more possibilities for a rewarding volunteer vacation.

There are opportunities for adults, teens, families with children, and groups, and time commitments anywhere from a half-day, one day, a week or two, one to four months, to six months or longer. National parks need assistance year-round, and you can find opportunities to match your interests and availability.

The national parks highlighted in this chapter may be in remote or unique locations, or offer unusual volunteer activities, recreational opportunities, or educational experiences. All regions of the country are explored, and it's easy to find volunteer positions in national parks on the government clearinghouse site (www.volunteer.gov/gov) and by using other resources found in this book.

Opportunities to volunteer in other federally protected areas abound. Most of the land owned by the government is managed by the Interior Department's Bureau of Land Management, Fish and Wildlife Service, National Park Service, and the Agriculture's Department of Forest Services, with the responsibility of protecting the country's natural, historical, and cultural resources while providing opportunities for recreation. National treasures include the National Wilderness Preservation System, National Wild and Scenic Rivers, American Heritage Rivers, National Estuarine Research Centers, National Marine Sanctuaries, National Wildlife Refuges, National Seashores and Lakeshores, the National Trails System, the National Register of Historic Places, National Scenic Byways, and National Parks.

Songbirds of the Tetons, Grand Teton National Park, Northwestern WY: Earthwatch Institute (3 Clock Tower Place, Suite 100, P.O. Box 75, Maynard, MA 01754; 1-800-776-0188; 978-461-0081; fax 978-461-2332; www.earth

watch.org; info@earthwatch.org; 9 days, contribution, $2,146). Live in Grand Teton National Park for nine days and help monitor resident and migratory songbirds. Early risers spend the morning identifying and banding birds and looking for previously banded birds, noting their GPS locations. After a lunch break, you will look for nests and banded juvenile birds.

Studies have shown that both resident and migratory songbirds, including chickadees, sapsuckers, grosbeaks, thrushes, warblers, woodpeckers, and vireos, have decreased over the last 30 years. Scientists are mist-netting (using fine, soft nets to safely capture and band songbirds), counting, and banding songbirds in several locations throughout Grand Teton National Park and Bridger-Teton National Forest, and you can help estimate songbird populations, understand how the songbirds use their habitats, and find out why populations are decreasing.

Volunteer accommodations are at either the Jackson or Kelly campus of the Teton Science School, and meals are included. The Jackson campus is just 2 miles from town, and residential lodges offer shared rooms and standard bathrooms, with a nearby dining lodge. The Kelly campus, located 45 minutes from Jackson, has rustic cabins and new meeting and dining facilities. Situated within Grand Teton National Park, it offers breathtaking views and an opportunity to live in the midst of park wildlife. Cabins are for 3–4 people, with a shared bathroom.

Evenings include dinner, followed by a speaker or time to socialize and relax. In your free time you can explore the area, tour national parks, or visit the National Museum of Wildlife Art. Jackson Hole, Wyoming, is bordered on the west by the Teton Mountain Range and to the south by the Snake River Range, with Yellowstone National Park to the north. You'll find detailed maps, locations, dates, and current information on the Earthwatch Web site.

Mary Jo's Story, Grand Teton National Park, WY

I love the volunteer opportunities that Earthwatch provides for those of us who do not have special skills to offer. My husband is 71 and I'm 65, and we've gone on 14 expeditions so far. My husband has a scientific background; I do not. They are looking for flexible workers willing to work.

We've been on projects where the researcher is trying to determine the impact of tourism on the native wildlife. Tourists are coming in and out for a half-day and we're actually living there for two weeks. It's very stimulating assisting these scientists, and our trip expenses are 100 percent tax deductible.

We just returned from the Songbirds of the Tetons project in Grand Teton National Park. The researcher was very clever. The first day, charts were put up on the wall for us to rate ourselves on different tasks we'd be doing that week: bird identification, bird banding, nest locating, GPS, Excel, and computer skills, among others. Most of us were at the 0 to 1 range, and at the end of our week we were asked to rate ourselves again. We all moved up to middle to high-end ratings.

I was doing things I'd never thought about before: reading satellite photos, documenting exactly where we were when we found a bird or nest, and noting the landmarks and description. They break the work down into manageable bits, and you come away with a great feeling of accomplishment.

Immersion Excursion: Visit Yellowstone and Grand Teton National Parks

Join **Wildlife Expeditions** (1-888-945-3567; www.wildlife expeditions.org) for wildlife viewing and natural history excursions to Yellowstone and Grand Teton National Parks. There are half-day, full-day, and multiday trips available, including a Wolf and Bear Expedition. Wildlife Expeditions is a nonprofit environmental education organization dedicated to educating people about wildlife and encouraging appreciation of wild places and wildlife. All expeditions are led by professional biologists, and vehicles are customized with multiple roof hatches and sliding side windows, which provide a safe and ethical means of viewing wildlife. Spotting scopes, binoculars, field guides, maps, snacks, and beverages are provided, and child seats are available. Travelocity rated Wildlife Expeditions as a top eco-travel destination and highlighted their Wolf and Grizzly trip.

Trails and Rails, Seattle, WA: Klondike Gold Rush National Historical Park, Seattle Unit (319 Second Ave., South, Seattle, WA 98104; 206-220-4240; volunteer program, Sean O'Meara, 206-220-4234; www.nps.gov/klse; sean_o'meara@nps.gov). If you live near or are planning to travel to the Seattle area, consider volunteering at Klondike Gold Rush National Historical Park, a partnership program between the National Park Service and Amtrak. People who love history and the rails are taught to provide a moving commentary aboard Amtrak's *Empire Builder* and *Coast Starlight* train routes. Trails and Rails Guides are needed between Memorial Day and mid-September.

A script outline will be provided with room to put the information into your own words describing historically, culturally, and geographically significant areas as seen from the trains. The position requires a uniform, which will be provided, and training begins in mid-March.

The Seattle Unit is located in Pioneer Square Historical District, which was the starting point for many of the stampeders who traveled to the Klondike region to prospect for gold. Klondike Gold Rush National Historical Park preserves the stories of the 1897–1898 Gold Rush and the stampede to the Yukon gold fields.

Immersion Excursion: The Chilkoot Trail

The only National Park Service hiking trail in Klondike Gold Rush Historical Park is the Chilkoot Trail, one of the main access routes to the Klondike in the late 1890s. The trail was in existence long before the gold rush, established by the Tlingit (indigenous people of northwestern America) as a trade route for seal oil and seaweed, moose and caribou hides, plants, and other goods. It takes three to five days to hike the 33-mile trail leading from Dyea, Alaska, to Bennett, British Columbia. Miners carried hundreds of pounds of gear, including food, cooking equipment, tools, trunks, and musical instruments. The Chilkoot Trail was designated a U.S. Historic Landmark in 1978, and in 1998, the centennial of the gold rush, Chilkoot National Historic Site in British Columbia joined the U.S. Park Service to form the Klondike Gold Rush International Historical Park.

Living History Volunteer, MD, WV, Washington, DC: Chesapeake and Ohio Canal National Historic Park (1850 Dual Hwy., Suite 100, Hagerstown, MD 21740; 301-739-4200; fax 301-739-5275; www.nps.gov/choh; Danny_filer@nps.gov). Combine a trip to Maryland, West Virginia, or Washington, DC, with a volunteer opportunity in the Chesapeake and Ohio Canal National Historic Park. The C&O Canal originally served communities along the Potomac River and was vital to the transport of coal, lumber, grain, and other agricultural products. Today, visitors hike or bike the 184+ miles of the canal, which never

High school students from St. Patrick's Episcopal Day School in Washington, DC, paint the entrance sign to Swain's Lockhouse.

reached its intended goal of linking Chesapeake Bay with the Ohio River. The park includes almost 20,000 acres, from densely populated Washington, DC, through farmland and forest to Cumberland, Maryland, and preserves floodplains and wetlands that contribute to the conservation of the Chesapeake Bay.

Consider being a Living History Volunteer as part of a boat crew, learn how a lock operates, travel along the canal, and relive America's history. Volunteers dressed in period costumes assist in the operation of the replica canal boats and may lead interpretive programs.

Learn about natural, historic, and recreational resources and work with a culturally diverse group of visitors. Good communication skills are required, and you must be physically able to carry out your responsibilities, which include mule care. Staff will provide orientation and on-the-job training in the handling of mules and operating the canal boat and lift locks.

Other volunteer positions include working at the Hagerstown, Maryland, headquarters as a visitor assistant, or as a summer assistant at the Williamsport or Hancock visitor centers, or the Brunswick Railroad Museum. There might be openings for a bike mechanic, a lockhouse and river docent, campground hosts, and bike patrol volunteers to assist visitors with information, first aid, and directions, and to identify towpath hazards.

Volunteer Billy Goat Trail Stewards educate visitors at the trailheads and help protect the natural resources of Bear Island. They make sure hikers are prepared for the strenuous hike, teach them Leave No Trace practices, and

C&O CANAL NATIONAL HISTORIC PARK

Volunteers move timber to be used as part of a water bar that will help prevent erosion of the River Trail at Great Falls, Maryland.

inform them about sensitive vegetation. If you volunteer for this position, you can hike the entire trail or just part of it, or connect with visitors near the trailhead, carrying an emergency radio and helping with basic first aid. The National Park Service and The Nature Conservancy (www.nature.org) co-own the island and help protect its diverse habitats.

Canal Pride Days is an annual event with over one hundred revitalization and stewardship projects. Volunteers paint signs, rebuild picnic tables, cut back vegetation, and construct trails. It's a great opportunity for a short-term volunteer project, where you meet new people and contribute your time and talents to a great endeavor. Individuals and groups of all skill levels are welcome.

The Chesapeake and Ohio Canal National Historic Park offers backpacking, bird-watching, boating and kayaking, camping, climbing, fishing, cross-country skiing, biking, horseback riding, wildlife viewing, nature walks, and interpretive programs to enhance your volunteer experience.

Immersion Excursion: From Town to Town

Beautiful countryside and river towns along the C&O Canal make this a great combination volunteering, touring, biking, hiking, and relaxation spot. Visit the stone aqueducts, downstream from Hancock on the eastern end of town, where the locktender and his family would have lived. At one time, people lived in every lockhouse, and today a few are still open to the public, thanks to volunteers. As you visit the towns along the canal, you're sure to meet residents with stories from grandparents, uncles, and cousins about life in the lockhouses. For more information on what to do and where to stay, visit the Hagerstown Washington County Convention & Visitors Bureau (1-888-257-2600; www.marylandmemories.org; info@maryland memories.com).

Accommodations and Dining

$ $ **America's Best Value Inn** (2 Blue Hill, Hancock, MD 21750; 301-678-6108; www.americasbvi.com), located on one of the hills of the Appalachian Mountains near the banks of the Potomac River, and recently renovated, has 22 guest rooms and offers a complimentary continental breakfast.

$-$ $ **Weaver's Restaurant** (77 West Main St., Hancock, MD 21750; 301-678-6346; info@weaversrestaurant.com). Weaver's has been in continuous operation since Gertie Weaver opened her restaurant in 1948. It is known for homemade soups, breads, and the best pies anywhere on the East Coast.

$-$ $ **Park-N-Dine Restaurant** (189 E. Main St., Hancock, MD 21750; 301-678-5242). With a view of the Potomac River and C&O Canal, this local landmark, open since 1946, serves breakfast, lunch, and dinner daily except on Christmas Day.

Karen's Story, C&O Canal, Hagerstown, MD

In 1977 I had just been through a personal crisis when friends called me and announced, "Get dressed to hike. We're picking you up at 8 AM on Saturday." I really didn't want to go, but they came anyway. It turns out that was the annual Douglas Hike at the Chesapeake and Ohio Canal National Historic Park. U.S. Supreme Court Justice William O. Douglas, in 1954, challenged the editors of the *Washington Post* to hike the entire canal. There was a plan to turn the canal into a parkway, and Justice Douglas was convinced that if people hiked the Canal, they'd never be able to support its demise.

I too fell in love with this all-natural park along the beautiful towpaths. I couldn't believe anyone would build a canal into mountains. I have a compulsive mind, and when I begin to have questions, I have to find the answers. I needed to learn everything I could about locks, waste weirs, drainage, and other important structures. At the time I was living in Washington, DC, only a half-mile from the beginning of the canal in the Foggy Bottom area. I volunteered there and came out to Hagerstown to a lovely B&B for many weekends. When I retired in 2001, I moved to Maryland to be closer to headquarters.

I am the volunteer librarian two days a week and participate in the Level Walker Program. People are assigned a section of the canal, about 1^1/$_2$ to 3^1/$_2$ miles, to be responsible for picking up litter and checking out the structures and paths. I've had my 2-mile section consistently since 1977. I leave my car at one end of my section and walk back. It's really fun and very interesting to watch how the level of the canal has changed over the course of the years, and year to year. The length of the levels depends upon where you can get into the canal. Some levels are very remote and access is difficult, making for very diverse and interesting volunteer work.

Visitor Services/Museum Operations, Murfreesboro, TN: Stones River National Battlefield (3501 Old Nashville Hwy., Murfreesboro, TN 37129; 615-893-9501; fax 615-893-9508; volunteer information, 615-893-9501; www.volunteer.gov; jim_b_lewis@ nps.gov). There are two internships available, with housing provided, for volunteers who commit to at least 32 hours of work per week over a four-week period. The difficulty level is average, and the positions are suitable for adults. Interns in the Visitor Services program learn how to do most of the tasks associated with being a park ranger, which is a great opportunity to try out a job as well as give something back.

Stones River National Battlefield, Murfreesboro, Tennessee, needs volunteers and interns to educate tourists and maintain the grounds.

As a Visitor Services intern you will learn how to research, develop, and give interpretive talks, take part in living history programs, and gain experience in visitor center operations and informal interpretation techniques. It may be possible to be involved in Web site development, research projects, PowerPoint program design, and development of temporary museum exhibits.

Interns in the Museum Operations program assist the park curator in management activities, including recording and cataloging objects, archives, and library items; monitoring environmental conditions; conducting research using the museum and library collections; preparing procedures, plans, and collection inventories; and doing routine housekeeping chores. Interns are asked to design and assemble at least one temporary exhibit, and offered the opportunity to learn visitor service skills.

Stones River National Battlefield is a 650-acre national park and cemetery dedicated to the memories of those who fought and died in one of the bloodiest battles of the Civil War. There were 80,717 Union and Confederate soldiers who fought at Stones River, and 23,517 were killed, wounded, or captured. The site was named a National Military Park in 1927, and transferred from the War Department to the National Park Service. It was designated as a national battlefield in 1960 and is listed on the National Register of Historic Places.

Immersion Excursion: The Legends of Country Music

Immerse yourself in Nashville, Tennessee, less than an hour's drive from Murfreesboro. Take time to explore historic Nashville, founded as a fort in 1779, home to two U.S. presidents, Andrew Jackson and James K. Polk, and the site of Civil War battles. Visit the Grand Ole Opry, the "home of American music" and "country's most famous stage," and hear music legends and rising new stars. Visit the Country Music Hall of Fame and Museum, with its rhinestone costumes, instruments and lyrics, interactive exhibits, films featuring county music's top performers, and private sessions with professional songwriters. Stop at Historic RCA Studio B, on Music Row, once the second home of Elvis Presley, Chet Atkins, Dolly Parton, and other legends. Take a stroll down the Music City Walk of Fame on Nashville's Music Mile and see the platinum-and-granite, star-and-guitar sidewalk markers that honor those with a connection to Music City who have made a significant contribution to the music industry. The Music Mile connects downtown Nashville to Music Row. Nashville is Music City, but the visual and performing arts are also represented. For art galleries, theater, sports and outdoor activities, science and nature attractions, and historical sites, log on to the Visitors Bureau Web site (www.visitmusiccity.com) to plan your Nashville adventure.

Restoration and Maintenance, Wildlife Monitoring, Visitor Services, Ranch Work, Point Reyes Station, CA: Point Reyes National Seashore (1 Bear Valley Rd., Point Reyes Station, CA 94956; 415-464-5145; fax 415-663-8132; www.nps.gov/pore; Doug_Hee@nps.gov). Volunteers at

NATIONAL PARK SERVICE

View of the Great Beach at Point Reyes National Seashore.

Point Reyes help restore natural habitats, monitor wildlife, maintain and repair trails, care for the park's horses, maintain cultural exhibits, patrol the park, educate visitors, and staff the park's visitor centers. Volunteering enables you to experience the park in a way that other visitors cannot, with more opportunities for fun, educational, and satisfying work while meeting interesting people and acquiring new skills.

Short-term opportunities include Adopt-a-Trail, with volunteers contributing six to eight hours a day clearing brush, removing downed trees, digging drainage ditches, and hiking on and off backcountry trails. Coho and Steelhead Monitoring asks for a six-hour commitment for as many days as you want, in order to collect data about stream habitat, water quality, and fish populations; help erect, repair, and check traps near creek mouths; record data during spring and fall surveys; and identify changes in habitat.

The Kule Loklo Workday is for a six-hour commitment on the second Saturday of every month; volunteers assist staff in maintaining the cultural exhibit and restoring and preserving traditional Coast Miwok structures and land-scaping. The Coast Miwok people inhabited what is now Marin and southern Sonoma Counties. "Kule Loklo," mean-ing "Bear Valley," is a recreated village that demonstrates the community's successful economy based on hunting, fishing, and gathering. Additional short-term opportunities include Habitat Restoration, the Native Plant Seed Collection, and the Stream Team.

Intermediate-term opportunities include Harbor Seal Monitoring, requiring a six- to eight-hour workday and a minimum of two survey days a month, for a total of 10 sur-vey days from March through July. Your contribution will help protect harbor seal colonies and assess the state of the marine ecosystem. Volunteers need to be able to hike off-trail to seal-monitoring sites and work independently, making detailed observations and notes.

Joining the Tule Elk Docents is another intermediate-term option. Docents work a seven-and-a-half-hour day, and contribute at least six weekend or holiday days from July through September. They assist staff in the protection of the park's tule elk population (a subspecies of North American elk found only in California) and help visitors view, under-stand, and appreciate the tule elk. Responsibilities combine identifying viewing areas, setting up spotting scopes, inter-preting elk behavior, and educating visitors about natural history. Other intermediate-term opportunities include the Snowy Plover Docent and Winter Wildlife Docent programs.

Longer-term volunteers are needed at the Morgan Horse Ranch, where you will experience all aspects of horsemanship, assist in ranch operations, greet visitors, and work with the horses. Additional longer-term opportunities are available with Visitor Protection, Museum Management, and Visitor Services.

Accommodations are available for some volunteer positions. You will find many lodging options in the area at usparks.about.com/blplanner-pointreyes7.htm, as well as the contact information for the West Marin Visitor's Bureau.

Camping at Point Reyes is limited to backcountry, hike-in-only sites located along the Pacific coast; they need to be reserved in advance. Car camping is available at nearby campgrounds. Find links to other nearby national parks, forests, and recreational areas at usparks.about.com/blplanner-pointreyes9.htm.

A Prize Volunteer

Frank is self-employed and often works seven days a week. He has also volunteered for the past 14 years at Point Reyes and has been involved in many projects, including being a docent for the Winter Wildlife, Snowy Plover, Summer Tule Elk, and Tule Elk monitoring programs. He was awarded the Point Reyes Volunteer-of-the-Year Award in 2003, and in 2004 he received the National Park Service Pacific West Region's Hartzog Award for Outstanding Individual Volunteer.

Frank's Story, Point Reyes National Seashore, CA

When the Spanish explorers arrived in central and northern California in 1769, they found over 500,000 tule elk roving in huge herds. During the Gold Rush, in 1849, there was a huge need for meat and they'd shoot two hundred elk at a time. Market hunting and

Frank (right) is a snowy plover docent, helping guests identify wildlife at Point Reyes National Seashore, Point Reyes Station, California.

conversion of rangeland to agriculture after the gold rush decimated the tule elk population. By the late 1860s they had disappeared and were believed extinct.

In 1875, workmen building a drainage canal in the Buttonwillow marsh near Bakersfield, California, found a single pair of tule elk hiding in the reeds on Henry Miller's cattle ranch. Miller recognized the value of saving the tule elk population and gave strict orders that the elk not be disturbed or hunted. The number of elk in the Buttonwillow marsh slowly increased and in 20 years reached a population of 28 animals.

By 1905 a population boom brought the number to 145, and efforts were begun to transplant some of the elk to areas of their former range. The Point Reyes herd was reestablished in 1978 with 10 elk and has grown to 650 now living in the park.

I like to read about the history of the park and the area. The more you know, the more you can pass on to other people. Having a volunteer docent standing next to the trail with a spotting scope, saying "I've got some tule elk in the scope. Would you like to see them?" can make a very big difference in a visitor's enjoyment of the park.

A tule elk docent as well, Frank uses telemetry to locate and follow the herd at Point Reyes National Seashore.

Accommodations and Dining

Ⓢ Ⓢ Ⓢ **Ten Inverness Way** (10 Inverness Way, P.O. Box 63, Inverness, CA 94937; 415-669-1648; www.teninvernessway .com; inn@teninvernessway.com) is a 1904 Craftsman-style B&B with five guest rooms on the Tomales Bay near the towns of Olema, Point Reyes Station, and Inverness Park.

Ⓢ Ⓢ Ⓢ **Point Reyes Station Inn** (11591 State Rte. 1, Pt. Reyes Station, CA 94956; 415-663-9372; www.pointreyes stationinn.com; prsi@mcn.org) is decorated to reflect life during the years when people visited the area by schooner, stage coach, or narrow-gauge railroad.

Ⓢ–Ⓢ Ⓢ **Café Reyes** (11101 State Rte. 1, Pt. Reyes Station, CA 94956; 415- 663-9493) is a 4-star (http://sanfrancisco .citysearch.com) indoor-outdoor Cal-Mex café.

Ⓢ–Ⓢ Ⓢ **Station House Café** (11180 State Rte. 1, Point Reyes Station, CA 94956; 415-663-1515; www.stationhouse cafe.com; sheryl@stationhousecafe.com) is known for creative use of local organic produce; the signature dishes match the beautiful views.

Habitat Restoration, Assateague Island, VA: Elderhostel: Access sections of the Chincoteague National Wildlife Refuge on the Virginia end of Assateague Island closed to the general public. Read the complete listing in Chapter 4, "Wildlife."

Wilderness Ranger, Information Specialist, or Trail Crew, Duchesne, UT: High Uintas Wilderness–Ashley National Forest (Eric R. Flood, Wilderness & Trails Coordinator, Duchesne/Roosevelt Ranger District, Ashley National Forest, P.O. Box 981, Duchesne, Utah 84021; 435- 781-5208; fax 435-781-5215; www.volunteer .gov/gov/ Featured.cfm?PRID=32; eflood@fs.fed.us). The High Uintas Wilderness is the largest federal wilderness in the state, covering 456,705 acres with 545 miles of trails. The Uinta Mountains rise from 7,500 feet to a height of 13,528 feet on the summit of King's Peak, the highest peak in Utah. Forests of spruce, fir, and pine grow below treeline, and tundra plant communities thrive above. At lower elevations, aspens and other species add to the stunning vistas. There are hundreds of lakes, streams, and meadows in beautiful basins, with rivers running into the canyons below.

Volunteer as a Wilderness Ranger and be responsible for visitor information and education, light trail maintenance, and natural-resource restoration and monitoring. Horseback positions may be available to qualified persons.

Wilderness Information Specialists provide information and education to visitors at busy trailheads. The position includes some light facility maintenance and would be a great volunteer opportunity for a couple seeking a remote and beautiful place to spend the summer.

Volunteer Trail Crew members are responsible for a full range of construction and maintenance activities, often in remote areas. The job is physically strenuous and requires heavy lifting, hiking several miles a day, and working in high altitudes.

All of these positions require good communication skills and the ability to work independently. The Forest Service provides equipment, housing or an RV pad, subsistence, and mileage reimbursement, if applicable. Temporary housing and a modest stipend and/or mileage reimbursement may be available for projects involving data entry, educational outreach, cleanup and restoration, and material and equipment transport (with stock). There are also opportunities for college students seeking internships or work-experience programs, upon request.

All volunteers are required to have Forest Service training and wear personal protective equipment, and those volunteers using chainsaws or crosscut saws must be certified by the Forest Service. Some volunteers may be asked to pass a work capacity test or provide proof of fitness. Contact Eric Flood, Wilderness & Trails Coordinator, to obtain more information or send a résumé with three references to express your interest in available volunteer positions.

Cynthia and Gregg's Story, Volunteer Park Rangers, Everglades National Park, Homestead, FL

> We read about a scientific research project that used student volunteers near where we live in Memphis, Tennessee. We thought it sounded great, called the researcher, began helping out, and continue doing it yearly. Friends returned from a winter as volunteer campground hosts in the Everglades National Park, and we were very excited by the thought of joining them the following year. Gregg had always wanted to be a park ranger. I wasn't as interested in working outdoors, but I liked the idea of learning all about the park and providing information to tourists. We just hadn't realized before that you don't have to be a park ranger to volunteer to do many of the park ranger's jobs. Gregg is an oral interpreter leading a variety of programs and works on the visitor-information desk. I work the telephones from the headquarters desk, providing information to callers. We have new careers doing things we always wanted to do but didn't know we could.

Ⓢ Study Moose and Wolves, Isle Royale, MI: School of Forest Resources & Environmental Science

(Michigan Technological University, Houghton, MI 49931; www.isleroyalewolf.org; lmvuceti@mtu.edu). Isle Royal National Park in Michigan is the most remote and least-visited national park in the lower 48 states. Isle Royale, 50 miles long and 8 miles wide, located in the northwest portion of Lake Superior, is one of the best places to learn about moose and wolves. Apply for a four-week internship (between early May and mid-June) and help researchers from Michigan Technological University with an ongoing project that studies the predator-prey system.

Work will be on- and off-trail and physically demanding. You may have to walk up to 10 miles a day carrying up to 60 pounds, and climate, insects, and terrain are all challenging. The schedule of 10 days on and 4 days off will vary, depending on project needs and other factors. Volunteers receive a food stipend of $15 a day, with no housing and transportation costs after you reach the island.

Responsibilities may include collecting wolf scat, measuring new growth on balsam fir trees, and collecting moose pellets and bones for analysis. Requirements include documented experience backpacking and camping, knowing how to use a compass and map for navigation, good physical condition, able to get along with others in a remote setting for an extended length of time, and enrollment in a Life Sciences curriculum at a college or university.

Volunteering Is Serious Business

This is an e-mail received from a volunteer coordinator:

My supervisor and I are very concerned about this park's volunteer opportunities being characterized as "volunteer vacations." The positions at this park are by no means vacations. We depend on our volunteers to do work and much of it is strenuous, hauling heavy gear a mile or more, and some is unpleasant, cleaning outhouses. We need our volunteers to be the first line of response in emergencies. Our island volunteers often work 10-hour days, with no days off during their tour of duty. We routinely weed out applications that indicate the applicant is looking for a vacation, more than looking to serve the park and its visitors.

Andrew's Story, Isle Royale National Park, MI

> There's no place else in the United States like Isle
> Royale. Untouched and unchanged, its remote, natu-
> ral beauty is exhilarating and exciting. My in-laws
> and my wife and I camped there last summer.
> Visitors arrive by ferry and need to carry in supplies;
> you step off of the boat into a different world. Just
> landing and breathing in the air you know you've
> found paradise.

Ⓢ **Resource Management, Interpretation,**
Protection, and Maintenance, "Downeast," ME:
Acadia National Park (P.O. Box 177, Bar Harbor, ME
04609; 207-288-8716; fax 207-288-8813; www.nps.gov/
acad). Almost 2,000 people a year volunteer in Maine's only
national park. Maintenance volunteers work in trail and
sign shops and join crews that maintain trails and carriage
roads. Opportunities in interpretation include welcoming
park visitors, maintaining slide files, answering information requests, and working in the library.

Volunteers in resource management monitor wildlife
populations, collect water quality data, catalog museum
collections, and assist with clerical and computer work.
Volunteers interested in protection can serve as campground hosts, assist with search and rescue, and patrol
trails and carriage roads.

Acadia, a cluster of islands on the Maine coast and the
first national park east of the Mississippi River, attracts visitors to hike, bike, kayak or canoe, swim, and enjoy the
stunning scenery. Cadillac Mountain, within the park, is the
highest point on the U.S. Atlantic coast.

Volunteers often stay for one to four months, with
many returning the next year. If you stay in the park, you
can expect to work three to five days a week. It is difficult
to get housing during the summer months, but campsites

Volunteers give Mr. Rockefeller's Teeth, the large granite stones that mark the edges of the historic carriage roads at Acadia National Park, Maine, a good flossing.

Acadia National Park volunteer workdays are for all ages and interests.

Volunteers work together to rebuild ocean paths in Acadia.

are available, and volunteers with their own RVs or trailers may be able to use a trailer pad with utility connections.

Short-term opportunities at Acadia National Park are available through Friends of Acadia (207-288-3934; www.friendsofacadia.org) and include volunteer work crews on Tuesday, Thursday, and Saturday mornings, June through Columbus Day, to work on park trails and carriage roads, clearing drainage ways, brushing, clipping, blazing, and rebuilding stone cairns.

Heidi's Story, Acadia National Park, ME

Born and raised in Ohio, I started tent camping in Acadia National Park about 20 years ago, then rented a weekend house, which led me to move there for a year. It's drop-dead gorgeous. My work as a scientific clinical program trials project team coordinator can be done remotely by telephone and computer.

Acadia is my home away from home. There are the mountains, ocean, and unlimited trails, and I've become part of the volunteer community; people who return year after year to contribute their time and skills, along with new visitors from all walks of life.

There are project days when people can volunteer for a morning or a day. We go out to work around 8:45 AM and return to eat lunch together about 11:30. There are jobs hauling gravel to build smoother walkways over bogs, or less strenuous projects trimming back branches or mowing and raking lawns.

What's great is you can see the difference between when you arrived and when you leave. Every hour I volunteer has an impact, and I like the fact that I'm helping to preserve something beautiful for the future.

Immersion Excursion: Total Immersion in National Parks

VIP: Volunteer-in-National Parks, Artists-in-Residence (www.nps.gov/archive/volunteer/air.htm) Apply to be an artist-in-residence at one of the 29 national parks that currently offer the program, including Buffalo National River, Arkansas; Cuyahoga Valley National Park, Ohio; Devils Tower National Monument, Wyoming; and Herbert Hoover National Historical Site, Iowa, among others. The artist-in-residence programs bring together professionals in the arts to publicize, share, and preserve resources in our national parks and to educate and communicate with the public. Visual artists, photographers, sculptors, performers, writers, composers, craftspeople, and other artists are invited to apply to live and work in the parks. Each participating park must be applied to individually, and each has its own eligibility requirements, application guidelines, timeline, and expectations.

Sheryl's Story, Everglades National Park, FL

I applied for and received a residency in the Everglades National Park, Florida. I loved every minute of living and writing within the park, soaking up the natural environment, learning from the park rangers, and interacting with guests. I developed, wrote, and delivered a program on the wildlife I met daily—alligators, crocodiles, anhingas, and amazing herons. The most exciting encounter was with the elusive and highly endangered Florida panther, which I spotted in my headlights on my second night in the Everglades. I shared a split second with a powerful, beautiful animal, and it was an integral part of the Everglades experience.

Historic Preservation and Renovation, The Greater Yellowstone Region, MT: Amizade (P.O. Box 110107, Pittsburgh, PA 15232; 304-293-6049; www.amizade.org; volunteer@amizade.org; group volunteer programs; 7-day trip, $792; 10-day trip, $1,037; 14-day trip, $1,318). As an Amizade volunteer, you will contribute to historic preservation projects and help renovate backcountry cabins in the greater Yellowstone Region of southwest Montana. Experience and explore a part of the country few tourists see and learn about our American heritage.

Amizade, a nonprofit organization founded in 1994, partners with the Gallatin National Forest Gardiner Ranger District on projects such as the OTO Dude Ranch and public campground improvements. The OTO Ranch, 10 miles north of Gardiner, in the Gallatin National Forest, is historically, environmentally, and architecturally significant. The 3,000-acre ranch is also a grizzly bear habitat and a corridor for elk.

Amizade volunteers help restore the residential cabins, rebuild the stables, water turbine cabin, and bunkhouse, and ensure the land can support animal habitats. Help with repairs to a backcountry cabin in the Bear Tooth Wilderness, or install fences and repair campground facilities.

Volunteers make their own travel arrangements to the site. Gardiner is located 5 miles from Mammoth Hot Springs and 55 miles from Old Faithful. The Yellowstone River runs through Gardiner, which is situated in Paradise Valley, at the north entrance to Yellowstone National Park.

There is an on-site orientation and full briefing upon arrival. Accommodations vary, depending on the project site, and volunteers should be prepared to camp with sleeping bags and a small tent, if recommended. Meals include local dishes, as you will be living as part of the community and experiencing new adventures. Bluegrass musicians often perform locally and there are opportunities for hiking and other outdoor recreational activities.

Amizade volunteers work together in Yellowstone National Park to renovate original backcountry cabins.

At sheepshearing time, everyone works.

Ellen and Jonathan's Story, Amizade Yellowstone

Friends invited me and my 17-year-old son, Jonathan, to join them on a volunteer vacation for an Amizade project. The OTO Dude Ranch is unbelievably rough, raw, and gorgeous, about 10 miles north of the entrance to Yellowstone National Park and about 2 miles back in the mountains. This is an amazing relic of the dude-ranch era of the 1920s and '30s.

When we were there, the days were about 100 degrees and it went down to 40 at night. We were living outdoors, working really hard cleaning up the original residential cabins, and totally roughing it. For the first three nights, Jonathan wouldn't speak to me.

I'm not a big camper either, but this wasn't an easy transition for a city kid. Fortunately Dan Weiss, the founder of Amizade, was there, and he put Jonathan to work. He invited him to help make pancakes, and that began a life-changing experience for both of us.

Our whole group was sent out to tear up a rail fence and replace it with another one. The adults were analyzing the task and debating how to do it. Jonathan got in there with two other guys and began pulling the rails off. Then they started competing to see who could hammer six-inch nails into the logs most quickly. The adults were still talking about it and the kids had already done the job. That kind of leadership is so very good for our children.

Archaeology and Historic Preservation, Multiple Locations: Passport in Time, USDA Forest Service (Passport in Time Clearinghouse, P.O. Box 15728, Rio Rancho, NM 87174; 1-800-281-9176; 505-896-0734; fax

LIBBY LANGSTON

Passport in Time (PIT) volunteers work on the Mineral Peak Fire Lookout restoration project in the Lolo National Forest, Montana.

505-896-1136; www.passportintime.com; volunteer@pass portintime.com). Volunteer with Passport in Time (PIT) and work with professional archaeologists and historians in national forests across the country. Help survey for historic sites in remote areas, excavate archaeological sites, monitor the condition of rock art, conduct oral history interviews, restore historic structures, or prepare artifacts for curation and research.

Past projects have included stabilizing the ancient cliff dwellings in New Mexico, excavating a 10,000-year-old village in Minnesota, restoring a lookout tower in Oregon, cleaning rock art in Colorado, surveying for sites in Montana, and excavating a historic mining site in Idaho.

PIT volunteers, fondly referred to as Pitheads, receive "PIT Passports," which are stamped each time a volunteer participates in a project. You can fill your passport with stamps from all over the country. The organization maintains an honor roll recognizing the top few hundred volunteers who contribute the most time to a wide variety of programs.

There is no fee to participate in PIT programs, but volunteers are responsible for transportation to and from the project site, and accommodations vary. Many trips involve backcountry camping, where you are responsible

U.S. FOREST SERVICE

PIT project excavation at Sucker Lake, Minnesota.

More Than 12 Million Acres

U.S. Army Corps of Engineers, Volunteer Clearinghouse (P.O. Box 1070, Nashville, TN 37202; 1-800-865-8337; www.corpslakes.us/volunteer; Volunteer.Clearinghouse@usace.army.mil). The United States Army Corps of Engineers is the steward of 12 million acres of land and water and operates more than 2,500 recreation areas at 456 lakes and waterways across the country. The Corps' mission at these locations is to protect natural resources and provide outdoor recreation areas.

There are many opportunities to volunteer at sites managed by the Corps. You can find currently open positions by contacting the Corps of Engineers Volunteer Clearinghouse by phone or checking for opportunities online. The Volunteer Clearinghouse links volunteers with park rangers at Corps lakes and waterways that need them. Volunteer opportunities include serving as a campground host, providing information at a visitor center, building and maintaining trails and park facilities, restoring fish and wildlife habitat, presenting educational programs, and more. A free campsite may be provided for long-term volunteers.

for your own food and equipment. On some trips RV hookups are provided. Projects range from two days to two weeks or more.

After you select a trip, you can apply online and will be notified of acceptance about three weeks after the application deadline. Group leaders try for a diverse mix of volunteers that includes men and women of different ages and experience levels from across the country. Many programs accept children so families can volunteer together.

⊛ Preserving the Trail System, Northwest Montana; Bob Marshall Wilderness Foundation
(P.O. Box 190688, Hungry Horse, MT 59919; 406-387-3808; fax 406-387-3889; www.thebmwf.org; shannon@bmwf.org). This nonprofit organization, tax-exempt since 1998, needs volunteers to help preserve the trail system

in the Bob Marshall Wilderness Complex, over a million acres of protected land with more than one thousand trails. By partnering with the U.S. Forest Service, youth groups, conservation organizations, university groups, volunteer packers, local businesses, and individual volunteers, the foundation provides opportunities to develop leadership skills, learn Leave No Trace ethics, and raise awareness about wilderness areas.

Help keep trails open and campsites in good condition. Explore an amazing wilderness area, one of the most completely preserved mountain ecosystems in the world. Trips range from weekend to weeklong backpacking trips. (These extended trips require previous backpacking experience.) Projects vary in difficulty and are rated from easy to strenuous. Many of them do not require any previous experience. You'll receive on-the-job training and be working with a group. Select a project that fits your time frame, abilities, and goals and download a registration form. There is a $50 deposit required, which will be returned to you at the end of the trip, or you may donate it to the Bob Marshall Wilderness Foundation.

 Volunteers-In-Parks (VIP) Program: Dry Tortugas National Park (P.O. Box 6208, Key West, FL 3304; 305-242-7700; fax 305-242-7711; www.nps.gov/drto/supportyourpark/volunteer.htm). Volunteer at one of the most unusual and remote parks in the country. Dry Tortugas has 64,657 acres of land above and below water, including coral reefs and wild bird nesting areas. Volunteers spend two to four weeks living on the island and working with staff on a variety of projects. Positions may include maintenance and operation of campgrounds, orientation for incoming campers, historic interpretation, operation of the park bookstore, beach cleanup, clerical work, and resource monitoring. It is a fabulous immersion experience in a subtropical marine environment.

Volunteers should be highly motivated, adventurous, and flexible. Skills such as carpentry, electrical work, boat repair, or operation of heavy equipment are a plus. Modest living quarters with access to laundry and fitness facilities, uniform shirts, and transportation to and from the park at the beginning and end of your assignment are provided. Meals are not included, but grocery service is available from Key West. The positions open are usually ideal for adult individuals, a couple, or a parent with one teen child.

The Dry Tortugas National Park, 70 miles west of Key West, is accessible by a four-hour ferry ride across the Florida Strait, which connects the Atlantic Ocean and the Gulf of Mexico. Its most noteworthy attraction is Fort Jefferson, a huge brick structure built to protect the southern coastline of the United States. During the Civil War, the fort was used as a prison for deserters and other criminals and, in 1898, by the navy during the Spanish-American War. In 1935 President Franklin Roosevelt designated Fort Jefferson as a national monument, and in 1992 President George H. W. Bush upgraded its status to a national park.

A Famous Inmate

One of the most famous inmates incarcerated at Fort Jefferson was Dr. Samuel Mudd, the physician who set John Wilkes Booth's leg after the assassination of President Abraham Lincoln. Mudd maintained that he did not know it was Booth he had treated, but he was convicted of complicity and, in 1865, received a lengthy prison sentence for his assistance to Booth and for misleading authorities. The panel that convicted Mudd had voted 5–4 to hang him along with other coconspirators, but a two-thirds majority was required for execution. He attempted an escape from the fort but was recaptured. During an outbreak of yellow fever, in 1867, Mudd took over the prison hospital after the death of the prison doctor and, in 1869, was pardoned by President Andrew Johnson.

344   Volunteer Vacations Across America

To view current openings and apply online, visit
www.volunteer.gov/gov and perform a zip-code search
for 33041.

Mike's Story, Dry Tortugas National Park, FL

> It seemed simple enough. I drove to Key West, Florida,
> and then took a seaplane to the Dry Tortugas National
> Park. It's a Civil War prison built like a giant pentagon,
> 100 yards in diameter, open in the middle with officers'
> quarters, prison cells, and armaments around the
> perimeter. During my visit I met three retired volunteer
> couples living on this beautiful island off the Florida
> Keys, in these amazing old Civil War quarters. Their job
> as volunteers was to keep the island clean and maintain
> everything in good order. What a life! There's snorkel-
> ing, swimming, a beautiful beach, and the National Park
> Service (NPS) provides the accommodations.

**Trail Work on Portage Trails, Boundary Waters Canoe
Area Wilderness, Superior National Forest, MN:
Wilderness Volunteers** (P.O. Box 22292, Flagstaff, AZ
86002; 928-556-0038; fax 928-222-1912; www.wilderness
volunteers.org; info@wildernessvolunteers.org; 1-week trip,
$259, ages 18+). Spend a week volunteering in this remote
and beautiful setting. The Boundary Waters Canoe Area
Wilderness (BWCAW) covers over one million acres of lakes,
streams, and forests along the Canadian border. It contains
several thousand portage-linked lakes and streams, carved
out by glaciers.

Volunteers improve the condition of the portage trails
so visitors can enjoy the natural beauty of the BWCAW, and
canoe, portage, and camp in this spectacular setting. Fish
species include walleye, northern pike, smallmouth bass,
lake and brook trout, rainbow trout, and brown trout. The

Proud Citizens

Take Pride in America (www.takepride.gov/voluntourism/tourism.html; takepride@ios.doi.gov) is a national partnership to increase service on America's public lands. Take Pride empowers volunteers across the country to protect, preserve, maintain, and enhance natural, cultural, and historic sites. Take Pride in America was established in 1985 by Interior Secretary Donald Hodel and reintroduced in 2003 under the direction of Interior Secretary Gale Norton. The "Take Pride in America and Voluntourism" interactive map on the Web site is a phenomenal resource for locating volunteer activities across the country. Click on any state and available opportunities will be listed with contact information, location, start and end dates, sponsoring partner, activities, suitability, difficulty, and the option of adding to your volunteer folder or applying online. Take Pride in America participates in Toyota's Voluntour Across America, offers assistance to plan volunteer vacations and Voluntourism grants through a partnership with Travelocity, and awards national recognition for outstanding volunteer travelers.

Superior National Forest is also home to deer, moose, the gray wolf, and black bear.

This trip is restricted to six volunteers with two staff. Paddle and portage four canoes to a remote campsite and cut wood with hand tools, since power tools are not permitted in the wilderness. Some canoeing experience is necessary. The Forest Service provides canoes, paddles, life jackets, tools, food, and all snacks. The trip rating is strenuous.

Completion, Maintenance, and Protection of the Continental Divide Trail, Multiple Locations, MT, ID, WY, CO, NM: Continental Divide Trail Alliance (P.O. Box 628, Pine, CO 80470; 1-888-909-CDTA; 303-838-3760; fax 303-838-3960; www.cdtrail.org/getinvolved; volunteer@cdtrail.org; fees, $19 per person per project to help cover

The first marker on the Continental Divide Trail.

project planning, food, and volunteer T-shirts; CDTA membership, $31 annually, covers unlimited project participation for 1 year). The Continental Divide Trail (CDT) was designated a National Scenic Trail in 1978. This designation was created to conserve the scenic, historic, natural, and cultural significance of the 3,100-mile route that travels from Canada to Mexico through Montana, Idaho, Wyoming, Colorado, and New Mexico.

The Continental Divide Trail Alliance (CDTA) is a nonprofit organization, founded in 1995, dedicated to the completion, maintenance, and protection of the CDT. The CDTA has identified the top five reasons people volunteer on the trail: to be outdoors, to give back, meet new people, experience public lands, and for physical fitness.

Help build and maintain trails; scout for missing trail links; become a crew leader; build bridges, trailheads, and kiosks; put up signs, or cook meals for volunteers. All volunteers receive a thank-you gift, a CDTA T-shirt, education on public-land issues, training on trail construction

BEN WATKINS

Volunteers enjoy the hard physical labor of creating uphill paths on the Continental Divide Trail.

techniques, exposure to new places and people, and the fabulously rewarding experience of contributing to a national treasure.

View the current CDTA projects, from one day to a week long, with either backpacking camping or vehicle-access camping, on the Web site, where projects are sorted by starting date and easy, moderate, difficult, and family-friendly levels, or request a Volunteer Guide by calling or e-mailing the CDTA office. You can also download the volunteer guide and project registration form. Once you decide on your projects, fax or mail the completed registration form to CDTA; responses take about six to eight weeks.

Gary's Story, Continental Divide Trail, CO and NM

My wife and I have hiked 710 of the 740 miles of the Continental Divide Trail in Colorado, and 500 of the 700 miles in New Mexico. Doing pieces of it at a time has taken us about 10 years. Once we finish these portions, we will tackle the CDT in Wyoming and Montana. We met two guys who started hiking the trail in April at the Mexico border and are doing the entire 3,000 miles of the trail in one summer, which is very impressive. The Continental Divide is not an easy trail. The CDTA has a very large summer program with thousands of volunteers working to improve the trail and make it better. The goal is to get off the roads, onto a clearly marked single-track trail without motorized vehicles.

The pleasure of the Continental Divide Trail is that it is much more of an adventure than most trails. We hiked about 150 miles above timberline through the Weminuche Wilderness Area, one of the longest sec-tions without any towns or roads breaking into it, which makes it quite spectacular. At age 65, I'm retired and I've put a lot of energy into climbing the top 100 mountains in Colorado, and now I'm working on the top-200 list.

We've participated in three CDTA service trips. They charge very little money, and almost everything is donated. We served as the cooks on one trip and were allotted $5 per person per day and fed everyone pretty well. The majority of people seem to fall in the 40 to 50 age range, but we always have a few on either end as well. This last trip a young man from France who is living in the States read about the program and decided to join us. He loved it. We all make our own contribution, and each and every one of us is highly appreciated.

Youth Corps Trail Building, Multiple Locations, MT, ID, WY, CO, NM: Continental Divide Trail Alliance (P.O. Box 628, Pine, CO 80470; 1-888-909-CDTA; 303-838-3760; fax 303-838-3960; www.cdtrail.org; volunteer@cdtrail.org; CDTA Youth Corps program, call office or e-mail Teresa Martinez at Teresa@cdtrail.org). People between the ages of 17 and 25 may join the CDTA Youth Corps, a 10-week trail-building summer program. Volunteers receive a living stipend and, with the successful completion of the program, an AmeriCorps Education Award. Become trained in the use of tools, trail-building techniques, emergency procedures, backcountry living skills, map and compass, and Leave No Trace principles. Projects range from several days to several weeks, and extensive hiking may be necessary to reach work sites, located at elevations of 7,000 to 13,000 feet.

For ten weeks you will live in a tent and share cooking and cleaning responsibilities. Weekends are for relaxing with your crew, swimming, hiking, and visiting historic, cultural, and scenic sites. During the last week of your commitment you and your fellow team members will prepare and give public presentations about your experiences on the trail.

👥 Family Service: Tahoe National Forest, CA; Sierra Club (85 Second St., 2nd Floor, San Francisco, CA 94105; 415-977-5500; fax 415-977-5799; www.sierraclub.org; information@sierraclub.org; 1-week; $545 adult; $445 teen, minimum age 15).

The Sierra Club, a nonprofit corporation, is the oldest, largest and most influential grassroots environmental organization in the country, founded in 1892 by John Muir, a naturalist, wilderness explorer, writer, and conservationist.

This is a great family-service trip, improving the health of the forest surrounding the Sierra Club's Clair Tappaan Lodge in the Tahoe Basin. Work may include brush and deadwood removal and opening up the canopy by removing smaller trees. The brush that is removed is mulched and returned to the land. Work varies depending on needs, weather, and ages and abilities of volunteers. On your day off, you can hike to Donner Peak and Mount Judah, visit the Donner Museum or historic Truckee, and see the petroglyphs, China Wall, and old railroad tunnels.

The lodge is about 12 miles west of Truckee, California, served by Amtrak and Greyhound as well as the Reno, Nevada, airport. Getting to the lodge is your responsibility. It's possible to walk to the work sites, but you may want a car for getting to trailheads and for your day off. Clair Tappaan Lodge is a rustic retreat located near the Donner summit.

Fees include accommodations and meals at the lodge, all tools and instruction. There are 2-bunk cubicles, family rooms for 5–12 people, a 10-person men's dorm, and a 23-person women's dorm. Bring your own sleeping bag or bedding; mattresses and pillows (for bunk beds) are provided. Bathrooms and showers are shared, and guests assist with kitchen chores. A detailed equipment list will be sent to registered participants.

Family Trail Work, Aspen, CO: Sierra Club (85 Second St., 2nd Floor, San Francisco, CA 94105; 415-977-5500; fax 415-977-5799; www.sierraclub.org; information@sierra club.org; 1-week; adult, $395; child, minimum age 7, $295). The Family Fun Trail Work trip to Maroon Bells, in the White River National Forest, Aspen, Colorado, is a perfect opportunity to introduce young people to the value of protecting their environment and to encourage their appreciation of nature.

Help build new trails, and hike, climb, ride a gondola, rent bicycles, ride horses, or relax on your day off. Volunteers meet in Aspen and are transported to base camp. A Forest Service ranger will provide a tool-safety orientation and explain your service project. There will be two days of work, a day off, followed by two days of work. The trip is rated easy to moderate.

Consider flying into Aspen, as you will not need a vehicle there. Aspen has free bus service, and almost everything is within easy walking distance. Bring your own tents, sleeping bags, and pads to camp on the banks of the Maroon Creek, in a beautiful wooded area. Meals will be provided beginning with lunch on the first day and breakfast on the last; food is mainly vegetarian.

Prairie Restoration, St. Croix National Scenic Riverway, WI and MN: Sierra Club (85 Second St., 2nd Floor, San Francisco, CA 94105; 415-977-5500; fax 415-977-5799; www.sierraclub.org; information@sierraclub.org; 1 week, $515). The Sierra Club sponsors service trips to the St. Croix National Scenic Riverway, in Wisconsin and Minnesota, where participants have removed invasive plants, constructed a timber-lined brick pathway, cleaned campsites, and assisted with living history events.

Explore the riverway by canoe and on foot and learn about the natural and cultural history of the area. Visit forests, parks, and waterfalls, ride the historic Osceola & St. Croix Valley Railway, and visit museums and interpretive centers. Travel on both land and water using canoes to reach various service projects along the river, and camp in both modern and primitive campgrounds.

Project work will be moderately strenuous, weather is unpredictable, and a current tetanus shot is required. Work clothes, canoeing clothing, rain gear, and camping equipment are essential. Basic canoeing knowledge is required, and whitewater experience is desirable but not necessary. The cost of the trip includes canoes, paddles, and life vests, work tools, campground fees, on-trip transportation, admission to cultural attractions, and most meals and snacks.

The St. Croix River is a tributary of the Mississippi, and forms a 125-mile boundary between Minnesota and Wisconsin. It joins the Mississippi River at Prescott, Wisconsin, about 20 miles southeast of St. Paul, Minnesota. The St. Croix National Scenic Riverway is one of the eight original rivers designated by Congress as a Wild and Scenic river in 1968.

Immersion Excursion: Fishing Hall of Fame

Plan a side trip to visit the **National Freshwater Fishing Hall of Fame** (10360 Hall of Fame Dr., Hayward, WI 54843; 715-634-4440; www.freshwater-fishing.org; fishhall@cheqnet.net; April 15–May, Sept–Oct., 9:30 AM–4 PM; June–Aug., 9:30 AM–4:30 PM). The museum is half a city block long and four and a half stories high, shaped like a leaping fish. Its open jaw is an observation platform. This unusual landmark is surrounded by a quarter-acre pond. The four-building complex has fishing artifacts, including over 5,000 lures, antique rods, reels and angling accessories, antique and classic outboard motors, and more than 400 mounts of different species of fish.

Trail Reconstruction, Guadalupe Mountains National Park, TX: Sierra Club (85 Second St., 2nd Floor, San

Francisco, CA 94105; 415-977-5500; fax 415-977-5799; www.sierraclub.org; information@sierraclub.org; 1 week, $395). Sierra Club partners with the National Park Service (NPS) on this trip that reconstructs and maintains trails in Guadalupe National Park. Volunteers remove large rocks, build or clean water control devices, regrade tread sur-faces, cut back vegetation, reroute trails, and erect retain-ing walls. There are more than 80 miles of trails in Guadalupe Mountains National Park.

The trip difficulty may be strenuous at times, but there is a variety of tasks related to trail work, and your team will be divided into several crews with at least one with minimal elevation gain. Tools are provided by the National Park Service; bring your own camping gear. NPS staff and your trip leader will ensure your volunteer experience is a safe and productive one.

Your team will have the opportunity to hike and explore the Chihuahuan Desert and see an amazing exposed fossil reef. In the Permian age, the last period of the Paleozoic era, the western portion of Texas was covered by a shallow sea; the Guadalupe Mountains are technically a massive coral reef. Surrounded by desert, the mountain range has ponderosa pine, bigtooth maple, Douglas fir, aspen, and many other trees.

Many outings are offered on your free day, including short, easy walking hikes, climbing Guadalupe Peak, and hiking to McKittrick Canyon to see fall foliage. McKittrick Canyon is considered one of the most beautiful places in Texas, with white cliffs, desert shrubs and cactus, canyon woodland, and high-country forest.

Accommodations may be indoors or at campsites, depending on availability. Meals are provided, and each team member will be on the cook crew for a day. Bring your own mess kit and utensils and hard plastic lunch contain-ers—no plastic bags are provided on this vegetarian-friendly trip.

A Wife's Volunteer Story

About 10 years ago my husband and I decided to take a yearly vacation together and a yearly one on our own. He is a runner and biker, and I'm a sitter and talker. We love traveling together, but it's been really nice for each of us to select something special for ourselves that we wouldn't do as a couple. Volunteer vacations are perfect for me. I must admit I put far more time into the planning and selecting stages than I ever did on any other trip.

On my last trip I decided to get outside and enjoy it at my own speed and in my own way. I planted flowers, helped children start a vegetable garden, and helped organize a library—the perfect combination for me. And when I return home, my husband is my greatest audience, eager to hear my tales and view my photographs, and then it's his turn to share.

Ⓢ Maintenance and Reconstruction, Multiple Locations in CA, OR, WA: Pacific Crest Trail Association (5325 Elkhorn Blvd., PMB #256, Sacramento, CA 95842; 916-349-2109; fax 916-349-1268; www.pcta.org; info@pcta.org). Join a trail crew on the Pacific Crest Trail (PCT) and help with the annual maintenance and reconstruction of this National Scenic Trail that runs from Mexico to Canada through California, Oregon, and Washington. The Pacific Crest Trail Association (PTCA) is a nonprofit public-benefit corporation founded in 1977 as the Pacific Crest Trail Conference.

Because the PCT has the greatest changes in elevation of any of the country's National Scenic Trails, it passes through six out of seven of North America's ecozones. Along the PCT are the Mojave Desert, the Sierra Nevada and

If all visitors learned to leave no trace behind, volunteers would have one less job to do.

Mt. Whitney, Yosemite National Park, Marble Mountain and the Russian Wilderness in Northern California, the volcanoes of the Cascades including Mt. Shasta and Mt. Hood, Crater Lake, Columbia River Gorge, Mt. Rainier, and the Northern Cascades. The PCT tempts great numbers of "thru-hikers," who try to cover the entire length of the trail in one season.

Volunteering along the PCT is challenging and fun as well as a way to contribute your time and services to protect one of America's national treasures. Trail crews perform a variety of necessary tasks, including clearing brush, repairing washouts, cutting back chaparral, repairing tread and rock walls, and constructing drainages.

Current Volunteer Trail Maintenance projects are listed by dates, project name, and location on the Web site,

Soon to be a widened path along the Pacific Crest Trail, thanks to the efforts of volunteer labor.

divided into six regions covering the length of the trail. Select a region and click on the project that interests you for a description, contact information, and how to apply. PCTA volunteer vacations are free of service or added charges. You pay for your transportation to the site; PCTA provides food, tools, training, and a complete list of the personal supplies, clothing, and camping gear you'll need.

Geppetto's Story, Pacific Crest Trail, Mexico to Canada

Out on the trail, hikers take on different names. My favorite character growing up was Geppetto, the kindly wood-carver who created a son for himself. My parents adored me like Geppetto cherished Pinocchio, even when he lied or was misguided.

Walking the Pacific Crest Trail from Mexico to Canada has been my goal for seven years now. Each time I've started, something has come up, and my plans changed. One year my father had a heart attack, one year I tripped and badly sprained my ankle, and another year the weather was against me.

This is my seventh summer out on some portion of the trail; I am completing it by walking into Canada. I am indebted to all the volunteers and workers along the way who repair and maintain trails so that dreamers like me can set a goal and achieve it.

John H.'s Story, Pacific Crest Trail, CA

My day job is very demanding. On weekends it's totally relaxing to be in charge of a group of people working together to clear or repair a section of the Pacific Crest Trail. I grew up in California and have been hiking the trail since I was a teen and volunteering on it for about 15 years.

The trail is world famous, and we have people from all over who plan their vacations around helping us with one- and two-day projects. We don't require any previous experience. It's all on-the-job training. As far as being in shape, as long as you can comfortably maneuver the trails and work hard for a day, we don't turn anybody away. There are plenty of jobs needing to be done by different people with different abilities. The closest thing to pure joy is being outdoors on your own with nature.

Ⓢ **Recreation Hosts, Sitka and Juneau, AK: Tongass National Forest** (Federal Building, 648 Mission St., Ketchikan, AK 99901; 907-225-3101; www.fs.fed.us/r10; mscholten@fs.fed.us). Volunteer in the nation's largest national forest, located in southeast Alaska, surrounding the Inside Passage. With 17 million acres, a rain forest, glaciers, mountains, waterways, and thousands of islands, Tongass Natural Forest is home to more than 400 species of wildlife.

There are openings in both Sitka and Juneau for Recreation Hosts. Each host position has different requirements, time commitments, reimbursements, and perks. Benefits usually include a host campsite with RV hookups for your own living unit, and at some locations there is a cabin with electricity, plumbing, phone, and water provided. Couples are usually preferred because of safety issues, but individuals may also apply.

Requirements include a desire to work with the public, committing to volunteering full-time for the dates specified, being in good health and physical condition in order to fulfill responsibilities, being able to lift wood rounds and handle split firewood, and agreeing to a background check. Duties include picking up litter; cleaning campsites, picnic areas, fire rings, and restrooms; opening and closing gates morning and night; light maintenance; monitoring use of trails; supplying split firewood to campers; and providing information as needed.

Immersion Excursion: The Inside Passage

The Inside Passage is a water route between mainland Alaska and the coastal islands, carved out by glaciers millions of years ago. The passage contains habitats for bald eagles, porpoises, sea lions, and whales, especially humpbacks, and there are whale-watch tours available in many places. Kayakers and canoeists love to explore its islands and coves, and anglers enjoy the great fishing for halibut, trout, and salmon. Ships can avoid the bad weather of the open seas and visit the communities along the route. Metlakatla has Alaska's only Indian reservation, and

Ketchikan was once known as the salmon capital of the world. It also has the world's largest collection of standing totem poles, and the highest zip code in the U.S.: 99950. Craig is another great fishing town, and kayakers go there for access to the caves on Prince of Wales Island. Wrangell is known for its petroglyphs, and Sitka is the only town facing the Gulf of Alaska. Juneau is the capital of Alaska, with a mountain tram, salmon hatchery, state museum, and the governor's residence. Hoonah is the home of the Huna, a Tlingit tribe indigenous to the Pacific Northwest Coast. Haines has a bald eagle preserve, and Skagway was the starting point for stampeders who traveled the Chilkoot Trail during the Klondike Gold Rush.

Volunteers-In-Parks Projects, Yorktown, VA: Colonial National Historical Park (P.O. Box 210, Yorktown, VA 23690; 757-859-1600; fax 757-898-6346; www.nps.gov/colo). Volunteer in this historic park that commemorates the beginning and the end of English colonial America. History buffs or those desiring to learn more about the colonial period have the perfect opportunity here, as well as the chance to help others enjoy their experiences.

The 8,677-acre park is located on the Virginia peninsula between the James and York Rivers, and includes the 23-mile Colonial Parkway, which connects Jamestown and Yorktown. Jamestown was the site of the first English settlement, and Yorktown was the site of the culminating battle of the American Revolution, in 1781. Colonial National Historical Park is listed on the National Register of Historic Places.

Volunteers-In-Parks (VIP) projects offer working in visitor centers, assisting with curatorial work, interpreting at archaeological sites and historic homes, doing administrative work, and helping with landscaping projects. Training and uniforms will be provided for certain positions.

Immersion Excursion: History Comes Alive

The **Jamestown Settlement and the Yorktown Victory Center** (Jamestown-Yorktown Foundation, P.O. Box 1607, Williamsburg, VA 23187; 1-888-593-4682; 757-253-4838; fax 757- 253-5299; www.historyisfun.org; 9 AM to 5 PM daily, until 6 PM June 15–Aug. 15; closed Christmas and New Year's days; tickets to Jamestown Settlement, $13.50 adults, $6.25 children over 6; tickets to Yorktown Victory Center, $9.25 adults, $5.00 children over 6; combination tickets, $19.25 adults, $9.25 children over 6; children under 6, free). The Jamestown-Yorktown Foundation (JYF), a nonprofit corporation exempt since 1999, operates the Jamestown Settlement and the Yorktown Victory Center, living history museums that educate visitors about the country's early history. Jamestown was America's first permanent settlement, an English colony established in 1607 (13 years before the Pilgrims arrived in Massachusetts) by 104 English men and boys. Jamestown Settlement presents a film, gallery exhibits, and a living history interpretation that chronicles the settlers' story, the culture of the Powhatan Indians, and the first century of life in the Virginia Colony. You can board replicas of the three ships that sailed from England to Virginia, walk through re-creations of the colonists' fort and a Powhatan village, and tour a riverfront area. Costumed historical interpreters recreate daily life in the early 17th century. The Yorktown Victory Center offers a timeline, a film, museum exhibits, and an outdoor living history interpretation educating visitors about the events that culminated in the American colonies gaining independence from Britain. Visit a re-created Continental Army encampment and 1780s farm to see how both soldiers and civilians lived during and after the Revolutionary War. Jamestown, Williamsburg, and Yorktown form "Virginia's Historic Triangle" and are linked by the scenic, 23-mile Colonial Parkway, a National Scenic Byway.

Ⓢ **Visitor Center Staffing, Central OR: Siuslaw National Forest** (4077 SW Research Way, P.O. Box 1148, Corvallis, OR 97339; 541-902-6943; fax 541-750-7234; www.fs.fed.us/r6/siuslaw; volunteer coordinator, Carole Wendler, clwendler@fs.fed.us). The Siuslaw National Forest, located along the central Oregon coast, includes 630,000 acres of diverse ecosystems. With its temperate rain forest, coastal mountains, the Oregon Dunes, and the beaches of the Pacific Ocean, the forest offers a wide variety of recreational options, including hiking, whale watching, mountain biking, horseback riding, and fishing.

It's a great place to volunteer, and opportunities at the Cape Perpetua Visitor Center, the Devil's Churn Information Center, the Oregon Dunes Day Use, or the Oregon Dunes Visitor Center at the Oregon Coast will enable you to help people get the most out of their visit to the Siuslaw National Forest.

Visitor and information center volunteers plan tours, provide information on recreational activities, and answer visitors' questions about the forest. Responsibilities involve operating video equipment, conducting book or recreation pass sales, answering questions and providing information at trailheads, leading hikes, or conducting programs for school groups.

Lodging at a campsite or in housing may be provided, depending on availability and location. At Cape Perpetua, there are two year-round sites (and one summer site) that hosts may use, and costs associated with the site (power, sewer, and basic phone) are covered. A basic stipend may be provided. Applications are available on the Web site; indicate your preferences as far as duties, locations, and time commitment. Three references are required.

Ⓢ **Lighthouse Keeper, Northern WI: Apostle Islands National Lakeshore** (415 Washington Avenue, Bayfield, WI 54814; 715-779-3397; www.nps.gov/apis; APIS_Volunteer_Coordinator@nps.gov; 18+). Be an island

APOSTLE ISLANDS NATIONAL LAKESHORE

The volunteer hosts at the Sand Island Lighthouse, Wisconsin, can count on numerous tourists visiting.

host or lighthouse keeper and spend several weeks to an entire summer working on an island at Apostle Islands National Lakeshore, located on the northern tip of Wisconsin on the shores of Lake Superior.

Lighthouse volunteers greet visitors, conduct interpretive guided tours of the light stations, and hike island trails to perform light trail work and pick up litter. Volunteers are responsible for notifying a supervisor when hazardous conditions exist, submitting work orders for routine maintenance needs, and serving as points of contact in the case of medical and marine emergencies. Duties include mowing lawns, routine grounds maintenance, light housekeeping, assisting Historic Structures Preservation maintenance workers with planned maintenance projects, maintaining visitation records, and monitoring visitor activities. Orientation and training are required and provided. Volunteers must be self-sufficient and ready to work for their entire tour of duty without restocking of supplies.

Devil's Island Lighthouse, at the northernmost point of Wisconsin, overlooks a formation of sea caves. It is one of the more heavily visited lighthouses, and you can expect

APOSTLE ISLANDS NATIONAL LAKESHORE

Volunteer hosts at Stockton Island greet visitors, provide information, and assist with routine maintenance.

to climb the tower stairs many times over a summer week-end. The keeper's house is located about 300 feet from the light tower, with two bathrooms, hot and cold running water, and limited DC electricity. Volunteers may be required to carry all of their gear 1 mile to a boat dock in case of rough seas.

Michigan Island Light Station has two towers—one is the oldest of the Apostle Islands lighthouses and the other is the tallest. There is no running water or electricity. Water needs to be filtered or boiled, and there is an out-house behind the quarters. Bring extra supplies, as the island is often inaccessible for days because of the dock's exposed location.

Sand Island Lighthouse occupies a scenic, rocky promontory. Visitor traffic is comparatively high, and the keeper will have frequent opportunity to share Sand Island's interesting stories. Monitoring of the island's camp-sites and assisting campers is a major part of this position and will require a great deal of hiking. Volunteers are housed 2 miles away from the lighthouse, accessible by a woodland trail. Housing has running water, stove, refrigera-tor, and indoor bathroom.

Volunteer island hosts on Oak and Stockton Islands greet and help orient tent and boat campers; clean camp-sites, the picnic area, and the boat dock; hike and perform light trail work; notify a supervisor when hazardous condi-tions exist; submit work-order requests for routine mainte-nance needs; provide visitor information and services; and serve as points of contact in the case of medical and marine emergencies. Orientation and training is required and provided.

All lighthouse keepers and island host volunteers must be in good physical shape and be able to hike and climb stairs. Help can be several hours or more away. Positions are usually for three to four weeks, with preference given to those who make longer commitments. There is an appli-cation online at www.volunteer.gov.

Gene's Story, Oak Island, WI

When my wife, Kandee, and I were both teachers, we took eight-week vacations all over the country where we would just go and play. Then I took a supervisory job and no longer had summers off. About nine years ago Kandee said she was going to volunteer at Apostle Islands National Lakeshore and would be staying on one of the islands for a few weeks at a time. Luckily for me, when she signed up for the training orientation they asked if she wanted to bring me along. That way, whenever I was available, we could both do the work. Last summer she volunteered 40 days and I managed 30. It's an 80-mile drive and a half-hour boat ride from our home.

It's worked very well for us. The first couple of years we worked cleaning up Oak Island, cleared and kept up 12 miles of hiking trails, cleaned and painted the cabin, maintained the campsites, and educated visitors about the history of the area. Kandee lives on Oak Island two weeks at a time then returns home for a week to restock supplies. She plans all of the meals ahead of time, and when friends want to come out to visit we remind them to bring their own food. We've got the best sunsets in the world, and deer and black bears come wandering through the yard.

Immersion Tip: Life in a Lighthouse

Lighthouse Keeper, Island Hosts, and Visitor Centers. *The Lighthouse News* (P.O. Box 19, Bristol, ME 04539; 906-387-3700; www.lighthouse-news.com) has the latest news, opinions, commentary, and feature articles on lighthouses worldwide, as well as current advertisements for volunteer lighthouse-keeper positions. The Web site was created to collect and dispense information about lighthouses and to promote the history, protection, and preservation of lighthouses everywhere. Sign up for the newsletter to find news reports, job openings, and everything that's happening at and around lighthouses all over the country.

Forest Volunteer, Northeastern MN: Superior National Forest (8901 Grand Ave. Place, Duluth, MN 55808; 218-626-4300; fax 218-626-4398; www.fs.fed.us/ r9/forests/superior; r9_superior_NF@fs.fed.us). The Superior National Forest, located in northeastern Minnesota, encompasses 3 million acres of land, water, rock, and trees. Clean, clear, and productive water is a major reason people come to the Superior National Forest to fish, swim, boat, camp, and enjoy the scenery.

The diversity of the Superior National Forest is reflected in the variety of volunteer opportunities available. Wilderness volunteers maintain and restore campsites, portages, and hiking trails. Recreation volunteers provide day-to-day maintenance of campgrounds, while campground hosts spend the summer greeting campers, maintaining the facilities, and answering visitor questions. The time commitments range from a day to a week or a month or longer. A camper or motor home is needed for the host position.

Wildlife volunteers assist wildlife biologists in improving habitats and conducting wildlife surveys. Botany volunteers survey and help control nonnative invasive species, and timber volunteers work on reforestation and timber-stand improvement. Naturalist program volunteers collaborate with local resorts and communities, providing interpretation through nature walks, talks, and ecology games. Heritage volunteers work on archaeological excavation and site interpretation and may also donate hours to historic building rehabilitation, artifact processing,

U.S. FOREST SERVICE

Volunteers assist with migratory bird surveys in the Superior National Forest.

Finding Volunteer Opportunities

Network for Good (7920 Norfolk Ave., Suite 520, Bethesda, MD 20814; 1-866-650-4636; fax 240-482-3215; www.networkforgood.org). Network for Good makes it easy to volunteer online with a search tool that matches your interests and location with organizations that need your help. Use the search tool to find volunteer opportunities near where you live, work, or in a location you will be visiting, and search for a charity by name, area (city and state, or zip code), how far you are willing to travel to volunteer, and area of interest. Indicate whether you are looking for placements that welcome kids, teens, groups, or seniors. There are also interesting tips, links, and information about America's volunteering tradition, and a section for nonprofits to register.

Volunteers clear debris to reclaim a boat launch area.

data entry, artwork, and completion of nonpublic site evaluations.

Superior National Forest has 445,000 acres of surface water, including almost 2,000 lakes, over 1,300 miles of major streams supporting cold-water fisheries, and more than 950 miles of major streams supporting warm-water fisheries. The northern forest is home to numerous wildlife species—eagles, deer, moose, and black bear—and Minnesota is one of the last habitats of the gray wolf in the lower 48 states.

Volunteer-In-Parks, Upper Peninsula, MI: Pictured Rocks National Lakeshore (N8391 Sand Point Rd., P.O. Box 40, Munising, MI 49862; 906-387-2607;

fax 906-387-4025; www.nps.gov/piro; Pamela Baker, volunteer coordinator, 906-387-3700; pamela_baker@nps.gov). Pictured Rocks National Lakeshore is located on the south shore of Lake Superior in Michigan's Upper Peninsula, between the communities of Munising (west) and Grand Marais (east). It was designated as America's first National Lakeshore in 1966. Most volunteer positions are for ski trail condition reporting and visitor services.

You can volunteer by assisting with backcountry patrol, monitoring, and informal interpretation, or as a campground host at Hurricane River and Twelvemile Beach Campgrounds. Volunteers are essential during the busiest tourist season, from May through October, but some volunteers also help with winter cleanup efforts, backcountry trail construction and maintenance, and at the visitor center. Other opportunities are available in interpretation at the Au Sable Light Station, photography projects, and manual labor to help stabilize and rehabilitate historic structures and landscapes.

There are one- or two-day projects, volunteer trail crews that usually work a week or more, and Student Conservation Association aides who stay about two months. Campground hosts are asked for a minimum four-week commitment and their own RV. Uniforms and gear are provided if required. A stipend may be available for travel and food expenses, with housing provided for long-term volunteers. Find more information on current openings, housing, and how to apply on the recruiting site bulletin at www.nps.gov/piro/supportyourpark/upload/VIPRecruiting.pdf.

Immersion Excursion: On the National Register

The **Au Sable Light Station**, built in 1873–1874, is located in the Pictured Rocks Lakeshore and is on the National Register of Historic Places. The tower's base diameter is 16 feet; the tower itself is 87 feet high. The lens focal plane is

107 feet above the lake, and the beacon, now solar-powered, shines 18 miles out on Lake Superior. Volunteers live at the light station and staff the museum and contact station. There is an apartment on the second floor of the keeper's quarters, with a kitchen, bathroom, living room, and bedroom. Submit your application at www.nps.gov/volunteer.

Interpretation/Visitor Services, Southeastern UT: Natural Bridges National Monument (H.C. 60, Box 1, Lake Powell, UT 84533; 435-692-1234, ext. 13; fax 435-692-1111; www.nps.gov/nabr; scott_ryan@nps.gov).

Natural Bridges National Monument, located in southeastern Utah, is named for three massive stone bridges formed by streams cutting through canyon walls. It is also designated as the world's first International Dark Sky Park: the night sky is amazing due to the lack of light pollution and the National Park Service's commitment to night skies as a natural resource. There are regularly scheduled nighttime astronomy talks, with telescopes, for visitors.

Volunteers staff the visitor center desk, greet visitors, provide information, and work in the gift shop. You may research and develop original interpretive programs, or present already-developed programs during walks or on the porch of the visitor center or at evening campgrounds talks. Volunteer assignments include archaeological and wildlife monitoring, backcountry conditions assessment, and exotic plant eradication. Volunteers are needed year round, with August through October being the busiest season for the park.

Volunteer commitments are usually two months, longer if desired. Shifts are four days a week, eight to nine hours a day. Three-day weekends are great for enjoying your surroundings and planning short trips. Housing and training are provided and reimbursement for meals is available.

Immersion Excursion: Visit Moab, Utah

Plan an excursion to **Arches National Park** (www.nps.gov/ arch), in Moab, Utah, along US Hwy. 191, to see more than 200 natural sandstone arches, the greatest density of natural arches in the world. People of all ages are mesmerized by the world-famous Delicate Arch. The park is located in a high desert, with elevations ranging from 4,085 to 5,652 feet. Rock layers throughout the park reveal millions of years of deposits, erosion, and other geological events. Enjoy viewing the unusual rock formations and colorations, hiking, biking, camping, climbing, photography, auto-touring, ranger-led tours, and backpacking.

Learning Center Host, Stanton, KY: Gladie Cultural-Environmental Learning Center (USDA Forest Service, Daniel Boone National Forest, 1700 Bypass Rd., Winchester, KY 40391; 859-745-3166; fax 859-744-1568; www.fs.fed.us/ r8/boone; evelynmorgan@fs.fed.us; open spring through fall). The Gladie Cultural-Environmental Center is located in the Red River Gorge Geologic Area of the Daniel Boone National Forest, in Stanton, Kentucky. Volunteer to staff the Learning Center information desk and greet visitors, answer questions, provide information, keep the brochure rack stocked, and assist with education and interpretive programs.

The Red River Gorge Geologic Area is a fabulous place to hike, climb, and view sandstone cliffs, natural stone arches, and unusual rock formations. A campsite will be provided with electric, water, and sewer hookups, or you may have a one-bedroom apartment. Volunteers need to be flexible, possess a positive attitude, enjoy working with people, and have basic map-reading and organizational skills. These are seasonal positions that require 24 work hours per week, including weekends in a variety of jobs.

The Daniel Boone National Forest is one of the most heavily used forests in the South, containing three large lakes, many rivers and streams, two wilderness areas, and a 296-mile National Recreation Trail. People come for the magnificent scenery, to fish, boat, hunt, ride, hike, climb, backpack, or relax. The Red River Gorge Geologic Area has a high concentration of prehistoric sites and supports a wide variety of plants and wildlife. The Gladie Cultural-Environmental Center offers exhibits designed to interpret the cultural heritage and natural resources of Red River Gorge.

Immersion Excursion: Forty-six Miles of National Natural Wonders

The Red River Gorge Scenic Byway (Kentucky, www .byways.org/explore/byways/2482) is an hour's drive or a five-hour tour to experience all the sites along the 46-mile route. Explore natural stone arches, caves, cliffs, ravines, and waterfalls in this National Natural Landmark, which has also been designated a National Wild and Scenic River and a National Geological Area. Stop to hike the many trails leading to the arches and waterfalls or try the area's excellent rock climbing with more than 1,200 routes for sport and traditional climbers of all skill levels (Red River Gorge Climbing Coalition, www.rrgcc.org).

Interpretive Ranger Aide, Central MO: Ozark National Scenic Riverways (404 Watercress Dr., P.O. Box 490, Van Buren, MO 63965; 573-323-4236; fax 573-323-4140; www.nps.gov/ozar; ozar_interpretation@nps.gov). Ozark National Scenic Riverways, the first national park area to protect a wild river system, has two of the clearest and most beautiful spring-fed rivers in the country, the Current and Jacks Fork Rivers. It is one of the best places to canoe, and there are numerous rentals and outfitters along the rivers.

YMCA TROUT LODGE & CAMP LAKEWOOD

Park ranger Kat instructs volunteers and visitors on what to look for when exploring this cave.

Volunteer to assist the National Park Service rangers by leading cave tours through Round Spring Caverns, or wear period clothes to help visitors experience the Ozark frontier of the 1890s. Staff a visitor information desk, or present a slide show on the history of the area or nature topics. Lead hikes, school programs, and field trips, and help with special events. Most of the work will be outdoors, interacting with the public. Housing and a small stipend may be provided. The time commitment is flexible.

Volunteer as a Campground Host and receive a free campsite with hookups. Your responsibilities cover meeting and greeting campers, answering questions, helping with the reservation system, checking people in and out, and making sure they've paid their fees. To apply, send a letter or résumé to the volunteer coordinator.

HawkWatch Volunteer, Coastal ME: Acadia National Park (Hawkwatch Volunteer Opportunities, c/o Raptor Ranger, Acadia National Park, P.O. Box 177, Bar Harbor, ME 04609; 207-288-8810; www.nps.gov /acad/nature science/hawkwatch.htm; lora_haller@nps .gov). Indivi-duals and couples can volunteer to be members of the Hawkwatch team, assisting rangers in spotting, identifying, and counting raptors when they migrate south for the winter season. The work schedule requires 32 hours per week, usually four days a week, which may include weekends and holidays from mid-August to mid-October. An RV pad with hookups is available.

The Acadia National Park Hawkwatch location is on Cadillac Mountain, the highest point on the North Atlantic seaboard. The numbers of raptors fluctuate, depending on whether they pass over the site, so the information collected in Acadia is added to the data collected at other hawkwatch sites. This knowledge helps scientists under-

Volunteer Partnership

Volunteer.gov/gov is a partnership among the U.S. Forest Service, U.S. Geological Survey, Cooperative State Research, Education and Extension Survey, Natural Resources Conservation Services, Corporation for National and Community Service, U.S. Army Corps of Engineers, Bureau of Land Management, National Park Service, U.S. Bureau of Reclamation, U.S. Fish and Wildlife Service, and USA Freedom Corps. Volunteer opportunities are searchable by keyword, zip code, state, activity or interest, agency, or date. Apply for positions or save them in a folder. View currently featured opportunities with project descriptions and find links to agency sites, contact information, and volunteer resources.

stand the status of raptor populations. Recent years have seen growth in the numbers of bald eagles, peregrine falcons, and osprey.

Hawkwatch volunteers help by interacting with park visitors and interpreting natural history and conservation relating to raptors, as well as counting and collecting resource data. You need to be proficient in public speaking, know about ornithology, natural history, and ecology, and have experience using computers. Weather can be variable and the terrain uneven and rocky. To apply, mail or e-mail a cover letter, résumé, three references, and contact information to the above address.

Restoration Projects, Mammoth Cave National Park, South-Central KY: Wilderness Volunteers (P.O. Box 22292, Flagstaff, AZ 86002; 928-556-0038; fax 928-222-1912; www.wildernessvolunteers.org;info@wilderness volunteers.org; 1-week trip, $259; ages 18+). Mammoth Cave National Park, in south-central Kentucky, contains the world's longest cave system. There are 365 explored miles with underground lakes and rivers, wildlife, and limestone formations. Wilderness Volunteers is a nonprofit organization created in 1997 to organize and promote volunteer service to wildlands.

Help the park staff remove invasive plants, do trail maintenance, or work on ongoing projects, including restoration of the American butternut, American chestnut, and dogwood; ginseng surveys; and prairie habitat restoration. Botanical surveys have found 25 species listed as endangered, threatened, or of special concern.

Accommodations are in a dormitory setting, with showers, and the trip is rated "active," with several miles of hiking to work sites; it also requires bending, pulling, lifting, and dragging. In your free time you can tour Mammoth Cave and go canoeing, kayaking, fishing, swimming, mountain biking, and horseback riding.

ⓢ **Trade Services for RV Site, Southwest OK: Wichita Mountains Wildlife Refuge** (32 Refuge Headquarters, Indiahoma, OK 73552; 580-429-3222; www.fws.gov/southwest/refuges/oklahoma/wichita mountains; wichitamountains@fws.gov; volunteer contact, danna_mallow@fws.gov; 580-429-2193). Couples and single individuals are needed to volunteer at the Wichita Mountains Wildlife Refuge in southwest Oklahoma. Established in 1901, and the oldest wildlife facility man-aged by the U.S. Fish and Wildlife Service, the 59,020-acre refuge provides habitat for American bison, Rocky Mountain elk, white-tailed deer, and Texas longhorn cattle. Over 50 mammal, 240 bird, 64 reptile and amphibian, 36 fish, and 806 plant species can be found in the refuge.

Volunteers work at the information desk at the refuge visitor center, and on maintenance projects, invasive species control, interpretation and environmental educa-

WICHITA MOUNTAINS WILDLIFE REFUGE

Snow-on-the-Mountain plants make a showy presentation at the end of summer, creating a sensation of snow on the Wichita Mountains.

tion programs, office and clerical work, computers, and general assistance. The refuge provides a trailer site and full hookups, plus propane, and access to a landline phone and Internet in return for a commitment of 24 hours of work per individual. The work is rated "not difficult" and is suitable for adults and seniors.

The refuge has 13 public-use lakes and many small ponds for both bank and boat fishing. The annual elk and deer hunts are two and a half days of some of the best managed

WICHITA MOUNTAINS WILDLIFE REFUGE

A still, bright, winter day in the Wichita Mountains Wildlife Refuge.

hunts in the country, regulated through a cooperative effort between the U.S. Fish and Wildlife Service and the Oklahoma Department of Wildlife Conservation. Careful management controls the numbers of elk and deer and ensures their survival. There are nine hiking trails and a variety of camping options, and the refuge's location in the Wichita Mountains and its mixed-grass prairies make it an important and beautiful conservation area.

A Single Woman's Story, Indiahoma, OK

Single and in my 50s, I opted for early retirement. I thought it was time to go somewhere and do something else. I'm a fulltime RVer, which is unusual. The vast majority of RVers are married couples, which makes it a bit easier to divide the labor involved. Traveling in your own home opens up a lot of possibilities in the volunteering world.

I've been to many beautiful places, but I was driving southwest, on the Oklahoma freeway, and took a secondary road south when I came through a range of slick hills and limestone outcroppings and over the top of weathered granite mountains; my heart went pitter-pat.

I like being here with biologists and other professionals around to interpret the environment and answer my questions about what I'm seeing and how things work. It's been a lot of fun getting involved and being appreciated for what I'm able to give.

Immersion Tip: For Rock Climbers

The Wichita Mountains Wildlife Refuge provides one of the best rock-climbing locations in the Southwest. Popular climbing sites include Mt. Scott, the Narrows, Elk Mountain, Crab Eyes, and Lost Dome. The hundreds of granite climbing routes are in the 5.6 to 5.11 difficulty range, and for many years technical climbing had been an unregulated activity in the refuge. In 1996, new management policies and regulations were put into effect to reduce the impact of climbers and protect the rock-climbing areas from soil erosion, trail degradation, and litter. Contact the Wichita Mountains Climbers (www.wichitamountains.org) for weather and conditions.

(S) **Visitor Center Aide, South-Central IN: Muscatatuck National Wildlife Refuge** (12985 East US Hwy. 50, Seymour, IN 47274; 812-522-4352; fax 812-522-6826; www.fws.gov/refuges/profiles/index .cfm?id=31530; volunteer contact, donna_stanley@fws .gov). Volunteer as a Visitor Center Aide in the Muscatatuck National Wildlife Refuge, located in south-central Indiana. Muscatatuck's mission is to restore, preserve, and manage forest, wetland, and grassland habitat for fish, wildlife, and

Great Birding in Eight States

The U.S. Fish and Wildlife Service is responsible for the management of migratory birds in American habitats. Out of the more than 800 species of birds that have been identified, about 500 species can be found in the U.S. Fish and Wildlife Service region that includes Illinois, Indiana, Iowa, Michigan, Missouri, Minnesota, Ohio, and Wisconsin. Management entails monitoring populations, research, wetland and grassland restoration and protection, bottomland hardwood restoration, developing hunting regulations, conservation planning, outreach programs, and partnerships with Native American tribes, state and local governments, nongovernment agencies, and individuals.

people. Each year about 185,000 people visit the refuge, which is known as an excellent bird-watching site.

Responsibilities include staffing the information desk, selling items in the nonprofit bookstore, restocking brochures, refilling birdfeeders, answering the phone, and possibly helping with educational programs. Work times are flexible, but at least four hours a day are required if you stay in available housing: a furnished double-wide trailer, a travel trailer with hookups, or a trailer pad with hookups. The position is rated not physically difficult and is suitable for adults and seniors.

The refuge was established in 1966 and covers 7,802 acres. Otters were introduced to the refuge in 1995 and trumpeter swans in 1998. Other wildlife includes seasonal visits by ducks, geese, eagles, great egrets, great blue herons, blue-winged teal, osprey, cormorants, and sandhill cranes.

ⓢ **Campground Host, Southeastern OH: Wayne National Forest** (Marietta Unit, 27750 State Rte. 7, Marietta, OH 45750; 740-373-9055; fax 740-373-8079; volunteer contact, 740-753-0862; www.fs.fed.us/r9/wayne;

gchancey@fs.fed.us). Volunteer as a Campground Host in the Leith Run Campground in Wayne National Forest, the only national forest in Ohio, with 300 miles of trails open to hiking, mountain biking, ATV use, and horseback riding, and 18 campground sites in the Leith Run Recreation Area.

Campground hosts are required to be on site seven days a week, with an RV pad, hookups, water, and sewer provided. Responsibilities involve checking in campers to ensure they are in compliance with the National Recreation Reservation system, mowing the campgrounds, and keeping the restrooms clean. The work is not difficult and is suitable for adults and seniors.

Wayne National Forest is located in southeastern Ohio, within a day's drive from Cincinnati, Columbus, and Cleveland, Ohio; Pittsburgh, Pennsylvania; Louisville and Lexington, Kentucky; and Charleston and Huntington, West Virginia. Leith Run is popular for boating, fishing, and seasonal float trips. The forest contains a wide variety of wildlife, including white-tailed deer, opossum, gray fox, woodchuck, and gray squirrel, and birds such as turkey, ruffed grouse, wood duck, and the pileated woodpecker.

Immersion Excursion: Canoe Along

Consider a canoe trip on the Little Muskingum River, which runs alongside forests, hills, and pastures next to the **Covered Bridge Scenic Byway**. At one time, Ohio had 2,000 covered bridges, more than any other state. The **Hills Covered Bridge** built in 1889 and four additional covered bridges are along the byway. Paddle under these century-old bridges and through beautiful rural landscapes with rock outcrops and overhanging shade trees, or take an auto tour of the Covered Bridge Scenic Byway, a self-guided 35-mile ride along the river. The complete tour takes about four hours with stops at 10 tour markers, and there is an option for a shorter tour.

Not the End: All That Comes Next

I always tell people that volunteer work is the best because, while it represents responsibilities one takes on, it is not an obligation, it's a choice, and that makes all the difference in the world.

—KAREN M. GRAY, C&O CANAL NATIONAL
HISTORICAL PARK LIBRARY VOLUNTEER

I t's common to have conflicting emotions at the end of an intense and highly active volunteer vacation: happiness that you'll soon be home surrounded by familiar comforts and family and friends, anxiety over returning to a demanding schedule, and sadness that the vacation itself has come to a close. Particularly if you've had a life-changing experience, you may not feel the same anticipation about returning home to your regular routine that you do after a typical vacation.

It's not easy leaving behind people you've come to know and really care about who might be in less-than-satisfactory conditions. Perhaps you didn't accomplish everything you wanted to and are feeling a pull to return even before you

PIT volunteers paddle along the western shoreline of Prince of Wales Island, Alaska, to record and monitor ancient Tlingit sites.

leave. Be kind to yourself and leave room to react, adjust, and process your volunteer vacation in different ways.

Experienced volunteer travelers report that their perspectives change: they've adjusted personal goals, reshuffled priorities, and look at life differently. "I always wrote checks to charitable causes," says Bernie, a volunteer from Minnesota, "but now that I have met the beneficiaries of well-meaning people like myself, I still send the checks but I've learned it's more important for me to show up."

You may be dealing with all of these feelings, including great pride in your achievement, exhilaration at doing something new and significant, and pleasure in learning new things about yourself. A lot of time and energy went into planning, selecting, and preparing for your trip. It was a major decision to embark on a volunteer vacation and share your skills and time to benefit others. You don't need to put quite as much time and energy into returning home, but it will help smooth your transition if you consider a few important steps.

There are basically four stages we all experience: anticipation, reality, modification, and acclimation. Anticipation is that high-flying stage of excitement that comes with returning home and to everything missed. When Dorothy arrived home after a three-month absence, her friends threw her a party and her children planned a weekend for all of them together. "I felt like the queen bee, with everyone eager for my attention." It's all great fun, but eventually the newness of your being back will dissipate.

Reality seeps in when you realize that your priorities are different from what they used to be, while other people are unchanged. "Many of my friends were very interested in where I'd been and what I'd done," said Emma following a service trip. "But I had no patience at all with the people who wanted to talk about weekend plans and what to wear." You gradually accept expressing what's important to you and tolerating what's not.

Modification involves readjustment to life at home and the way you want your life to be. Making limited changes and adapting to the changes you have experienced will help with the process. Maintain an active awareness of the new priorities you've chosen and the personal growth you've made and continue to make.

Everyone needs a little time and space to decompress from the intensity of a volunteer vacation, which is more meaningful, more emotional, and has a greater impact on you than a typical vacation. "The smartest thing we did was extend our volunteering week with a few days on each end to adjust to our new surroundings," said Kathy after her trip with her husband and two children to Rock Point, Arizona. "The few days before gave us a chance to anticipate and prepare for the experience, and the few days at the end allowed us to wind down, relax, and regroup before returning home." Rather than flying home on Sunday night for work and school on Monday, Kathy scheduled their return flights for Friday to ease reentry.

Fitting back into the old routine can be uncomfortable at first. Things happened in your absence, only a few of which you will hear about, and this might make you feel out of sync. As you were expanding your awareness of other people and places and meeting new challenges, coworkers continued tackling daily chores.

One way to transition the gaps is to bring a few photos or mementos from your volunteer vacation. Sharing your stories will invite others into your experience and could build interest in future excursions.

Step four is acclimation. That's when what you've learned and accomplished is adapted into your daily life. You are comfortable with who you are and how you do things in a slightly new and different way. Reaching this stage is a very good sign that you are ready to embark upon another volunteer vacation.

Share Your Experiences

Incorporate what you've learned from your volunteer vacation to expand your daily life and interests. "With every trip I make," says Patricia, "I identify one significant but not necessarily major something that I observed elsewhere and can change the way I do things at home. On my last trip a nine-year-old taught me a no-fail way to tie my boots so they never come untied while hiking, but with a secret trick pull to untie them in a hurry."

In this book you read about the Mission of Love, an organization that has been growing for over 20 years because people have used their experiences to inspire others to volunteer. Talk about what you've done. Share your volunteer vacations with people in your community through Web sites, press releases, articles for your local newspaper, a slide show at the library, or by speaking at community, school, and other local meetings. Perhaps you volunteered with an organization that you want to raise funds for and educate others about. Volunteers return to their communities and make a difference by connecting with and engaging others.

Consider partnering with local businesses and organizations, particularly those with similar interests and goals, in other parts of the country. Find out if your employer offers matching donations that would be applicable, or if there are educational, research, or private grants available to benefit the group you worked with, or to sponsor your next trip.

Decisions

This is where reviewing your guestbook and the journal you kept while you were away will give you perspective and valuable information about the impact of your trip. It will also help you review and assess your experiences. What did you like most about your volunteer vacation?

AMIZADE

The perfect family vacation, working together to provide others with a roof.

What experiences would you like to repeat? What didn't you do that you'd like to try next time?

You might not know the answers yet, but you probably have a list of possibilities garnered from the people you've met and worked with. A great way to decide what you want to do next is to read about other trips that are being offered and talk to other people who have taken volunteer vacations. Your new approach to travel might very well take you into exciting territory, creating a willingness to do things you hadn't considered before.

Some volunteers who booked their first volunteer vacation through a sponsoring organization opt to make their own arrangements for follow-up trips.

"As an actor and musician I've always used agents, paying for their knowledge and expertise with the security that they know what they are doing," says one volunteer. "I really knew nothing about volunteer vacations, so it made sense for someone else to plan it for me. Now that I've had my learning experience, and paid a huge amount of money for the services, I will go about it in a different way next time." In this particular case, the two organizations she volunteered with can be contacted by private individuals putting together their own trips. Arrangements need not be made through a sponsoring organization.

There are others who stay with an organization that offers appealing trips, returning to the same place or enjoying a wide variety of offerings. One volunteer feels strongly that the organization he travels with arranges opportunities he wouldn't have access to otherwise and adds, "I like having other people take care of the details."

An e-mail that arrived from a traveler sums up how the vast majority of us feel after a volunteer vacation: "I'm sitting here back home with a million things vying for my attention, thinking I need to plan my next trip."

Throughout *Volunteer Vacations Across America* we've gotten to know many different people through their personal stories. Gary and Teresa volunteered as cooks for a group working on the Continental Divide. Gene and Kandee volunteered to clean up an island they now call home every summer. Anthony documented nesting puffins in Maine. Donna sewed costumes at the Pioneer Playhouse Summer Theater. Fiona left her job and home to travel to the United States from the United Kingdom to volunteer with primates and wolves. Claudia has participated in 14 different Earthwatch trips (so far) and volunteers her time as a spokesperson for the organization in her own community.

I've made a master list of volunteer vacations I hope to take within the next two years, all of which are included in this book. I want to volunteer one week of my summer as a camp counselor with the Camp AmeriKids in Warwick, New York. I'd like to work on the Heritage Conservation Network project rehabilitating abandoned shotgun-style houses in Cairo, Illinois, to provide quality affordable housing.

I have two must-do projects from the wildlife chapter. I'm passionate about whales and have always wanted to work with an independent researcher at the Hawaii Whale Research Foundation on Maui, and I'm intrigued by the volunteer opportunities with the Gibbon Conservation Center in Santa Clara, California. In addition, a one-week trip with the American Hiking Society is something I'd love to do with my two daughters, to work on building and maintaining trails across the country. I have volunteered extensively in national parks and hope to experience the diversity of the Siuslaw National Forest in Corvallis, Oregon.

What about you? What would you love to do?

New Friends in New Places

The best part of traveling is the people you meet. "I made two forever friends on my volunteer vacation," says Ann. "We bonded immediately and that was it."

The second best part of completing a volunteer vacation is planning the next. "My volunteering experiences left me feeling intensely high, energized, and excited," said Louise, "more so than after any other travel experience." When the awareness of how much is accomplished during a volunteer vacations fully hits, use it as motivation and inspiration to consider and plan future trips.

Volunteers tend to fall into two groups: those who get hooked on one activity and return to it year after year, and those who like to explore diverse choices in a variety of locations on each successive trip. Carolyn's volunteering at the American Bear Association led to a dream come true to secure full-time employment as program coordinator. A volunteer vacation offers a great opportunity to explore a career change or a desire to gain more education or training in a particular field.

One purpose of writing this book was to celebrate and focus on the multitude of volunteer opportunities throughout the United States that are providing great services and need our support. Another goal was to offer people who have never volunteered an informative, easy-to-use tool for planning and taking volunteer vacations, and to provide those who have already explored volunteer possibilities, and participated in volunteer activities, a wealth of additional suggestions for exciting new experiences. I hope readers in both categories will return to volunteering over and over again, building on each experience, finding new and exciting opportunities, and planning future volunteer vacations.

Please share your experiences with our broader community by contributing your volunteer story, observations, and tips at www.volunteervacationsacrossamerica.com. Let me know where you've been and where you're going. Happy volunteering, traveling, enjoying the people and places you visit, and appreciating the true beauty of this wonderfully caring country.

General Index

A

airline tickets, 35

Alaka'i Wilderness Preserve (HI), 273

Alexandria Archeology Museum (VA), 161–62

Alpine Lakes Wilderness (WA), 261

altitude and elevation shifts, 40

Amistad National Recreation Area (TX), 151

Amtrak, 150–51, 314

Anasazi people, 198

Anchorage (AK), 263–64

Angel Canyon (UT), 197, 198

Animas River (CO), 124–25

Annual ReRun Benefit Trail Ride (NY), 227

Appalachian Trail, 261, 265–66, 291, 303

Arches National Park (UT), 371

Arizona Wind-Song Leadership Center (AZ), 99

Assateague Island (MD, VA), 268–69, 328

Au Sable Light Station (MI), 369–70

B

Badlands (SD), 122

Bandelier National Monument (NM), 54, 55, 308

Baxter State Park (ME), 264

Bear Butte (SD), 122

Bear Island (MD), 317–18

Bear Tooth Wilderness (MT), 336

bears, 72, 162, 168, 177, 199–203 220, 231, 264, 314, 336, 345, 365, 368

Beasley, Jean, 182

Berkshires (MA), 303

Big Dipper Eco-Farm (MI), 60–61

Biloxi-Chitimacha people, 152

birds, 238–44, 311–14, 374–75

Black Hills (SD), 122

Blanchard River (AK), 123

Boundary Waters Canoe Area Wilderness (MI), 230, 344–45

Bridger-Teton National Forest (WY), 312

Bryce Canyon (UT), 197

Burning Man Festival (NV), 292, 294

C

Caladesi Island State Park (FL), 267–68

Cameron Trading Post (AZ), 85

Canal Pride Days (MD), 318

Cannery Row (CA), 281

Canyon de Chelly (AZ), 140

Carmel-by-the Sea (CA), 281

Cascade Mountains (WA), 299, 354

Catalina Botanical Museum (CA), 253

Organizations Index

Organizations by Region Index

Activity Index